Women
and Indian
Shakespeares

SHAKESPEARE AND ADAPTATION

Shakespeare and Adaptation provides in-depth discussions of a dynamic field and showcases the ways in which, with each act of adaptation, a new Shakespeare is generated. The series addresses the phenomenon of Shakespeare and adaptation in all its guises and explores how Shakespeare continues as a reference-point in a generically diverse body of representations and forms, including fiction, film, drama, theatre, performance and mass media. Including sole authored books as well as edited collections, the series embraces a mix of methodologies and espouses a global perspective that brings into conversation adaptations from different nations, languages and cultures.

Series Editor:
Mark Thornton Burnett (Queen's University Belfast, UK)

Advisory Board:
Professor Sarah Hatchuel (Université Paul-Valéry Montpellier 3, France)
Dr Peter Kirwan (University of Nottingham, UK)
Professor Douglas Lanier (University of New Hampshire, USA)
Professor Adele Lee (Emerson College, USA)
Dr Stephen O'Neill (Maynooth University, Ireland)
Professor Shormishtha Panja (University of Delhi, India)
Professor Lisa Starks (University of South Florida, USA)
Professor Nathalie Vienne-Guerrin
(Université Paul-Valéry Montpellier 3, France)
Professor Sandra Young (University of Cape Town, South Africa)

Published Titles:
Adapting 'Macbeth', William C. Carroll

Forthcoming Titles:
Lockdown Shakespeare
Edited by Gemma Allred, Benjamin Broadribb and Erin Sullivan
'Romeo and Juliet', Adaptation and the Arts:
'Cut Him Out in Little Stars'
Edited by Julia Reinhard Lupton and Ariane Helou
Shakespeare, Ecology and Adaptation: A Practical Guide
Alys Daroy and Paul Prescott
Shakespeare and Ballet, David Fuller

Women and Indian Shakespeares

Edited by
Thea Buckley, Mark Thornton Burnett, Sangeeta Datta and Rosa García-Periago

THE ARDEN SHAKESPEARE
LONDON • NEW YORK • OXFORD • NEW DELHI • SYDNEY

THE ARDEN SHAKESPEARE
Bloomsbury Publishing Plc
50 Bedford Square, London, WC1B 3DP, UK
1385 Broadway, New York, NY 10018, USA
29 Earlsfort Terrace, Dublin 2, Ireland

BLOOMSBURY, THE ARDEN SHAKESPEARE and the Arden Shakespeare logo are trademarks of Bloomsbury Publishing Plc

First published in Great Britain 2022
This paperback edition published 2024

Copyright © Thea Buckley, Mark Thornton Burnett, Sangeeta Datta, Rosa García-Periago and contributors, 2022

Thea Buckley, Mark Thornton Burnett, Sangeeta Datta, Rosa García-Periago and contributors have asserted their right under the Copyright, Designs and Patents Act, 1988, to be identified as the authors of this work.

For legal purposes the Acknowledgements on pp. xvi–xviii constitute an extension of this copyright page.

Series design by Ben Anslow and Tjaša Krivec.
Cover image: Parvathy Baul in the movie Arshinagar (2015) directed by Aparna Sen (© courtesy of SVF Entertainment Pvt Ltd)

All rights reserved. No part of this publication may be reproduced or transmitted in any form or by any means, electronic or mechanical, including photocopying, recording, or any information storage or retrieval system, without prior permission in writing from the publishers.

Bloomsbury Publishing Plc does not have any control over, or responsibility for, any third-party websites referred to or in this book. All internet addresses given in this book were correct at the time of going to press. The author and publisher regret any inconvenience caused if addresses have changed or sites have ceased to exist, but can accept no responsibility for any such changes.

A catalogue record for this book is available from the British Library.

Library of Congress Control Number: 2022933843

ISBN: HB: 978-1-3502-3432-1
 PB: 978-1-3502-3436-9
 ePDF: 978-1-3502-3434-5
 eBook: 978-1-3502-3433-8

Series: Shakespeare and Adaptation

Typeset by Integra Software Services Pvt. Ltd.

To find out more about our authors and books visit www.bloomsbury.com and sign up for our newsletters.

CONTENTS

List of illustrations viii
List of tables ix
Notes on contributors x
Acknowledgements xvi
A note on references xix

Introduction
Thea Buckley, Mark Thornton Burnett, Sangeeta Datta and Rosa García-Periago 1

Part One: Histories

1 The 'woman's part': Recovering the contribution of women to the circulation of Shakespeare in India
   Poonam Trivedi 21

2 Framing femininities: Desdemona and Indian modernities
   Paromita Chakravarti 43

Part Two: Translations

3 Indian Shakespeares in the British Library collections: Translation, indigeneity and representation
   Priyanka Basu and Arani Ilankuberan 65

4 Women translating Shakespeare in South India: *Hemanta Katha* or *The Winter's Tale*
   Thea Buckley 91

Part Three: Representations

5 'I dare do all that may become a man': Martial desires and women as warriors in *Veeram*, a film adaptation of *Macbeth*
   Mark Thornton Burnett and Jyotsna G. Singh 113

6 'You should be women': Bengali femininity and the supernatural in adaptations of *Macbeth*
   Taarini Mookherjee 131

7 *Romeo and Juliet* meets rural India: *Sairat* and the representation of women
   Nishi Pulugurtha 149

8 Dy(e)ing hands: The hennaed female agent in Vishal Bhardwaj's tragedies
   Jennifer T. Birkett 167

Part Four: Critics and creatives

9 Embattled bodies: Women, land and contemporary politics in *Arshinagar*, a film adaptation of *Romeo and Juliet*
   Rosa García-Periago 187

10 Where the wild things are: Shifting identities in *Noblemen*, a film adaptation of *The Merchant of Venice*
   Mark Thornton Burnett 207

11 Women punctuating Shakespeare: Campus theatrical experiment, the Shakespeare Society and the insider/outsider dialectic
N. P. Ashley 225

12 Adapting Shakespeare: Directors and practitioners in conversation
Bornila Chatterjee, Sangeeta Datta, Annette Leday, Sreedevi Nair and Preti Taneja 243

Appendix
A selection of Shakespeare translations/adaptations from the British Library North Indian Languages Collection
Priyanka Basu and Arani Ilankuberan 262

Index 285

LIST OF ILLUSTRATIONS

3.1 Image of *Tales from Shakespeare* by Charles and Mary Lamb (1852), British Library VT 1623(b). Courtesy of © British Library Board   68
3.2 Image of the title page and translator's note from *Jhanjha* (1913), a translation of *The Tempest* by Nagendra Prasad Sarbbadhikari, British Library VT 3285(b). Courtesy of © British Library Board   71
3.3 Image from *Sushila-Chandraketu* (a translation of *Twelfth Night*) by Kantichandra Bidyaratna, British Library VT 963(l). Courtesy of © British Library Board   73
3.4 Image of a scene from a production of *A Midsummer Night's Dream*, from S. A. Hirematha, *Vasantayamini Svapnacamatkara Natakavu* (1925), British Library 14176.e.28(7). Courtesy of © British Library Board   78
3.5 Title page of A. Madhaviah's Tamil translation of *Othello* (1902), British Library 14171.i.1.(1.). Courtesy of © British Library Board   81
3.6 Image of Adriana threatening Dromio with violence in *Viprama Vihasam* (1905–6), A. Venkatacharyar's Tamil translation of *The Comedy of Errors*, British Library, 14172.m.1. (vols 1–2). Courtesy of © British Library Board   84
4.1 *Hemanta Katha: A Malayalam Translation of The Winter's Tale*, trans. O. M. Lakshmy Amma (1892), flyleaf dedication. Courtesy of © British Library Board   98
9.1 The tragic *dénouement* of *Arshinagar* (dir. Aparna Sen, 2015). Courtesy of Aparna Sen and Shree Venkatesh Films   195

LIST OF TABLES

3.1 Table of manuscripts and proscribed publications in North Indian collections by language   66
3.2 Table of South Indian collections by language   76

NOTES ON CONTRIBUTORS

N. P. Ashley, dramaturge, translator and socio-political commentator, teaches English at St Stephen's College, Delhi. His research interests are in performance studies and New Historicism, and he teaches Shakespeare, literary theory and Text and Performance courses. He was President of the Shakespeare Society of St Stephen's College for five years and was the production supervisor for five Shakespeare plays staged as part of a tradition that started in 1926. The plays he has worked on as dramaturge have been performed at theatre festivals including the Edinburgh Fringe Festival, UK (*Blind Spots*, Delhi University production); Brisbane World Theatre Festival (an adaptation of Ibsen's *Lady from the Sea*); and Australia and Bharat Rang Mahotsav, Delhi (*The Museum of Lost Pieces*). He is co-consultant editor of the Pearson ICSE English textbook series, 'Lighthouse'. He writes on socio-political issues in Malayalam and English and comments on Malayalam TV. He translates between English and Malayalam and is the translator and editor of the *Selected Works of O. Henry* in Malayalam.

Priyanka Basu is a Lecturer in Performing Arts at King's College, London, and was previously the Project Curator on the 'Two Centuries of Indian Print' project at the British Library. She received her PhD degree in South Asian Studies from SOAS. She is currently working on a monograph based on her doctoral thesis (forthcoming from Routledge). Her research interests include folklore, theatre and film histories, book history, gender and dance studies. Her current project examines histories of dancers as trans-national cultural workers between South Asia and the UK in the context of decolonization.

Jennifer T. Birkett is a Presidential Fellow and PhD candidate at the University of Notre Dame. She studies early modern literature with a specific interest in linguistic intimacy and representations of marriage. Her current work considers the function of pet names and endearments in early modern drama. Characteristically, her scholarship magnifies quirky details and contradictions to arrive at new affordances for both the page and the stage.

Thea Buckley is a Research Assistant in the School of Social Sciences, Education and Social Work at Queen's University Belfast, where she was previously a Leverhulme Early Career Fellow in the School of AEL. Her research project 'South Indian Shakespeares: Reimagining Art Forms and Identities' examines Shakespearean productions across boundaries of language, caste, media and place in South India, where she grew up. She previously worked for the Royal Shakespeare Company; the British Library; the University of Birmingham and the Shakespeare Birthplace Trust and has published work in *Reviewing Shakespeare*; *Cahiers Élisabéthains*; *Theatre Notebook*; *A Year of Shakespeare* (London and New York: Bloomsbury Academic, 2013); *Multicultural Shakespeare*; *Shakespeare and Indian Cinemas: 'Local Habitations'* (London and New York: Routledge, 2019); and, most recently, *Shakespeare Jahrbuch*, *Revista Canaria de Estudios Ingleses* and *Indian Theatre Journal*.

Mark Thornton Burnett is Professor of Renaissance Studies at Queen's University Belfast. He is the author of *Masters and Servants in English Renaissance Drama and Culture: Authority and Obedience* (1997), *Constructing 'Monsters' in Shakespearean Drama and Early Modern Culture* (2002), *Filming Shakespeare in the Global Marketplace* (2007; 2nd ed. 2012), *Shakespeare and World Cinema* (2013) and *'Hamlet' and World Cinema* (2019).

Paromita Chakravarti is Professor, Department of English, Jadavpur University, and has been Director, School of Women's Studies, Jadavpur University. She completed her doctoral studies on early modern discourses of madness at the University of Oxford, UK. She teaches Renaissance drama, women's writing, queer and film studies. She has been a Visiting Fellow at the universities of Oxford, Liverpool, Hyderabad, Delhi and Birmingham. She has published widely on Shakespeare and early modern studies in *Renaissance Studies*, *Shakespearean International Yearbook* and other journals and volumes. Her book, *Women Contesting Culture*, co-edited with Prof Kavita Panjabi, was published in 2012. Her anthology, co-edited with Poonam Trivedi, *Shakespeare and Indian Cinemas: 'Local*

Habitations' was published in 2018. A further anthology, co-edited with Poonam Trivedi and Ted Motohashi, *Asian Interventions in Global Shakespeare: 'All the World's His Stage'*, was published in 2021.

Bornila Chatterjee is a filmmaker. She earned her BFA in film and television from NYU's Tisch School of the Arts and was a Fellow of the Sundance Institute/Mumbai Mantra Screenwriters Lab in 2014. Her debut feature, *Let's Be Out, The Sun Is Shining*, won the Audience Award at the 2012 New York Indian Film Festival. Her film adaptation of Shakespeare's *Titus Andronicus*, *The Hungry* (2017), was screened in the Special Presentations section at the 2017 Toronto International Film Festival and has also been screened at the New York Indian Film Festival.

Sangeeta Datta is a writer/director, independent filmmaker and cultural commentator. She is director of Baithak – a non-profit arts company – and Stormglass Productions, which, also dedicated to making meaningful cinema and theatre, draws on narratives which have an international appeal. Trained and published in Tagore music, Datta has been a Research Fellow at the University of Sussex and SOAS and is the co-editor, with Kaustav Bakshi and Rohit K. Dasgupta, of *Rituparno Ghosh: Cinema, Gender and Art* (London and New York: Routledge, 2016). Her critically acclaimed work includes the award-winning feature film adaptation of *King Lear*, *Life Goes On* (2009), the stage productions *The Dying Song* (2008) and *Gitanjali 100* (2013–14), and the documentary, *Bird of Dusk* (2019).

Rosa García-Periago completed her doctoral studies on Shakespeare, Bollywood and beyond at the University of Murcia, where she is a Senior Lecturer. She was formerly an EU Marie Curie Individual Fellow ('Shakespeare and Indian Cinematic Traditions') at Queen's University Belfast. She is co-editor of *Jane Austen and William Shakespeare: A Love Affair in Literature, Film and Performance* (2019) and has published extensively on Indian Shakespeares in *Adaptation*, *Atlantis*, *Borrowers and Lenders*, *Cahiers Élisabéthains*, *Indian Theatre Journal*, *SEDERI Yearbook*, *Shakespeare* and other journals.

Arani Ilankuberan is the Head of South Asian Collections at the British Library. Previously, she held the post of South Indian Collections Curator at the British Library. Before she joined the library, she worked as a researcher of the Tamil Hindu community in London as part of an ESRC-funded project on London faith communities at Goldsmiths, University of London. She has recently submitted her PhD at Goldsmiths that examines the faith literacies and identities of the UK Tamil diaspora through viewing Tamil Hindu film.

Annette Leday, a dancer and choreographer, studied at the Institut des Langues Orientales, Paris, and, with a scholarship from the Indian government, at the Sadanam and at the Kalamandalam institutions, Kerala. She participated in many performances in Kerala and abroad with the troupes of these two institutions. After about ten years' immersion in the traditional form of Kathakali, she created the Annette Leday/Keli company. In 1988, she invited her masters, Shri Keezhpadam Kumaran Nair and Shri Padmanabhan Nair, to take part in adapting Shakespeare's *King Lear* into Kathakali. The two masters played the role of Lear, and the full team toured with her around the world. Leday directed the production along with Dr David McRuvie and performed the role of Cordelia.

Taarini Mookherjee is currently a Lecturer in the Discipline of English and Comparative Literature at Columbia University, New York. Prior to this, she was a Visiting Assistant Professor in the Department of English at SUNY, New Paltz. She received her PhD in English and Comparative Literature in 2020 from Columbia University, where she was also affiliated with the Institute for Comparative Literature and Society. Her dissertation, '*Desifying* Shakespeare: Performing Contemporary India in Adaptations', focused on contemporary Indian adaptations of Shakespeare in film and theatre. By mobilizing the bilingual portmanteau *desify*, a word that simultaneously references the abstract and aspirational nation and the quotidian process of making local or native in popular culture, this project argues that these self-consciously Indian productions or '*desified* Shakespeare' disclose contemporary Indian ideas about and enquiries into the nation, rendering visible how the nation is imagined, constructed and performed. Her broader research and teaching fields include early modern drama, global Shakespeare, translation theory, postcolonial theory and theatre and performance studies.

Sreedevi K. Nair, academic, translator and editor, works at the Samyukta Research Centre, Thiruvananthapuram, Kerala, India.

She was formerly head of the Department of English at NSS College for Women, Thiruvananthapuram. Her research interests include Translation Studies, Women's Writing, Education and Shakespeare Studies. She recently guest edited a special issue of *Indian Theatre Journal* (2021) on 'Indian Othellos: Shakespeare Adaptations in India'.

Nishi Pulugurtha is Associate Professor, Department of English, Brahmananda Keshab Chandra College, Kolkata. Her areas of interest are British Romantic literature, Indian writing in English, the diaspora and Shakespeare film adaptations. Dr Pulugurtha has published in refereed international and national journals and collections – in the *Coleridge Bulletin, The Encylopaedia of Postcolonial Studies, Shakespeare and Indian Cinemas: 'Local Habitations'* (2019), *The Cambridge Companion to British Romanticism and Religion* (2021) and elsewhere. She has a monograph on *Derozio* (2010) and a collection of travel essays, *Out in the Open* (2019), an edited volume of essays on travel, *Across and Beyond* (2020), a volume of poems, *The Real and The Unreal and Other Poems* (2020), and a collection of short stories, *The Window Sill* (2021). She has edited a special issue of *Muse India* on 'Shakespeare in Indian Cinema' (July/August 2021).

Jyotsna G. Singh is Professor of English at Michigan State University. She teaches and researches early modern literature and culture, colonial history, travel writing, postcolonial theory, early modern histories of Islam and gender and race studies, often exploring the intersections of these different fields. Her published works include numerous articles, book chapters and works such as the following: *The Weyward Sisters: Shakespeare and Feminist Politics* (1994), co-authored; *Colonial Narratives/Cultural Dialogues: 'Discovery' of India in the Language of Colonialism* (1996), authored; *Travel Knowledge: European 'Discoveries' in the Early Modern Period* (2001), co-edited with Ivo Kamps; *A Companion to the Global Renaissance: English Literature and Culture in the Era of Expansion, 1559–1660* (2009), edited; *The Postcolonial World* (2016), co-edited with David D. Kim; and *Shakespeare and Postcolonial Theory* (2019), authored.

Preti Taneja is a writer, activist, and Professor of World Literature and Creative Writing at Newcastle University. Her novel, *We That*

Are Young (2017), a translation of Shakespeare's *King Lear* set in contemporary India, won the 2018 Desmond Elliott Prize for the UK's best debut of the year, and was listed for awards including the Folio Prize; the Shakti Bhatt First Book Prize (India); the Republic of Consciousness Prize (UK); and Europe's premier award for a work of world literature, the Prix Jan Michalski. It was a book of the year in *The Guardian*, *The Sunday Times* and the *Spectator*, and a top 10 Book of the Decade for India's *The Hindu* newspaper. It has been translated into seven languages and is published in the USA by Alfred A. Knopf. Her second book is *Aftermath* (2021), a lament on the language of terror, prison, trauma and grief.

Poonam Trivedi was Associate Professor in English at Indraprastha College, University of Delhi. She was the Secretary of the Shakespeare Society of India (1993–9) and has directed college Shakespeare plays and is currently the Vice-Chair of the Asian Shakespeare Association (in which capacity she convened its biennial conference in Delhi, 2016). Her latest publications (co-edited) are *Shakespeare and Indian Cinemas: 'Local Habitations'* (2019) and *Shakespeare's Asian Journeys: Critical Encounters, Cultural Geographies, and the Politics of Travel* (2017). She has also co-edited *Fields of Play: Sport, Literature and Culture* (2015), *Re-playing Shakespeare in Asia* (2010) and *India's Shakespeare: Translation, Interpretation and Performance* (2005). She has authored a CD-ROM, *'King Lear' in India* (2006), and has published on Shakespeare in India, on performance and film versions of Shakespeare, on women in Shakespeare and on Indian theatre in *Borrowers and Lenders*, *Hamlet Studies*, *Literature/Film Quarterly*, *The Shakespearean International Yearbook*, *Shakespeare Survey* and other journals.

ACKNOWLEDGEMENTS

This book represents one of the outputs of the collaborative research project, 'Indian Shakespeares' (2018–22), at Queen's University Belfast. Funded by Being Human, the EU and the Leverhulme Trust, 'Indian Shakespeares' aimed to explore and identify the significances of Shakespeare's presence in India, and India's engagement with Shakespeare, across a variety of media, including cinema, translation and stage performance. Over the course of the project, we hosted a conference, an exhibition, film screenings, book launches, talks and discussions. Details can be accessed at https://www.qub.ac.uk/schools/ael/Research/ResearchinEnglish/ResearchProjectsinEnglish/INDIANSHAKESPEARES.

For supporting this book and bringing it to fruition, we would like to acknowledge the following:

Thea Buckley: working on this book has been a gift. Having grown up mostly in India, which like the rest of the world has been rent by the pandemic, I am especially grateful to our publisher, The Arden Shakespeare, for the opportunity right now to bring together and to the world so many voices on women in Indian Shakespeares. While I owe a debt of encouragement to too many to name here, for this volume in particular I thank my mother, the ever-supportive Leverhulme Trust, and my three generous and vibrant co-editors, Mark Thornton Burnett, Sangeeta Datta and Rosa García-Periago. This collection's theme was crystallized by the latter's focus on gender as part of our 'Indian Shakespeares' project, and it benefitted from the thriving academic community of the School of Arts, English, and Languages at Queen's University Belfast (including work by Ramona Wray and Edel Lamb), even though the topic had also been gelling for some time. Moments stand out. London, 2015, watching Jatinder Verma's brilliant Indian *Macbeth* with *hijra*-witches. London, 2016, hearing Poonam Trivedi, Diana Henderson, and Deanna Rankin speak inspirationally on feminism in the field of

Indian Shakespeares. Belfast, 2019, discussing Arya's 1888 Hindi-language *Merchant of Venice* translation across consecutive papers, including Anandi Rao's searching exploration, and appreciating how Kimberlé Crenshaw's 'intersectionality' a century later still aptly describes what Arya faced as an Indian woman translating Shakespeare: interlocking obstacles of racism, classism, sexism and colonialism. The films, papers and conversations that autumn, ranging from lived experiences and revisitations of Judith Butler's 'performative' gender to discussions of the recent decriminalization of same-sex unions in both India and Northern Ireland, fundamentally informed the undergraduate course I taught the following semester, and the way in which I now work on women, India and Shakespeare. While it is impossible to contain that entire festival of lights in this one volume, it marks a start.

Mark Thornton Burnett: I would like to thank, at Queen's University Belfast, Thea Buckley and Rosa García-Periago for a rich and rewarding professional relationship and manifold courtesies, conversations and kindnesses. I am also grateful to Richard Dutton, Edel Lamb and Ramona Wray for their friendship and collegiality as members of a thriving Shakespeare/Renaissance community. I am greatly indebted to Sangeeta Datta for her wisdom, scholarship and creative example. I acknowledge the support of the School of AEL for grants from the Research Fund and a period of sabbatical leave which enabled the completion of the collection. Further afield, I would like to thank Jyotsna G. Singh, Poonam Trivedi, Alexa Alice Joubin and N. P. Ashley (who invited me to teach and lecture at St Stephen's College, Delhi) for their support, fellowship and generosity over the years. Finally, at The Arden Shakespeare, many thanks to Mark Dudgeon and Lara Bateman, for believing in and commissioning the collection, and to Tjaša Krivec for her wonderful design work.

Sangeeta Datta: I would like to thank my co-editors, Mark Thornton Burnett, Thea Buckley, Rosa García-Periago, who invited me to the 'Women in Indian Shakespeares' conference at Queen's University Belfast and who make up the team behind the 'Indian Shakespeares' collaborative research project. It is an appropriate moment to thank my teachers in school and University who taught us Shakespeare so passionately, inspiring theatre practitioners in India including the late actor-directors Utpal Dutt and Soumitra Chatterjee from Kolkata and imaginative screenplay adapters of

Indian Shakespeare, Gulzar and Vishal Bhardwaj. Finally, I thank my father for my exposure to hybrid Shakespeare productions in theatre and the indigenous *jatra* traditions.

Rosa García-Periago: my first gratitude goes to the European Union for granting me a Marie Skłodowska-Curie Fellowship titled 'Shakespeare and Indian Cinematic Traditions' (Project ID 752060) that enabled me to work with outstanding colleagues such as Mark Thornton Burnett and Thea Buckley at Queen's University Belfast. Any success this collection achieves will be due to the depth of this fabulous and enriching collaboration. This fellowship partly funded the conference we hosted, 'Women and Indian Shakespeares', where I met the superb filmmaker, scholar and co-editor of this collection, Sangeeta Datta. I also wish to thank my colleagues from the University of Murcia, especially those involved in the research project, 'Shakespeare and the 20th Century: War, Cultural Memory and New Media' (FFI2015-68871-P), led by Clara Calvo. I sincerely thank Clara Calvo for her mentorship and constant support.

Gratitude beyond words goes to my amazing and loving husband, my parents and my brother. And, of course, to my incredible and inspiring daughter, Nora, who remains my constant reminder of the necessity of a collection like this so that she has powerful women to look up to.

Collectively, we thank all the contributors for their patience, participation, collegiality and insights, generously offered in challenging times, and the anonymous readers for corrections and suggestions for improvement.

A NOTE ON REFERENCES

The edition used for quotation from Shakespeare's plays is *The Arden Shakespeare: Complete Works*, ed. Richard Proudfoot, Ann Thompson, David Scott Kastan and H. R. Woudhuysen, 3rd series (London, New York, Oxford, New Delhi and Sydney: Bloomsbury, 2021).

We have not used diacritical marks in this book nor have we standardized spelling of Indian names/places across the board, retaining in several instances varying orthographical practice.

Introduction

Thea Buckley, Mark Thornton Burnett, Sangeeta Datta and Rosa García-Periago

The study of Shakespeare in/and India has often been conducted without explicit reference to gender and inside wider debates about 'Shakespeare and Asia' and Global Shakespeare. Ground-breaking, originary studies include Jyotsna G. Singh's article, 'Different Shakespeares' (1989), which illuminates the place of Shakespeare on eighteenth- and nineteenth-century Calcutta stages, D. A. Shankar's collection, *Shakespeare in Indian Languages* (1999), on adaptations and translations of Shakespeare into different Indian languages, Nandi Bhatia's article, 'Different *Othello(s)*' (2007), an exploration of responses to, and debates about, productions of *Othello* at key moments in India's history, and Poonam Trivedi's article, 'Filmi' Shakespeare' (2007), a discussion of Shakespeare's repeated iterations in popular Hindi-language cinema. Similarly, Poonam Trivedi and Dennis Bartholomeusz's agenda-setting collection of essays, *India's Shakespeare: Translation, Interpretation and Performance* (2005), was a key intervention, canvassing the earliest engagements with Shakespeare in Parsi theatre, trajectories in translation and appropriation inside folklore.

If these first forays identified the field, they also demonstrated what was possible in terms of argument, approach and scope, paving the way for subsequent investigations. As criticism on Indian Shakespeares has proliferated, both the spectrum of examples and the historical reach have broadened and extended. Suddhaseel Sen's recent book, *Shakespeare in the World: Cross-Cultural Adaptation in Europe and Colonial India, 1850–1900* (2021), focuses on the latter half of the nineteenth century in fascinating discussions of a long and diffuse history of Indian adaptive practice. There is now a more finessed sense both of Shakespeare theatre performances that use India in diasporic contexts (Loomba 2005: 121–37; Trivedi 2020: 113–23) and Shakespeare theatre performances in India that deploy dance, parody and local/global staging praxes (Chakravarti and Ganguly 2010: 271–90; Trivedi 2021: 15–32). If these studies point up tensions between colonial legacies and the will to postmodern experiment, related studies turn to concepts of performance to reflect on 'Indianness'. Exemplary is Shormishtha Panja and Babli Moitra Saraf's collection, *Performing Shakespeare in India: Exploring Indianness, Literatures and Cultures* (2016), which singles out theatre, festival culture, Indian cultural icons and Shakespearean texts 'as catalysts for the entrance of the Indian nation into modernity' (Panja and Saraf 2016: 11–12). Such a reorienting has allowed for recalibrations of methodology, with Thea Buckley's discussion demonstrating the virtues of applying intercultural paradigms to Indian Shakespeare performances in international venues (2016: 77–91).

As concepts and expressions of performance have opened out for critique, so, too, has cinema. Covering mainly Hindi-language Shakespeare film adaptations, and broaching issues of definition, identity and cultural capital, Craig Dionne and Parmita Kapadia's collection, *Bollywood Shakespeares*, confirmed the Shakespearean significance of India's Mumbai-based film industry when it was published in 2014. Since then, however, 'Bollywood', as an instrument for the adaptation of Shakespeare, has increasingly been set against other film industries in India, such as 'Mollywood' or Malayalam-language cinema (Burnett 2013: 55–86), while recent collections attend both to the history of Shakespeare on film in India and to Shakespeare's presence in regional and independent film forms and 'local habitations' (Trivedi and Chakravarti 2019: 1–19). Simultaneously, the move to recognize the role of the regional has had a transformative effect in work on theatre. Criticism has become more readily attuned to matters of regional variety and to the contribution of 'indigenous' traditions, such as Bengal's *jatra* theatre, to processes of cultural exchange (Kapadia 2008: 91–104).[1] Indeed, if there is a single critical direction in Indian Shakespeares, it is towards a greater recognition of the specifics of expression, place and diversity. Language has an important place in this shift. As a nation-state, India, according to the census of 2001, comprises 122 major languages, with films being made in up to 35 languages annually. It is perhaps not surprising, then, that, as work on Indian Shakespeares has progressed, a deeper appreciation of the linguistic choices available in the adaptive encounter has presented itself. Recent work, such as Vikram Singh Thakur's *Shakespeare and Indian Theatre: The Politics of Performance* (2020), moves from the eighteenth century to the contemporary to point up the significance of adaptations of Shakespeare in Hindi, Kannada, Malayalam and Marathi, while associated studies of theatre and film have attended to ideas of *masala*, highlighting the cultural impact of linguistic admixture (Harris 2018: 31–2, 35–6, 53–65).

Growing numbers of studies demonstrate the energizing effect of the embrace of the specific; they also illuminate the rapidity of developments in the field. To pinpoint only one example: *Haider* (dir. Vishal Bhardwaj, 2014), a film adaptation of *Hamlet*, has attracted a plethora of interpretive treatments, from the adaptation's immersion in affective poetics and legal debates (Taneja 2018: 46–65; Singh 2019: 177–94) to its relationship to the 'global south' and 'the idiom of the War on Terror' (Young 2019: 49–78; Dadabhoy 2021: 19). And, across the field as a whole, clusters of thematic concern are growingly apparent. The role of the Shakespearean text in Indian education, both in its colonial and postcolonial manifestations, is one returned-to topic (Loomba 1993: 227–50; Banerji 2012: 29–42); another is the Shakespearean text's multilayered relationship to Indian genres, mythologies and poetics (Panjwani 2018: 110–19). If one thematic focus continues to gravitate to instances of postcolonial resistance, attention also increasingly falls on the continuing play of cultural authority and national identity, the valences of intercultural and intracultural conversations, and the extent to which Shakespeare speaks to the anxieties and ambitions, pressures and projections, of the subcontinent.

Inside this burgeoning and exciting field, issues around gender have not as yet received sustained treatment. This is despite the multiple ways in which women, and those identifying as women, are, and have been, engaged with Shakespeare in India. Women's engagements encompass the full range of media, from translation to cinematic adaptation and from early colonial performance to contemporary theatrical experiment. But the singular contributions of women, and the ways in which women are envisaged in representational registers, continue to be largely critically neglected. Discussion of women in performative contexts is limited: for example, no historically comprehensive account exists of the Shakespearean actress on Indian stages. The work that does exist is piecemeal and most often centred around individual women film directors in India and the diaspora. For example, to support her broader argument about 'female authorship' and the ways in which, as makers of Shakespeare, women experience a 'process of estrangement' in 'encroaching on' a sphere of 'male entitlement' (2016: 433, 434), Courtney Lehmann highlights the importance of Deepa Mehta's *Water* (2005), a film adaptation of *Romeo and Juliet*. Other work explicitly concerned with Indian women as directors/practitioners has singled out thematics around the gendered legacies of Partition and the idealized role of the Indian mother figure (Földváry 2020: 93–100). Several studies highlight the extent to which film directors working in India (such as Aparna Sen) have adapted Shakespeare to reflect on inter-community Muslim-Hindu enmities (Chakravarti 2019: 308; Mookherjee 2019: 1–22; Panja 2020: 573–92). Perhaps most suggestively, recent studies are attentive to issues of intersectionality, to, in the words of Patricia Hill Collins and Sirma Bilge, the ways in which the 'major axes of social division in a given society at a given time, for example, race, class, gender, sexuality, dis/ability and age operate not as discrete and mutually exclusive entities, but build on each other and work together' (2016: 4). Forms of attention are beginning to reflect on representations of 'third gender' identities, such as that of the *hijra*, suggesting possibilities for dialogue with studies attentive to transgender and non-binary identities in Asian adaptations and performance modes (Burnett 2019: 229; Joubin 2021: 114). As a whole, these interpretive instances suggest the promise of placing in dialogue 'women' and 'Indian Shakespeares' – to do so is to reorient existing lines of investigation, to extend the disciplinary field, to bring into visibility still occluded subjects of representation and to open up the potential for radical and alternative readings.

I

As critical studies begin to grow and diversify, Indian women, and women in India, have been making and creating Shakespeare in unprecedented numbers. The most cursory glance at Indian Shakespeares and women's creative activity reveals a contemporary energy and compulsion to engage Shakespeare across a variety of media (a force we attempt to capture in this collection through the incorporation throughout of practitioners with a purchase on Indian Shakespeares present and future). There has been a diverse range of authorial interventions, from novels by women which repurpose *Macbeth* and *King Lear* (Bharati Mukherjee's *Wife* [1987] and Preti Taneja's *We That Are Young* [2017] are exemplary) to solo performances in which women draw on Shakespeare to mock present-day corporation culture and motivational workshops (Trivedi 2021: 25–8). As practitioners, women in India and the diaspora have turned to Shakespeare as an instrument of ideological mediation and an imaginative opportunity. Hence, puppeteer and artist, Maya Krishna Rao, conceived, performed and directed an art piece/cross-media show, *Are You Home Lady Macbeth?*, in 2008, using changing colours and back projection to simulate a witch's invention of Lady Macbeth in multiple manifestations, while Rani Drew has consistently turned to Shakespeare (in works such as *The III-Act Hamlet* [1992], *Shakespeare & Me* [1995] and *Caliban* [2001]) to promote emancipatory, gendered and postcolonial perspectives.[2] Deepa Mehta's film adaptation, *Water* (2005), set in an *ashram* on the banks of the Ganges, interweaves *Romeo and Juliet* with reflections on the historical taboo against widow remarriage. Meanwhile, in her 2019 theatrical production of *The Merchant of Venice* at B. A. M. Khalsa College, Garhshankar, Punjab, Vijeta Saini enlisted the *Nukkad Natak* street play form, and distinctive foot stamping routines, to generate conflicting interpretations of British and Indian cultures.[3] This much will indicate that, despite geographical, cultural and social variations, authorial interventions touch on questions particular to Indian womanhood and gender roles, including patriarchally arranged marriage, female foeticide and infanticide, honour killing, dowry death and ritual impurity. Issues around same-sex female desire and non-binary sexuality are also part of this social and cultural landscape, although more often than not represented only in diasporic Indian Shakespeare productions.[4] A revealing instance is Jatinder Verma's Tara Arts production of *Macbeth* (2015) in London which staged the witches as 'third gender' *hijras*, making extensive use of elaborate choreographies and hand gestures and demythologizing the play's generic contours.

If Indian women, and women in India, are making, they are simultaneously being made – as the Tara Arts example suggests – with at least as much vigour and energy. Indian film industries and performance traditions remain overwhelmingly male. But, in spite of this, or possibly because of this, they remain charged repositories for the negotiation of constructs and images of womanhood. Recurring thematics around gender in Indian cinemas include the restriction of bodily autonomy, the circumscription of sexual desire, the attrition of feminine agency and the persistence of gender-linked economic and educational inequalities. So, a Malayalam-language film such as *Kannaki* (dir. Jayaraj, 2002), an adaptation of *Antony and Cleopatra* set amidst Kerala's flooded paddy fields and rivers, recasts Cleopatra as a desiring village priestess and snakebite healer. Comparable dynamics are held in play in *Maqbool* (dir. Vishal Bhardwaj, 2003), a Hindi-language adaptation of *Macbeth* unfolding in Mumbai's underworld; here, the Lady Macbeth figure, Nimmi, is berated for her child's uncertain paternity, with masculine anxieties about the perpetuation of lineage contributing to breakdown, death in childbirth and the murder of both potential fathers. Beyond the filmic, in a Tamil-language theatre adaptation of *King Lear*, *Iruthiattam* (dir. R. Raju, 2001), which adopts a non-illusionist style, draws on *terukkuttu* motifs and invests in heightened physicality, we are made aware of the cultural importance of a politicized and outspoken Cordelia who, unmarried, escapes death at the production's close.[5] As Sangeeta Datta has argued, the weight of representation is such that the time is ripe for appraisals that attend to how Indian representations challenge 'masculine concoction[s]', making available 'alternate subjective vision[s]' (2000: 75). Her call is echoed in assessments of the film adaptations of Vishal Bhardwaj and their enlistment of the woman as avenger figure (Trivedi 2019: 25) and in arguments that highlight the ideological freight attached to representations of women and agency (Chatterjee 2019: 93–110; García-Periago 2021: 349–66). In the parallel processes of creation and challenge, it is possible to see a transformed Shakespeare, a playwright who appears differently when seen through the gendered eyes of a new Indian, diasporic and global generation of critics, historians, archivists, practitioners and directors. The terms of this collection's title, we hope, will spark fresh ways of thinking even as they interrogate existing modes of thought.

II

Part One (**Histories**) explores the vibrant history of women's involvement with Shakespeare in India. Chapter 1 by Poonam Trivedi ('The "woman's part": Recovering the contribution of women to the circulation of Shakespeare in India') establishes, for the first time, a pantheon of many of the 'invisibilized' Indian women who were instrumental in creating and circulating the entity of 'Shakespeare' in India. Introducing obscured but representative figures of colonial India's earliest Shakespearean actresses (English and Indian), her essay moves on to examine the role of selected local female scholars, translators and directors of Shakespeare, tracing their life histories through the socio-political upheavals surrounding India's Independence to today's Shakespearean offerings with their 'decolonized' yet hybrid sources of modernity. Trivedi foregrounds a revisionist perspective while recording and reviewing these women's stories and their public achievements, hitherto neglected or erased. This first chapter serves as both an introduction to women who shaped Indian Shakespeares and an overview of women's wide-ranging contributions to the field across text, performance and cinema.

Chapter 2, 'Framing femininities: Desdemona and Indian modernities', by Paromita Chakravarti, traces echoes of Desdemona through several post-colonial works and their afterlives, dwelling on a moment in which the journeys of a Shakespearean heroine help to mark significant shifts in India's social, cultural, political and cinematic histories. It sets out how Tarashankar Bandyopadhyay's Bengali novel, *Saptapadi* (1959), and its cinematic adaptation, *Saptapadi* (dir. Ajoy Kar, 1961), in turn influenced the Tamil language film, *Ratha Thilagam* (dir. Dada Mirasi, 1963), and the Hindi Bollywood thriller, *Hamraaz* (dir. B. R. Chopra, 1967). These works cite Desdemona's murder scene from *Othello* to articulate ideas of transgressive love, partnership, marriage and communal conflict, suggesting how these may be negotiated within the modern vision of the emerging post-colonial nation. The imaginary of the new nation is sited on the construction of Desdemona's character and draws from as well as frames notions of normative Indian femininity as it emerges through a dialectic of tradition and modernity. In closing, the chapter contemplates *Saptapadi*'s legacy half a century on, considering intertextual allusions in the Bengali love tragedy, *Hrid Majharey* (dir. Ranjan Ghosh, 2014), a film that deploys *Othello* in narrating a private story of heartbreak, jealousy and spiralling unreason to examine a very different conception of Indian neoliberal modernity.

Part Two (Translations) looks at women as both authors and subjects of Indian-language translations of Shakespeare. In Chapter 3, British Library Curators Priyanka Basu and Arani Ilankuberan guide us through Indian-language Shakespeare translations in the 'Two Centuries of Indian Print' project and South Indian Collections respectively, examining their prefatory material, illustrations and content to illuminate 'Indian colonial ... socio-historical and political attitudes towards women in the nineteenth and early twentieth centuries' (p. 66). The chapter first studies Bengali-language Shakespeare translations and adaptations, discussing how translators 'Indianize' or indigenize Shakespeare to harmonize with local nationalist and Hindu sentiments and the manners and customs of colonial India. Furthermore, the chapter provides an overview of Shakespeare translations in the four main South Indian languages of Tamil, Telugu, Kannada and Malayalam. It compares 'Tamilized' tragic Shakespearean heroines to powerful and agential female protagonists from Hindu epics and investigates the 'performative' nature of gender in depictions of comic Shakespearean heroines (often male-acted), which differentiate 'demure' and 'shrewish' women by their clothing, bearing and hairstyles. The chapter equally analyses these texts' prescribed roles and behaviours for women in the social and domestic spheres according to the ideals of chastity, honour and duty these colonial-era 'Indianized' Shakespearean women are meant to represent. This chapter is supported by an Appendix, 'A selection of Shakespeare translations/adaptations from the British Library North Indian Languages Collection'.

Chapter 4 sustains this focus in 'Women translating Shakespeare in South India: *Hemanta Katha* or *The Winter's Tale*', delineating how early local women translators both typify and problematize colonial-era hierarchies and codes of femininity. Thea Buckley explores O. M. Lakshmy Amma's 1892 Malayalam-language prose version of Shakespeare's late play, a rare nineteenth-century female-authored translation from the Lambs' *Tales From Shakespeare*. Buckley locates Lakshmy Amma's position as a female translator amid intersections of feminism, casteism, colonialism and Marxism, linking her preface's emphasis on female education to local matrilineal rulers' literacy initiatives with translations of Shakespeare. *Hemanta Katha*'s onomatopoeic localization and Hinduization of character names and locales are here contextualized in relation to contemporary strategies of translation, including the use of Shakespeare to introduce Western literary ideals of womanhood and female sexual agency in works such as O. Chandu Menon's 1889 romance, *Indulekha*, the first major Malayalam-language novel and one that advocates free marital choice over arranged marriage for its titular heroine. Overall, the chapter demonstrates that these Malayali translators use Shakespeare to both underline and modernize South Indian ideals of femininity in emphasizing gender equality.

The four chapters of **Part Three** (**Representations**) focus on women and their representation in Indian Shakespeares. In Chapter 5, '"I dare do all that may become a man": Martial desires and women as warriors in *Veeram*, a film adaptation of *Macbeth*', Mark Thornton Burnett and Jyotsna G. Singh analyse the destabilization and realignment of gender in Jayaraj's *Veeram* (which translates as 'courage'), a 2016 radical filmic appropriation of *Macbeth* set amid warring Puthooram and Kotha Baidya *kalarippayattu* martial arts clans in medieval Malabar (today's Kerala). *Veeram* foregrounds empowered female warriorhood to unravel *Macbeth*'s tropes of martial masculinity, drawing on matrilineal Malabar's folkloric 'Northern Ballads' to interweave the epic story of Chandu Chekavar/Macbeth, his betrothed Unniyarcha/Macduff and Kuttimani/

Lady Macbeth. In this Hindi/English/Malayalam retelling, these characters form a love triangle of seduction, ambition and betrayal whose divided loyalties cause Aaromal/Duncan's death and bring about Chandu's downfall. *Veeram* mingles martial conflict with aggressive sexual sparring so that even *Macbeth*'s supernatural is eroticised: scenes of snake-worship mix with those of seduction by a dagger-wielding Unniyarcha; a sorceress and trance-bound virgin deliver the prophecy; Kuttimani's un-sexing is replaced by a seduction scene where she gains agency, later absorbing the goddess' *shakti* (female power) and decapitating the *kalari* idols with her *urumi* (flexible sword). Filmed against the fantastical background of North India's Ajanta and Ellora caverns and rock-carvings, and enhanced with ahistorically elaborate costumes, makeup and CGI effects, Jayaraj's vigorous doubly-gendered revision of *Macbeth* fits the new 'turn' in global Shakespeares that Burnett and Singh identify, where adaptations are increasingly debated in terms of both their deployment of local cultures and their international ambitions. In its spectacles of athletic sensuality and ritualized violence, ultimately, the film's titular *veeram* belongs to female warriors.

In Chapter 6, '"You should be women": Bengali femininity and the supernatural in adaptations of *Macbeth*', Taarini Mookherjee continues the previous chapter's exploration of how the play 'troubles an easy separation between gendered identities' (p. 143) while further investigating how two cultural archives – the classical Sanskrit Hindu epics, and the colonially inherited Shakespearean canon – intersect in contemporary Indian cultural production. Framed by Douglas Lanier's theory of the Shakespeare rhizome, Mookherjee's chapter utilizes a wide range of literary and performance texts – particularly Bharati Mukherjee's novel, *Wife* (1987); Kalyani Kalamandalam's 2016 theatrical production, *Macbeth Mirror*; and Vikram Iyengar's 2004–11 dance performance, *Crossings* – to illustrate intertextual connections between 'contemporary Indian engagements with Lady Macbeth and Hindu mythological models of idealized and monstrous femininity' (p. 135). These late twentieth- and early twenty-first-century Bengali Shakespeares appropriate and subvert Indian models of idealized womanhood, which Mookherjee situates in the Hindu *Ramayana* and *Mahabharata* epics and goddess-centric traditions. Through *desification* – Mookherjee's term for *desi* (Indian) adaptation – these three works engage with what *Macbeth* does not, the question of what it means to *be* a woman. In closing, the chapter alludes to West Bengal's contemporary political contexts, analysing how and whether these indigenous representations of Shakespearean femininity remain relevant.

Chapter 7, Nishi Pulugurtha's '*Romeo and Juliet* meets rural India: *Sairat* and the representation of women', analyses the portrayal of tabooed romance across caste and class differences in Nagraj Manjule's 2016 Marathi film adaptation, *Sairat*, set in Maharashtra. Archi/Juliet is a wealthy local politician's daughter from the Maratha caste, while Parshya/Romeo is a Dalit who faces discrimination as the lower-caste son of a poor fisherman. By featuring an upper-caste, dark-skinned female protagonist and a handsome, fair-complexioned young Dalit hero, Manjule's film flips conventional societal stereotypes of beauty. Explaining how *Sairat* innovatively draws attention to ideologies of social and racial equality, Pulugurtha further locates Manjule's adaptation within the Dalit cinema movement, where Dalit filmmakers represent Dalit subjectivities. The film also challenges gender norms; whereas Parshya is passive, Archi drives tractors and makes the first move, displaying striking female agency, even if her character later endures domestic abuse and control. *Sairat*'s violent ending evokes contemporary Indian socio-political issues, from Hindutva anti-Romeo squads that beat up would-be lovers, to 'honour killings' carried out to maintain the social balance of patriarchal power and reinforce caste and class hierarchies.

Chapter 8 looks conversely at deadly female agency, as Jennifer T. Birkett sheds light on how tragic Bollywood Shakespearean heroines kill/are killed with hennaed hands in 'Dy(e)ing hands: The hennaed female agent in Vishal Bhardwaj's tragedies'. Birkett analyses visual henna motifs in *Maqbool/Macbeth* (2003) *Omkara/Othello* (2006) and *Haider/Hamlet* (2014), looking in turn at heroines Nimmi/Lady Macbeth, Dolly/Desdemona, Indu/Emilia, Arshia/Ophelia and Ghazala/Gertrude, to propose that Bhardwaj imbues henna with new symbolism as a token of violent feminine volition. Reading these figures in the tradition of Ugaritic myth's vengeful hennaed goddess Anath and drawing upon Poonam Trivedi's work on female avengers (2019: 23–44), Birkett links henna with the blood of virginity, fertility and death in analysing how Bhardwaj's trilogy deconstructs the Bollywood trope of wedding spectacle by overlaying it with Shakespearean tragedy to conflate marital merriment and misfortune. As henna morphs here from a marital custom to a marker of toxic sensuality, it triggers both female agency and violence, crucial to restoring justice and resolving domestic tragedy.

Part Four (Critics and creatives) considers women as agents, creators, directors and practitioners. In Chapter 9, 'Embattled bodies: Women, land and contemporary politics in *Arshinagar*, a film adaptation of *Romeo and Juliet*', Rosa García-Periago conducts an in-depth examination of Aparna Sen's 2015 Bengali-language film, set in fictional Arshinagar (Mirror-ville). García-Periago argues that Sen's woman-helmed film marks a departure in Indian cinematic representations of women, juxtaposing female bodies and political instability to feature women as long-term victims of senseless violence, without Bollywood's oft-attendant consumerist reification. Through its puppeteer-narrator, *Arshinagar* foregrounds a female voice and representational authority, even as it adds to, nuances or expands Shakespeare's women characters to reveal female bodies as centres of crisis. Sen transposes the Capulet-Montague strife to a longstanding conflict between the town's Muslim (Khan) and Hindu (Mitter) families. The lovers meet cross-dressed during a costume party, where Julekha Khan/Juliet substitutes her veil for a turban while Ronojoy Mitter/Romeo dresses as a Muslim woman; this interchange of signifiers of gender and religion represents loving the mirror 'Other'. *Arshinagar's* mirroring includes generational Juliets – Ronojoy's mother's parents had barred her marriage to Julekha's father. Beyond societal divides, Sen's film explores controversial political issues, such as West Bengal's land acquisition, played out on the nurse-character's (Fatema) body. Amidst chaos, female spaces and support networks of sorority emerge as the antidotes to turmoil in *Arshinagar*.

Chapter 10 continues to centre woman-directed Shakespeare, exploring tabooed same-sex desire in 'Where the wild things are: Shifting identities in *Noblemen*, a film adaptation of *The Merchant of Venice*'. Here, Mark Thornton Burnett delves into Vandana Kataria's 2018 English-language reworking of Shakespeare's play of intolerance, set in Mount Noble High, a fictional North Indian exclusive Christian boys' boarding school. Burnett analyses how Kataria's resetting portrays the wider gamut of intolerance and toxic masculinity latent in residually colonial environments – institutionalized abuse, sadism, sexism, bullying, homophobia and indifference to resulting suicidal levels of psychological suffering. Simultaneously, his chapter reveals what can occur with the absence or exclusion of Shakespeare's female archetypes and qualities such as tolerance and mercy. The catalyst for *Noblemen*'s central tragedy is a school production of *Merchant* in which shy and bullied tenth-grader Shay/Shylock wins the romantic lead. Here, the casket scene is foregrounded as Shay's sexual awakening while watching male drama teacher Murali deliver the Prince of Morocco's speech, 'Mislike me not for my complexion' (2.1.1). Kataria's film further examines race, caste and gender discrimination through Shay's ostracized friends Ganesh/Gratiano, designated the 'fat dark boy', and Pia/Portia, who desperately chops her hair to fit into the boys' club. Ultimately, tortured and sexually assaulted by Bassanio/Baaadal and rejected romantically by Murali, the sensitive schoolboy externalizes his former sufferance of an elite society of corrupted 'noblemen' finally to find himself.

Chapter 11 also looks at student Shakespeare theatricals, but from a different angle. In 'Women punctuating Shakespeare: Campus theatrical experiment, the Shakespeare Society and the insider/outsider dialectic', St Stephen's College professor and dramaturge N. P. Ashley uncovers the work of the Delhi institution's formerly all-male Shakespeare Society (instituted in 1896 as the 'Falstaff Club') and its ninety-four-year-old tradition of staging an annual Shakespeare play. The Society's first Staff Advisor, Ashley provides anecdotes and performance analysis to chart the history of the Anglophilic Indian academy and its gradual evolution to accommodate female guests, members, players and directors. He outlines the process of bridging the Society's split between a fluid, unofficial performance tradition, with the capacity to infiltrate spaces of gender stratification, and a fixed, mainstream textual tradition that framed women in limiting ways. Analysing three of the Society's recent Shakespeare offerings – 'The Blue Pencil', an all-female-directed ensemble piece featuring Shakespeare selections (2011); a full-length *Tempest* (2013); and a slimmed-down version of the same play (2015) – Ashley highlights these adaptations' importance in developing an understanding of college theatre productions, the spaces women occupy and their contributions to the field of Indian Shakespeares, including their potential to counter hyper-masculine rhetoric and majoritarian ideologies with a politicized, representative feminism.

This potential is realized in Chapter 12, 'Adapting Shakespeare: Directors and practitioners in conversation', which features several of the leading women artists and practitioners working at the intersections of adaptation, Shakespeare and India today, in a conversation originally recorded as part of a roundtable at the 'Women and Indian Shakespeares' conference (Queen's University Belfast, 2019) and updated and expanded for publication. Here, filmmakers Bornila Chatterjee and Sangeeta Datta, director-performer Annette Leday, translator Sreedevi Nair and author Preti Taneja respond to five main questions in relation to their distinctive and varied reworkings of Shakespeare's plays for film, translation, theatre, dance and fiction: *The Hungry* (2017), *Life Goes On* (2009), *Kathakali-King Lear* (1989, 2018–19), *The Stars Still Shine on Desdemona* (2019), and *We That Are Young* (2017), respectively. Each contributor reflects in turn on Shakespeare's significances; the challenges of adapting Shakespeare to a new medium; decisions made in relation to the Shakespearean image and language; and the extent to which adaptation enables the emergence of a different kind of 'Shakespeare', including female characters. The final part of the chapter branches out to allow contributors to reflect, variously, on the national, political and gendered aspects of the work of adaptation.

Women and Indian Shakespeares makes visible the ways in which women are variously figured as resistant agents, martial seductresses, redemptive daughters, victims of caste discrimination, conflicted spaces and global citizens. And it identifies how, in Indian Shakespeares on page, stage and screen, women increasingly possess the ability to shape different futures across patriarchal and societal barriers of race, caste, religion and class. In repeated iterations, the collection turns our attention to localized modes of adaptation that open opportunities for women while celebrating Shakespeare's gendered interactions in India's rapidly changing, and increasingly globalized, cultural, economic and political environment. Radically imagining Indian Shakespeares with women at the centre, *Women and Indian Shakespeares* interweaves history, regional geography/regionality, language and the present day to establish a record of women as creators and adapters of Shakespeare in Indian contexts.

Notes

1. The 'Global Shakespeares Video and Performance Archive' web resource (https://globalshakespeares.mit.edu/region/india) features extracts from a range of regional Indian theatre adaptations of Shakespeare (accessed 15 April 2021). See also Rosa García-Periago, 'Database of Indian Shakespeare Films', at: https://www.qub.ac.uk/schools/ael/Research/ResearchinEnglish/ResearchProjectsinEnglish/INDIANSHAKESPEARES/shakespeare%20and%20indian%20cinematic%20traditions%20qub (accessed 4 June 2021).
2. Images from the art piece/cross-media show can be consulted at 'Maya Krishna Rao', available at: http://mayakrishnarao.blogspot.com/p/multi-media.html?m=1 (accessed 14 November 2021). For a wonderful account of her work, see 'Rani Drew', available at: https://ranidrew.wordpress.com/plays (accessed 14 November 2021).
3. The production can be viewed on the 'Global Shakespeares Video and Performance Archive' web resource at: https://globalshakespeares.mit.edu/the-merchant-of-venice-saini-vijeta-2019 (accessed 1 April 2021). See also here Varsha Panjwani's exciting podcast series, 'Women and Shakespeare', available at: http://womenandshakespeare.com (accessed 3 June 2021).
4. Consensual homosexuality was decriminalized in India only in 2018. See Safi (2018: 27).
5. The production is available for view on Trivedi (2006).

References

Banerji, R. (2012), '"Every College Student Knows by Heart": The Uses of Shakespeare in Colonial Bengal', *The Shakespearean International Yearbook*, 12: 29–42.

Bhatia, N. (2007), 'Different *Othello(s)* and Contentious Spectators: Changing Responses in India', *Gramma*, 15: 155–74.

Buckley, T. (2016), 'Indian Shakespeare in the World Shakespeare Festival', in S. Panja and B. M. Saraf (eds), *Performing Shakespeare in India: Exploring Indianness, Literatures and Cultures*, 77–91, New Delhi and London: SAGE.

Burnett, M. T. (2019), 'Gendered Play and Regional Dialogue in *Nanjundi Kalyana*', in P. Trivedi and P. Chakravarti (eds), *Shakespeare and Indian Cinemas: 'Local Habitations'*, 221–37, London and New York: Routledge.

Burnett, M. T. (2013), *Shakespeare and World Cinema*, Cambridge: Cambridge University Press.

Chakravarti, P. (2019), 'Interview with Aparna Sen', in P. Trivedi and P. Chakravarti (eds), *Shakespeare and Indian Cinemas: 'Local Habitations'*, 304–16, London and New York: Routledge.

Chakravarti, P. and S. Ganguly (2010), 'Dancing to Shakespeare: Crossing Genre and Gender in the Tragedies', in P. Trivedi and M. Ryuta (eds), *Re-playing Shakespeare in Asia*, 271–90, New York and London: Routledge.

Chatterjee, K. (2019), '"Where art thou Muse that thou forget'st so long, / To speak of that which gives thee all thy might?": *Qayamat Se Qayamat Tak* (1988) – A Neglected Shakespearean Film', in P. Trivedi and P. Chakravarti (eds), *Shakespeare and Indian Cinemas: 'Local Habitations'*, 93–110, London and New York: Routledge.

Collins, P. H. and S. Bilge (2016), *Intersectionality*, Cambridge and Malden: Polity.

Dadabhoy, A. (2021), 'Something's Rotten in Kashmir: Postcolonial Ambivalence and the War on Terror in Vishal Bhardwaj's *Haider*', *Shakespeare*, 17 (1): 15–28.

Datta, S. (2000), 'Globalisation and Representations of Women in Indian Cinema', *Social Scientist*, 28 (3–4): 71–82.

Dionne, C. and P. Kapadia, eds (2014), *Bollywood Shakespeares*, Basingstoke and New York: Palgrave.

Földváry, K. (2020), *Cowboy Hamlets and Zombie Romeos: Shakespeare in Genre Film*, Manchester: Manchester University Press.

García-Periago, R. (2021), 'Localizing *Romeo and Juliet*: *Ram-Leela*, Female Agency, and Indian Politics', *Adaptation*, 14 (3): 349–66.

Haider (2014), [Film] Dir. Vishal Bhardwaj, India: UTV Motion Pictures.

Harris, J. G. (2018), *Masala Shakespeare: How a Firangi Writer Became Indian*, New Delhi: Aleph Books.

The Hungry (2017), [Film] Dir. Bornila Chatterjee, India/UK: Cinestaan/ Film London.

Joubin, A. A. (2021), *Shakespeare and East Asia*, Oxford: Oxford University Press.

Kannaki (2002), [Film] Dir. Jayaraj, India: Neelambari Productions.

Kapadia, P. (2008), 'Jatra Shakespeare: Indigenous Indian Theater and the Postcolonial Stage', in C. Dionne and P. Kapadia (eds), *Native Shakespeares: Indigenous Appropriations on a Global Stage*, 91–103, Aldershot and Burlington: Ashgate.

Lehmann, C. (2016), '"An élan of the soul"? Counter-cinema and Deepa Mehta's *Water*', *Shakespeare Bulletin*, 34 (3): 433–50.

Life Goes On (2009), [Film] Dir. Sangeeta Datta, UK/India: Stormglass Productions.

Loomba, A. (1993), 'Hamlet in Mizoram', in M. Novy (ed.), Cross-Cultural Performances: Differences in Women's Re-Visions of Shakespeare, 227–50, Urbana and Chicago: University of Illinois Press.
Loomba, A. (2005), 'Shakespeare and the Possibilities of Postcolonial Performance', in B. Hodgdon and W. B. Worthen (eds), A Companion to Shakespeare and Performance, 121–37, Malden and Oxford: Blackwell.
Maqbool (2003), [Film] Dir. Vishal Bhardwaj, India: Kaleidoscope Entertainment.
Mookherjee, T. (2019), 'Theorizing the Neighbor: *Arshinagar* and *Romeo and Juliet*', Borrowers and Lenders, 12 (2): 1–21. Available online: https://openjournals.libs.uga.edu/borrowers/article/view/2374 (accessed 15 March 2021).
Mukherjee, B. (1987), Wife, New York: Penguin.
Nair, S. (2019), The Stars Still Shine on Desdemona, Thiruvananthapuram: Samyukta Research Foundation.
Panja, S. (2020), 'Critiquing Globalization: Transnational Technologies in *Arshinagar*, Aparna Sen's Bengali Adaptation of *Romeo and Juliet*', Shakespeare Bulletin, 38 (4): 573–92.
Panja, S. and B. M. Saraf (2016), 'Introduction', in S. Panja and B. M. Saraf (eds), Performing Shakespeare in India: Exploring Indianness, Literatures and Cultures, 1–21, New Delhi and London: SAGE.
Panjwani, V. (2018), 'Juliet in *Ram-Leela*: A Passionate Sita', Shakespeare Studies, 46: 110–20.
Safi, M. (2018), '"A Great First Step": Elation in India after Gay Sex is Legalised', The Guardian, 7 September: 27.
Sen, S. (2021), Shakespeare in the World: Cross-Cultural Adaptation in Europe and Colonial India, 1850–1900, New York and London: Routledge.
Shankar, D. A., ed. (1999), Shakespeare in Indian Languages, Shimla: Indian Institute of Advanced Study.
Singh, J. G. (1989), 'Different Shakespeares: The Bard in Colonial/Postcolonial India', Theatre Journal, 41 (4): 445–58.
Singh, J. G. (2019), Shakespeare and Postcolonial Theory, London and New York: Bloomsbury.
Taneja, P. (2018), 'Breaking Curfew, Presenting Utopia: Vishal Bhardwaj's *Haider* Inside the National and International Legal Framework', in A. I. Devasundaram (ed.), Indian Cinema Beyond Bollywood, 46–65, London and New York: Routledge.
Taneja, P. (2017), We That Are Young, Norwich: Galley Beggar Press.
Thakur, V. S. (2020), Shakespeare and Indian Theatre: The Politics of Performance, London and New York: Bloomsbury.
Trivedi, P. (2007), '"Filmi" Shakespeare', Literature / Film Quarterly, 35 (2): 148–58.

Trivedi, P. (2020), 'Fooling around with Shakespeare: The Curious Case of "Indian" *Twelfth Night*s', in C. Desmet, S. Iyengar and M. Jacobson (eds), *The Routledge Handbook of Shakespeare and Global Appropriation*, 113–23, London and New York: Routledge.

Trivedi, P. (2021), 'Making Meaning between the Local and the Global: Performing Shakespeare in India Today', in P. Trivedi, P. Chakravarti and T. Motohashi (eds), *Asian Interventions in Global Shakespeare: 'All the World's His Stage'*, 15–32, London and New York: Routledge.

Trivedi, P. (2006), *Shakespeare in India: 'King Lear'*, a multimedia CD-ROM.

Trivedi, P. (2019), 'Woman as Avenger: "Indianising" the Shakespearean Tragic in the Films of Vishal Bhardwaj', in P. Trivedi and P. Chakravarti (eds), *Shakespeare and Indian Cinemas: 'Local Habitations'*, 23–44, London and New York: Routledge.

Trivedi, P. and D. Bartholomeusz, eds (2005), *India's Shakespeare: Translation, Interpretation and Performance*, Newark: University of Delaware Press.

Trivedi, P. and P. Chakravarti (2019), 'Introduction', in P. Trivedi and P. Chakravarti (eds), *Shakespeare and Indian Cinemas: 'Local Habitations'*, 1–19, London and New York: Routledge.

Water (2005), [Film] Dir. Deepa Mehta, Canada, India and USA: David Hamilton Productions.

Young, S. (2019), *Shakespeare in the Global South: Stories of Oceans Crossed in Contemporary Adaptation*, London and New York: Bloomsbury.

PART ONE

Histories

1

The 'woman's part': Recovering the contribution of women to the circulation of Shakespeare in India

Poonam Trivedi

It is unfortunately true that, despite the radicalizing energies released by feminism, women's full contribution to society and its development, especially in the arts, continues to remain largely hidden from history in India, undocumented and undervalued. While the position of women in India in all fields over different time periods in the many separate regional and linguistic cultures has received substantial academic investigation in the postcolonial period, gaps in our knowledge remain. Indian theatre history is one such area and recouping the 'woman's part' (*Twelfth Night*, 1.4.34) in it, especially in the niche, but significant, interest area of Shakespeare studies, presents particular challenges. The historiography of India's performing arts in general, and of theatre in particular, continues to remain a nascent and contested area of enquiry. Several studies have emerged in recent decades, but they are necessarily confined to regional/linguistic/generic/ periodization specificities, which often throw up competing points of view and give little space to women's contributions (Gokhale 2000; Dharwadker 2005; Dalmia 2006; Sathe 2015; and Kosambi 2015). Studies of women in theatre too show similar selectivity (Bhatia 2010 and Mangai 2015). Within these, Shakespeare gets at the most a brief acknowledgement of his influence in the early stages on the growth of regional drama, but almost nothing on the performance of his plays and the participation of women in them, unless attention focuses on the colonial period (Sengupta 2005; Majumdar 2005; Chatterjee 2007; Singh 2009; Dutt and Munsi 2010; Gooptu 2015; and Bhattacharya 2018). Hence, locating the largely invisible contribution of Indian women to the circulation of Shakespeare in India is, firstly, an urgent matter of establishing the archive: of uncovering and documenting, largely for the first time, the role of Indian women – performers, directors, scholars, translators, teachers and critics from all around the country who were instrumental in creating and sustaining the larger entity of 'Shakespeare' in India. In the attempts to retrieve evidence, however, we need to be alert to the power politics inherent in the processes of archive making, of the implications of selectivity and of the silences and erasures inevitably inherent in the archives, and to foreground a revisionist perspective by embedding women's stories within their cultural and economic materialities which both stimulate and contain their agency, resisting the tendency to simply reproduce a galaxy of exemplary women. This sensitization would be especially helpful in tracing the Shakespearean strand in Indian performative and literary cultures, which is often relegated as marginal and tangential, but was in fact foundational and continues to remain potent. Research on Shakespeare often meets with quizzical looks in India: 'Why this obsessing with Shakespeare?' is not an infrequent question. Local, indigenous perception can be dismissive of the effort, putting it down to being locked in a residual colonial hangover. These attitudes, however, reflect the ongoing but incomplete decolonization which has swerved from seeing colonial influence in everything, to rejecting it altogether, to a slow recognition of the hybrid sources of our modernity, especially in our theatre histories. It therefore becomes doubly important to take a more discriminating perspective to estimate the nature of influence, its absorption and evolution, tracing interpretative communities in which the grand narratives comprise micro-histories, particularly where women in the 'Shake-story' in India are concerned.

Hence, to begin with, it would be apt to exploit the multiple significations of Shakespeare's phrase, 'a woman's part', and openly side with women, pick them out and try to recoup, as far as current research allows, their part in the circulation of Shakespeare in India. And to stretch the implied pun, to show how in theatre history women won the right to perform the woman's part in India, what they learnt from and contributed to the interpretation of these Shakespearean roles through their playing of their own body languages, and finally how, in what 'semblative' ways, with 'lip ... smooth and rubious' and with 'small pipe ... shrill and sound' (*Twelfth Night*, 1.4.31-4) or with bold moves and dancing steps, women in India have continued to play out and play with Shakespeare. It is of course impossible to document all women over the nearly 250 years that Shakespeare has been present in India, so the focus will be on the obscured but representative figures of the earliest actresses (English and Indian), of a scholar, a translator and a director – each of whose work is symptomatic of key moments in the development of the Shakespearean presence.

The English actress

Shakespeare came to India as an entertainer. Theatres were among the earliest buildings erected by the English traders in the three settlements of Calcutta – in *c.* 1753/7, Bombay 1776 and Madras 1780 to provide for their 'divertissements'. The earliest performers were all amateurs, English and male, volunteering from the army, company and other civilians. Female impersonation by men on stage was the norm, women being proscribed by convention from performing their own parts until 3 January 1788, when, as the *Calcutta Gazette* (18 December 1788) has it, the 'novel appearance of a lady whose condescension to grace the Calcutta stage' (Das Gupta 2002: I, 207) changed things forever. Western-style theatre, of a text being enacted on a black box proscenium stage, was first witnessed in Calcutta (founded 1690), which therefore provided the space, and the opportunity, for the emergence of the earliest actresses, English, and later, Indian, of the modern period in India. Names of actresses of ancient India do not survive, though it is well known that women had a sanctioned role as *nati* (actress) in Sanskrit theatre which flourished *c*. 400BCE-1000CE. Women performers, like dancers, singers and musicians, flourished through the ages, but the identifiable 'actress', enacting a scripted role, comes into being only with the emulation of Western theatre practice in India. Hence, it becomes imperative in this archival reconstruction to explore the circumstances which incentivized the English actresses and impacted their talents, and to redress a strand of narrow postcolonial parochialism in Indian theatre historiography which is apt to undermine, even erase, the fundamental formative influence of the early English actresses.

In the 1780s, Calcutta was a small settlement comprising the officers and servitors of the East India Company and its attendant army, and the lives of the early English actresses are part and parcel of these twin pillars of the colonial and expatriate society. The need for entertainment was paramount and, paradoxically, the army was more instrumental in this. Mrs Emma Bristow, who was the one to boldly grace the Calcutta stage in 1788, and who can be termed the first amateur actress of modern India, was the daughter of a soldier, born Amelia Wrangham, who had earlier made her way from St Helena, an EIC and army outpost, to Calcutta, and had so charmed the society of Calcutta that she was feted in the gossip columns which were agog with speculation about her many suitors. In May 1782, at the young age of nineteen, she married a merchant almost twice her age, John Bristow. In January 1788, she appeared at the Old Courthouse assembly to sing and perform, transforming in the process from being the 'toast of Calcutta' to becoming its 'prima donna'. Such was the frisson created by this event that the established Calcutta Theatre (1775–1808) was free to follow suit. Several women performers were soon formally engaged to add to the pleasures of theatre going.

Mrs Bristow was more than a femme fatale: her social ambitions led her to set up a private theatre of her own in her Chowringhee house to 'entertain their wide circle of friends' which was described in the *Calcutta Gazette* (7 May 1789) as giving 'the most perfect gratification ... in a perfect theatre differing only from a public one in its dimensions' (Das Gupta 2002: I, 211–13). She even organized a troupe of all-female amateurs who were emboldened to perform virile parts: her own role of Lucius in *Julius Caesar* caused quite a flutter.

Even though Mrs Bristow had a brief acting career – she left for England in 1790 – this bold and enthusiastic young woman broke the genteel barrier, exploiting male voyeurism to pioneer a public space for other female performers, English, and later, Indian, in Calcutta. Through such indirections did women's performance of Shakespeare find a starting direction in India.

It was with the next generation of theatres that the actress and the performance of Western drama and Shakespeare came into its own in Calcutta. This may be ascribed to the singular talents of Esther Leach (1809–1843) who was the undoubted star of the main Chowringhee Theatre (1813–1839), earning the sobriquet of the 'Siddons of Bengal' (Shaw 1958: 304). Her stellar position was underlined in Emily Eden's (sister of the Governor General) observation in October 1841 that she had 'for eighteen years been the only professional actress in India' (Nair 1989: 747). Her induction into the theatre, like that of her predecessor Mrs Bristow, the first amateur actress, reveals much about the position of the 'theatricals' in the social complex of early Anglo-India.

Like Mrs Bristow, Esther Leach, too, was the daughter of an English soldier, Mr Flatman, but born and bred in India, in 1809. She was married at an early age to a non-commissioned officer, John Leach, a widower and seventeen years her senior, like Mrs Bristow's husband, almost twice her age. But there were crucial class differences between the two: Mrs Bristow married into the ruling elite, and her husband John Bristow, a senior merchant, was an ally and close friend of Sir Philip Francis, a rival of the Governor General, Warren Hastings. Hence, she could 'host' theatricals. Esther Leach's success, on the other hand, was entirely due to her innate talents. J. H. Stocqueler, journalist and amateur actor who performed alongside Esther Leach, brings her to life in his *Memoirs*. We are told that her scholastic training may not have been of a high order but developed her 'natural aptitude for getting pieces by heart' (Stocqueler 1873: 92). She had distinguished herself as a child in *Tom Thumb* and *Little Pickle* and was gifted a copy of Shakespeare, a turning point:

> She became a devotee of the mighty bard, and thenceforth devoured everything in the shape of dramatic poetry and prose which happily came in her way. Her fame traveled to Calcutta, and

she, nothing loath, accepted an engagement at the Chowringhee Theatre. This necessitated her husband's transfer to Fort William as garrison sergeant major. He was not the first man who owed his advancement to his wife.

(Stocqueler 1873: 92)

She joined the Chowringhee Theatre in 1827 and for eleven years reigned as the Queen of the 'Calcutta Drury' (as the English press called the Chowringhee Theatre), the cachet legitimating hers as a serious histrionic talent. In Stocqueler's words:

> Esther Leach ... was singularly gifted. Extremely pretty, very intelligent, modest, and amiable, possessing a musical voice and good taste, she adapted herself to all the requirements of the drama. The *ingénue* and the *soubrette*, the leading parts in such plays as *Othello*, the *Wife*, the *Hunchback*, and the *Lady of Lyons*, the highest flights in comedy, the pantomimic action of *La Muette* ... were all alike to this clever child of nature.
>
> (Stocqueler 1873: 91)

Such was the admiration that, when she played Katherine, the critics exclaimed 'this is the shrew that Shakespeare drew', forgetting that the play was actually Garrick's *Catherine and Petruchio* (Shaw 1958: 306)! In 1836, she lost her husband, and, with her health failing, she undertook a visit to England, from January 1838 to June 1839. On her return she found that the Chowringhee Theatre had burnt down to the ground a month before.

Esther Leach displayed another talent of the actress-manager: she immediately leased another building, fitted up a temporary theatre, under the name of the Sans Souci, which opened in August 1839, and sent out an appeal for subscription of a larger theatre. Contributions poured in, including a handsome amount from a new Governor General, Lord Auckland, and many Indians including Dwarakanath Tagore, grandfather of Rabindranath, who had also bailed out the debt of the Calcutta Theatre earlier. Other actresses, 'general utility' actors and a scene-painter from England were hired. The Sans Souci thus augmented and consolidated the foundational role of the early English theatre in India by employing professional actors both female and male. Until then, both male and many female roles had been performed by 'gentlemen actors', mainly from the army.

Esther Leach may thus be seen as the first successful actress-cum-theatre manager in India. In fact, having been born and brought up indigenously, she may even be considered as the first modern Indian actress, especially since she died tragically, in 1843, when during a performance of *The Merchant of Venice* her dress caught fire, and now she lies buried at the Military Cemetery, Bhowanipore.

Esther Leach's daughter, Mrs Anderson, has a notable place in the performance of Shakespeare in India too. She was the Desdemona to Vaishnav Charan Auddy's 'real unpainted n****r Othello' (Raha 1978: 13), as an English newspaper report had it, the only performance of an Indian actor with an English actress in the colonial period, in 1848, at the Sans Souci Theatre.

Thus, we find that, though English theatre in India begins to thrive only when women come out to participate in it, right from the beginning, the English colonial actress is enmeshed in a nexus of gender, class, politics, pleasure and imperialism, factors which affect the later reception and participation of the Indian actress too. The women were pushed to perform and professionalize through a combination of factors of visibility, social mobility and economic circumstances. Though feted and courted in the press, they were always addressed as 'Mrs' to maintain a veneer of respectability. Calcutta had its share of puritan theatre haters too inveighing against it as a 'house of sin' and the actresses had to bear this stigmatization. Their financial status was usually precarious, 'benefit' performances were arranged frequently and, when the Chowringhee Theatre suddenly burnt down in 1839, many female actors were so distressed that the proceeds of the opening night of the Sans Souci went to their repatriation.

Moreover, the theatre along with its attendant actresses was co-opted into a propagandist role for the empire: in a speech made at the dinner celebrating the opening of the Sans Souci Theatre, on 6 March 1841, Sir John Peter Grant, Supreme Court judge, remarked that he attended the theatre as much from a sense of public duty as from the motives of private entertainment, and he looked upon drama on a well-organized stage as, according to the *Asiatic Journal* of May 1841, a great instrument of civilization and refinement (Das Gupta 2002: I, 270).

English theatre and staging practice in Calcutta had a profound impact on the elite Indians who began frequenting performances, especially of Shakespeare, whose plays had begun to be taught in schools and colleges set up by the English. Not only did they actively support the theatre with substantial financial aid, but they were also inspired by it to create their own theatres in direct imitation. In Bombay, English theatre started later than in Calcutta, but went through similar phases of development. Here, since the expatriate community was smaller and the audience was not quite so homogeneous, theatrical activity was limited, and no outstanding name among the amateurs is recorded. Here too, women only performed privately, in home theatricals. The first actress of note is Mrs Deacle, who left the Calcutta Sans Souci to take up the position of the manager of the newly opened Grant Road Theatre, which was inaugurated in 1846 with a performance of *The Merchant of Venice*. Here too, local communities of the Marathi and the Parsis were deeply impacted by this Western style of playgoing. More so than in Calcutta, the elite of Bombay saw in the theatre a new area of influence and participated in theatre building with gifts of land and capital. They too soon set up their own theatres and companies.

The British army records reveal another actress, Mrs Cuppage, a lesser known but talented amateur. As noted earlier, the army played a major role in promoting theatrical activity: it set up theatres in all cantonment towns and started Amateur Dramatic Clubs to organize the entertainments. Officers along with civilians and their families participated in concerts, recitals and plays. Among the hundreds who performed, the name of one representative amateur female actor, Mrs Cuppage, has survived.[1] She was one of those who dared to take on Shakespeare and who performed the role of Nerissa at the only Shakespeare production at the Simla Gaiety, called the 'Mecca of amateur theatre', which was a 1898 burlesque, *The Merry Merchant of Venice*. She was the wife of Major Willie Adam Cuppage (who acted as Lorenzo) of the Indian Army posted in the north, 1881–1905, and the Cuppages were a talented couple, much in demand for their singing and histrionic skills. They debuted in a Simla Gaiety production in 1894–5 of the play *Women's Wrongs*. Their thespian status and success were further confirmed with their inclusion in the one and only Shakespeare, albeit a burlesque. Mrs Cuppage's pinnacle of success came when she was cast as the lead in *San Toy* at the Rink, Mussoorie, 9–14 September 1904 and was complimented with a gift by no less than the Maharajah of Kapurthala (Trivedi 2016: 103–20). Amateur theatricals too had a seminal impact in India: soon, ordinary Indians organized themselves into ADCs (amateur drama companies) and emulated role-playing of the histrionic kind.

The Indian actress

Recovering the presence of the Indian performers of the woman's part is more complicated, with several competing strands of narrative from different regions and languages coming into play. The earliest Indian actress emerges predictably in Calcutta, in the very first Bengali public play, Herasim Lebedeff's twin bill in translation, 1795, advertised as being performed by actors of 'both sexes', though nothing more is known about them. The next recorded instance is in 1835 of a performance from *Vidyasundar*, a quasi-*Romeo and Juliet* eighteenth-century narrative poem, which had as many as four female roles performed by women and was staged as a private affair. In 1873, Michael Madhusudan Dutta's *Sharmistha* (said to be influenced by *As You Like It*) at the Bengal Theatre included actresses. This performance, which is held as pioneering the introduction of women as professional performers on the public stage in Calcutta and in India, was both welcomed and reviled for its inclusion of women, triggering a huge debate on their suitability as public role models, since these women came from red-light or courtesan households. This controversy soon raged all over India, peaking at different times with varying inflections wherever Western style theatres were developing. As Rimli Bhattacharya has put it, 'the changing equations from between occupation and marital status, between sexual and aesthetic codes and the contradictions therein, were visibly embodied' in the actress, questioning 'the legitimacy of impersonation' (2018: 4–5). Indian society, while deeply attracted to Western theatre, was not quite ready to accept its ramifications, especially with regard to female performers. Morality, idealism and nationalism were also brought to bear on this issue in the early twentieth century.

These debates have been extensively documented and analysed, as have the stories of the most well-known actresses of this early period, especially from Bengal. To recall those with a particular relation with Shakespeare, Teenkori acted as Lady Macbeth in Girish Ghosh's Scots *Macbeth* in 1893, and Tarasundari performed

Lady Macbeth, Ophelia (1896), Desdemona (1919) and Cleopatra (1913) in Bengali adaptations over a career of forty-six years. However, the most celebrated of the early Bengali actresses, Binodini Dasi, did not directly perform any Shakespearean roles, but was hugely influenced by their example. Her autobiography, a rare account, states that 'I would be anxious to see the performance of any British actor or actress who happened to come to the city' (1998: 78) and that she learnt her craft inspired by the stories that her mentor Girish Ghosh would narrate about Mrs Siddons, Ellen Terry, and other famous British actresses. In fact, the model of the English theatre was repeatedly held up by critics not just as an ideal for honing the performative skills of these early actresses but also for endowing those who were commonly perceived as 'fallen women' with respectability and legitimacy.

Almost around the same time, in 1872, in Bombay, a singer and dancer, Latifa Begum, was engaged to act by the Parsi Theatrical Company only to be immediately abducted from the theatre. This caused a furore, but such was the novelty of the female performer that it did not prevent other companies from vying for actresses, and female-oriented plays began to be written. The British army supplied actresses for the Indian stage too: Mary Fenton (known as Mehar Bai), country-born daughter of an Irish soldier, trained in song and dance and well versed in Gujarati, Hindi and Urdu, became Parsi theatre's most successful professional actress when she married Kavasji Khatau, a Parsi actor and theatre manager. She is said to have performed in *Khudadad*, an Urdu adaptation of *Pericles*, in 1898, and might be the first female performer in a Parsi Shakespeare play, but the existence of multiple versions of this play precludes confirming her position. As is well known, Parsi theatre (1860–1930) adapted and amalgamated around twenty-five Shakespeare plays and popularized them in its characteristic flamboyant and spectacular manner, but the names of the actresses who performed in them represent an archive waiting to be consolidated.

The appearance of the actress in Marathi and Gujarati theatres, which were also happening simultaneously in Bombay, came later in the early twentieth century and was also deeply contested by audiences and critics. Here the popularity of the female impersonator, men playing female roles in the *sangeet nataks* (musical plays), who overlapped with the actresses for a decade or so, added another layer to the debate on the actress, now on 'authentic Indian femininity' and whether cross-dressing was a more effective means of achieving it. However, as with the case of the Parsi theatre and Latifa Begum, the scopophilic pleasures of a more naturalistic performance, feminine singing voices, the ageing of the female impersonators and, significantly, the advent of cinema (talkies, 1931) soon swept aside these male moralizings.

A close scrutiny of the archives of performance in Bombay reveals that the very first Marathi stage actress, Kamalabai Gokhale (1900–1998), also the first star of the silver screen, has a Shakespearean connection. She had begun her film career acting with Dadasaheb Phalke in *Mohini Bhasmasur*, but significantly her first stage appearance was in *Vikar Vilasita*, Agarkar's Marathi translation of *Hamlet*, in 1905, at the age of five, playing the role of a boy in the play-within-the-play, along with her mother Durgabai, who was also in a bit role. Kamalabai is also said to have acted in Marathi adaptations of *Hamlet, Romeo and Juliet* and *Othello*. Women began performing the female parts in the many Marathi translations of Shakespeare from the early twentieth century onwards, but the life stories of many have yet to be recovered.

It is only by the mid-twentieth century that educated women joined theatre, more out of serious interest than economic necessity, and as in Calcutta, in Bombay too, many proved their skills in Shakespearean roles. Durga Khote, for example, a well-known Bollywood actress who began acting in the theatre, played Lady Macbeth in *Rajmukuta*, a Marathi translation/adaptation by V. V. Shirwadkar, alongside the legendary actor Nanasaheb Phatak as Macbeth in 1954. Another, Vijaya Mehta, a doyen of later Marathi theatre, also played Desdemona opposite Nanasaheb Phatak in *Zunzarrao*, Deval's translation of *Othello*, also in 1954. Vijaya Mehta, of a later generation, recalls how her experience of performing a classical role like Desdemona at the age of eighteen was a learning experience, as was acting with Nanasaheb, who had great physical presence: 'he had absolutely hypnotic piercing eyes … one could hardly look into those dark satanic eyes … remember, the [last] scene … is itself frightening for the actress who plays Desdemona … Othello was an education for me which has remained like an island in my career' (Paul 1989: 14). Shakespeare's influence on Indian drama was not confined to scripting and dramaturgy; the performance of his strong characters enabled many actresses, earlier Binodini, later Vijaya Mehta, for instance, to mature as artists; the strengths they gained went into the shaping of other roles in Indian plays, 'pointing to the forging of a tradition of female performance ... through Shakespeare' (Sengupta 2005: 256).

The scholar

Theatre is a group activity: performers, especially the actresses, always garner immediate attention, but they are the final flowering of an elaborate process. We need to look behind the scenes for those who put them there: the scholars who unearthed their histories, the translators who shaped their scripts, the directors who visualized their performances and the critics who estimated and promoted them.

First and foremost among the invisible women is Dr Kumudini Arvind Mehta (1925–89), who has been adjudged by writer and theatre critic Shanta Gokhale, 'an extremely important presence on the theatre scene in the city (Mumbai) during the seventies and eighties' (2016: 76) Ironically, it is Mehta's home and hospitality which created a meeting point – a salon of sorts – for theatre persons, artists, writers, academics, politicians and so on, providing a breeding ground for the experimental theatre movement in Bombay, which is most talked about now. However, Mehta's most significant contribution is her extensive and painstaking research undertaken towards her PhD thesis for the University of Bombay, titled *English Drama on the Bombay Stage in the late Eighteenth Century and in the Nineteenth Century* (1960), which has been until now relegated to the stray citation in the footnotes of a few theatre historians. This thesis, unfortunately not published till 2021, is the single most comprehensive and authoritative source of information about the growth and development of the Western form of theatre in Bombay, including the beginnings of the performance of Shakespeare. It marks several firsts: beyond its invaluable documentation, it takes a decidedly postcolonial view when it states in the synopsis that it 'examines theatre concepts planted on Indian soil from the outside – concepts at variance with the traditions of the indigenous and classical theatre of India'.[2] It therefore does not confine itself to English drama but also charts the beginnings of Marathi playwriting, Parsi theatre and amateur theatricals in Bombay in the mid-nineteenth century under the influence of English drama. Most significantly, the thesis, much ahead of its time, and perhaps the first in India, treats 'drama' not as literary texts to be read but as plays to be performed. Mehta's work charts the development of 'playgoing' in Western India which, as Sharmistha Saha has put it, was the critical development of a 'society' of playgoers and the 'sociabilities' (2021: 9–10) consequent to it – a cultural formation new to Indians in the eighteenth century. Further, this reconstruction of the growth of theatre in Western India in the thesis provides a much-needed comparative corrective, since the history of early Indian theatre has been dominated by its initial growth in Bengal.

When I began my work on Shakespeare in India almost twenty-five years ago, before the days of laptops and internet, a chance encounter with this thesis in a foreign university library was like stumbling upon a gold mine, so full of detailed information it was, not just about performances, but also about the playhouses; their patrons and their politics; the economies of theatre-going; the visiting companies; the development of amateur groups; their acting styles; their reception; the audiences; and, most crucially, the interactions between the English theatre and that in the Indian languages, Marathi, Gujarati and Urdu, all what led to theatre becoming an indelible part of the literary, social and commercial life of the city of Bombay. A wondrous new world was opened up in the thesis, and I devoured it hungrily, filling whole notebooks with precious references, which I later followed up for a fuller picture. It was not just a fortuitous discovery, but also a timely one; many of the early newspaper collections which I rushed to consult were crumbling in my hands. Kumudini Mehta's work has had a foundational impact on my research. Several studies of theatre in Western India have since been written, but none has the range and breadth of Kumudini Mehta's work, and Shakespeare figures prominently, laying the ground for and proving the seminal impact his work has had in the early stages of the development of different Indian theatres.

What was the motivation behind this meticulous research? Who were her mentors, and why English drama? Paradoxically, for an influential public personality, not too much is known about Kumudini Mehta's personal life and career. We know that she studied English Literature at Elphinstone College in Bombay, where she met her husband, Arvind Mehta. She accompanied him for further study to the UK, where she took a degree in Library Science, acquiring skills which explain her meticulous theatre research. On her return she taught at colleges of the University of Bombay even while she was pursuing her PhD research. Meantime, she became increasingly involved with theatre, encouraging many young artists in their experimental ventures. Her home was a central – an *adda* – meeting point: Girish Karnad, Vijay Tendulkar, Satyadev Dubey and so on, major playwrights, all gathered to discuss and debate threadbare recent presentations. Amol Palekar recalls these meetings as a 'bounty' (Gokhale 2016: 75) he received as a young man at her hands. Later, Kumudini moved into translating Marathi poetry and plays. Her commitment to the arts along with her intellectual capabilities was recognized when she was appointed the first Joint Director of the newly established National Centre for Performing Arts in 1972, and she was singularly responsible for giving Marathi theatre, seen as plebeian by the Westernized elite, a place at the NCPA. She was also the editor of their influential journal, the *NCPA Quarterly*, for several years. Called the 'Constant Supporter' (Gokhale 2016: 75), she played a major role in preventing Vijay Tendulkar's controversial play, *Sakharam Binder*, from being banned. She fought for theatre practitioners to be included in the Censor Board and went out of her way to provide opportunities for talented artists.

While her singular contribution to collating the cultural history of English drama and Shakespeare in Western India, which marked many firsts, remains virtually unknown in comparison, Kumudini Mehta's intellectual trajectory is representative of many postcolonial scholars whose in-depth study of Western theatre was a starting stimulus, and who turned their attention to their more immediate environs, exploring the intricacies of Indian theatres in new ways. The NCPA commemorated Kumudini Mehta's immense contribution to the institution by planting a tree in her name. The tree has flowered and will thrive once the printed version of her thesis is available.[3]

The translator

Another woman I would like to foreground is Hansa Jivraj Mehta (1897–1995), better known, more eminent, than Kumudini Mehta, but like her, with her contribution to Indian Shakespeare disregarded till now. Hansaben, as she is commonly referred to (not to be confused with Hansa Wadkar/'Hansabai', Marathi film and stage actress, 1923–1971), was a freedom fighter, reformist, activist, educationist, writer and translator. She is that rarity, an Indian female translator of Shakespeare. She translated *Hamlet* and *The Merchant of Venice* into Gujarati verse, which were published in 1942 and 1944, respectively. Her translations, largely faithful to the original, have been rated highly by many critics and, more importantly, have proved their worth on stage, often chosen for performance. Hansaben was a committed translator; she rendered Molière, portions of Valmiki's Sanskrit *Ramayana* and children's literature into Gujarati. She believed that translation was essential in a multilingual country like India, for 'mutual understanding', to access our ancient knowledges from Sanskrit, and most of all for 'east west understanding' (1963: 158–9). She also published travelogues and even a collection of articles in English, titled *Indian Woman*, in 1981.

Hansaben was a remarkable, even radical, woman, and translation was only a part of her many activities. She was one of the earliest Indian women to travel to England for education, doing journalism in London after her graduation in philosophy from Baroda in 1918. She met Sarojini Naidu in London, and later, Gandhi, and was inspired by them to join the freedom struggle. On her return she entered an inter-caste marriage, Brahmin to Vaishya, which sparked an uproar in her community in Baroda, but was supported by her father and the reformist Maharaja of Baroda. She and her husband moved to Bombay and plunged into politics. They were both arrested for leading protest marches and spent time in jail in 1932. She then contested and won two terms in the Bombay Legislative Council, was elected President of the All India Women's Conference (1946–7) and instituted their charter of Indian Women's Rights. She was appointed to the Constituent Assembly, the committee for drafting the Constitution of independent India. Here too, her commitment to equal rights regardless of religion and gender made her argue for a Uniform Civil Code, something on which she clashed with Nehru and Ambedkar. Her championship of equality was recognized, however, when she was appointed by Nehru in 1948 to the UN Human Rights Conference. Here she is credited for arguing for a fundamental change in the wording of Article 1 of the UN Declaration of Human Rights, a change from 'all men are created equal' (Eleanor Roosevelt's preferred phrase) to 'all human beings'. This intervention gives us a clue as to why she chose to translate *The Merchant of Venice* – an early disquisition on equality in human rights and interfaith marriage, as seen between Jessica and Lorenzo. Incidentally, during the drafting of the Constitution of India, Hansaben had also argued for interfaith unions to be included in the fundamental rights, again an issue which was resisted then and which is on fire currently, with laws being promulgated against it.

There is no end to the list of Hansaben Mehta's achievements: called a staunch feminist, her advocacy of women's rights and women's education bore fruit when she was appointed the Vice-Chancellor of SNDT (Shreemati Nathibai Damodar Thackersey), the first women's university in the country. Later she functioned as Vice-Chancellor of Baroda University, where she is known to have actively supported theatrical activities including the performance of Shakespeare. She was honoured with a Padma Bhushan in 1959.

I have enumerated Hansa Jivraj Mehta's many achievements to emphasize the fact that in the midst of a very public life of politics, in the thick of the freedom struggle, and the championing of equality, she found the time and inclination to translate Shakespeare. It reveals to us today, how far Shakespeare is embedded in Indian culture and how women and men wish to prove themselves with and/through him, Shakespeare being both a cause and an effect of their larger interests.

The director

Among the women theatre directors who have given us radicalized interpretations of Shakespeare are Amal Allana, Anuradha Kapoor, Tripurari Sharma, Maya Rao and others. Amal Allana's production of *King Lear* in 1989 in Delhi was outstanding among them for its ground-breaking performative and interpretative creativity.

This *Lear* was an extraordinary production, which deployed environmental staging, alienation techniques, and a feminist interpretation. It was performed at the Crafts Museum in Delhi's Pragati Maidan and utilized its spaces and the structures to materially position the localization of the play in a mediaeval Rajasthani ambience. An open-air square, backed by replica structures of traditional houses of stone and wood, bamboo doorways, sand and brick floor, helmed by large trees, with huge earthenware urns lurking in the background, it physically projected a primeval vast space to present the epical sweep of the play. A canvas canopy painted in fiery colours overhung the main acting area, its shades suffusing the stage intermittently. Smaller stages/acting spaces were located at other points, and the audience had to swivel around and reposition themselves to view the action. Electronic speakers, hidden from view, produced a stereophonic effect – action, audience and ambience were all enveloped in a surround effect.

The staging, however, consciously deconstructed the 'staginess' of this setting. Rapid movements, fast pacing, the shifting locus of the action, audience movement and acting techniques all combined to distance the performer from the performed. Manohar Singh, who played Lear, was a bulky actor who could have easily been the overbearing monarch. But Allana chose to make him mock court decorum to highlight Lear's inner contradictions: he entered playing ball with the Fool, giggling, with no semblance of understanding the serious business at hand. Many such reinterpretative touches were added: Allana saw Lear's story as the trauma of 'divestment' – *tyaga* – of power, and the difficulties that 'attachment' – *mohah* – (both well-known concepts of Indian philosophy) results in. This attachment to power was symbolically localized not in the turban or the crown but in the sword, which he held in his hand, alternately brandishing it with vigour or clutching it like 'a security blanket' (Allana 2011: 254) in the hovel scene. The knights were envisioned as Lear's bodyguards, his black cats, who were constantly on the move, surrounding and shielding him.

The most original aspect, radical for its time in the context of Indian stagings of *Lear*, was Allana's interpretation of Lear's relationship with his daughters as one full of a suppressed 'sexual charge ... Lear, though old, is unable to still his senses ... The sexual charge manifests itself in his will to subjugate, despite the fact that he feels he should abdicate', explained Allana in an interview with the author. Cordelia was clearly the favourite: when Lear fell playing with the ball in the opening scene, and the courtiers froze, it was Cordelia who rushed trippingly to help him get up. This interaction between Lear and Cordelia, with embracing, fondling, touching, suggested an almost sexual, incestuous relationship (Allana 2011: 255).

Goneril and Regan were dressed in traditional dark, ornate skirts, heavy with embroidered mirror work with an overload of jewellery – the large *bore* (forehead) ornament, the bulky necklaces and bangles, and heavy head scarves, *chunnis*, all of which seemed to encase them like straitjackets, signifying the continuing oppression both of a patriarchy which prescribed such dress codes and of the tenacity of their own appetites. They were seen as sexually frustrated and, like their father, expressed their unused sexual energy in 'curdled wrath' (Allana 2002: n.p.). In 2.2, when Goneril asks Lear to curtail his hundred knights, Amal devised a circular choreography to illustrate this. With Lear and the Fool in the centre, surrounded and guarded by the knights in a circle, Goneril coldly baited and mocked him. The circle of knights reacted by moving closer to Lear. Goneril tried to break this wall; they held her at bay; Lear cracked his whip, hitting out at her. This repeated back-and-forth movement suggested a sexual excess; when Goneril finally penetrated the circle, both father and daughter were sweating and panting.

The Lear-Cordelia relation climaxed in 4.7 when Lear awakens from his delirium in her lap. This moment Allana graphically visualized as a 're-birth' of Lear (Allana 2011: 255). Cordelia sat on bare earth, cradling her father's head in her lap, while he lay curled up foetus-like, as she rocked him, humming a lullaby. When suddenly Lear woke from his delirium, he screamed, pummelling his legs in the air, while Cordelia simultaneously parted her legs, throwing her head back in a birthing movement. Lear convulsed his body once more, tumbling off her lap, panting. Cordelia too, exhausted, moved towards him to cradle him in her arms on the floor. At the end, both father and daughter lay, locked in an embrace, at the exact spot where once had lain the crumpled map of the kingdom at the end of the first scene.

Amal Allana's directorial work is well known for its radical exploration of gender relations and questions of self-identity. This particular production, her only Shakespeare venture, has, however, not quite found a place in the annals of landmark Indian Shakespeare performances. Its experimentalism was perhaps too alienating; it brought the soul-searching angst of Lear too close to the audience. It was also critiqued for exoticizing and pandering to a tourist gaze. However, no other production of Shakespeare in India has taken such innovative risks, or applied a feminist perspective, least of all by a female director.

This selective account of the 'woman's part', spotlighting the emergence of the actress in modern India along with the intersecting figures of a scholar, a translator and a director, all connected by their engagement with Shakespeare, is but an introduction to the wide-ranging contributions of women in the theatre arts. Their individual journeys are significant for the breakthroughs they achieved, which served to build up the modern theatre as also instrumental in changing societal attitudes. The narrative has confined itself to establishing facts and materialities which conditioned their work, touching upon their efforts in the public sphere. It does not venture into the private and personal: the trials and tribulations confronted and the trade-offs between the personal and the public. Much more needs to be recovered and foregrounded; the challenge of a gendered history of Indian theatre, and the Shakespearean strand in it, has just begun. Recouping the efforts of women is not just filling in the gaps, it is also re-ordering the historiography of Indian theatre and balancing out the critical estimations of their work, which continues to be a contested terrain.

Notes

1 For further information, see the archival material at the British Library, IOL Mss Eur B418.
2 The quotation is from the synopsis of the 1960 thesis and is not numbered.
3 Much of the information about Kumudini Mehta's life is based on the writings of Shanta Gokhale (she has a Preface to the published thesis too) and on Sharmistha Saha's Prologue to it. I am grateful to them for sharing their work before publication.

References

Allana, A. (2002), interview with author.
Allana, A. (2011), 'Spatial Dynamics in the Staging of *King Lear*', in V. Chopra (ed.), *Shakespeare: The Indian Icon*, 249–56, New Delhi: Readers Paradise.

Bhatia, N. (2010), *Performing Women/Performing Womanhood: Theatre, Politics and Dissent in North India*, New Delhi: Oxford University Press.

Bhattacharya, R. (2018), *Public Women in British India: Icons and the Urban Stage*, London and New York: Routledge.

Chatterjee, S. (2007), *The Colonial Staged: Theatre in Colonial Calcutta*, London: Seagull Books.

Dalmia, V. (2006), *Poetics, Plays and Performances: The Politics of Modern Indian Theatre*, New Delhi: Oxford University Press.

Das Gupta, H. N. ([1944–46] 2002), *The Indian Stage*, 4 vols, New Delhi: Munshiram Manoharlal.

Dasi, B. ([1913] 1998), *My Story*, ed. and trans. R. Bhattacharya, New Delhi: Kali for Women.

Dharwadker, A. (2005), *Theatres of Independence: Drama, Theory and Urban Performance in India since 1947*, Iowa City: University Iowa Press.

Dutt, B. and U. Sarkar Munsi (2010), *Engendering Performance: Indian Women Performers in Search of an Identity*, New Delhi: SAGE.

Gokhale, S. (2000), *Playwright at the Centre: Marathi Drama from 1843 to the Present*, Calcutta: Seagull.

Gokhale, S., ed. (2016), *The Scenes We Made: An Oral History of Experimental Theatre in Mumbai*, New Delhi: Speaking Tiger.

Gooptu, S. (2015), *The Actress in the Public Theatres of Calcutta*, New Delhi: Primus.

Kosambi, M. (2015), *Gender, Culture and Performance: Marathi Theatre and Cinema before Independence*, London and New York: Routledge.

Majumdar, S. (2005), 'That Sublime "Old Gentleman": Shakespeare's Plays in Calcutta, 1775–1930', in P. Trivedi and D. Bartholomeusz (eds), *India's Shakespeare: Translation, Interpretation and Performance*, 260–9, Newark: University of Delaware Press.

Mangai, A. (2015), *Acting Up: Gender and Theatre in India, 1979 Onwards*, Delhi: Leftword Books.

Mehta, H. J. (1963), 'Quality in Literary Translation', in E. Cary and R. W. Jumpelt (eds), *Quality in Translation: Proceedings of the IIIrd Congress of the International Federation of Translators*, 158–9, New York: Pergamon Press/Macmillan.

Mehta, K. (2021), *English Theatre in Colonial Bombay in the Late Eighteenth and Nineteenth Century*, Manipal: Manipal University Press.

Nair, P. T. (1989), *Calcutta in the Nineteenth Century: Company Days*, Calcutta: Firma KLM.

Paul, S., ed. (1989), *A Tribute to Shakespeare 1989*, New Delhi: Television and Theatre Associates.

Raha, K. (1978), *Bengali Theatre*, New Delhi: National Book Trust.
Saha, S. (2021), 'Prologue', in K. Mehta (ed.), *English Theatre in Colonial Bombay in the Late Eighteenth and Nineteenth Century*, 9–15, Manipal: Manipal University Press.
Sathe, M. (2015), *A Socio-Political History of Marathi Theatre: Thirty Nights*, New Delhi: Oxford University Press.
Sengupta, D. (2005), 'Playing the Canon: Shakespeare and the Bengali Actress in Nineteenth Century Calcutta', in P. Trivedi and D. Bartholomeusz (eds), *India's Shakespeare: Translation, Interpretation and Performance*, 242–59, Newark: University of Delaware Press.
Shaw, D. (1958), 'Esther Leach, "The Mrs. Siddons of Bengal"', *Educational Theatre Journal*, 10 (4): 304–10.
Singh, L., ed. (2009), *Play-House of Power: Theatre in Colonial India*, New Delhi: Oxford University Press.
Stocqueler, J. H. (1873), *Memoirs of a Journalist*, Bombay: Times of India.
Trivedi, P. (2016), 'Garrison Theatre in Colonial India: Issues of Valuation', in C. Cochrane and J. Robinson (eds), *Theatre History and Historiography: Ethics, Evidence and Truth*, 103–20, Basingstoke: Palgrave.

2

Framing femininities: Desdemona and Indian modernities

Paromita Chakravarti

Shakespeare's contribution to the theme and content of Indian films is only one aspect of his influence which works at the multiple levels of shaping representational protocols, characterization, generic conventions, visual codes and socio-cultural norms as well as regional, national and global identities of Indian cinema. Many of these Shakespearean interventions in Indian films are mediated and manifested through the figure of the Shakespearean heroine. This chapter will dwell on a post-colonial moment in which the journeys of a Shakespearean female protagonist mark significant shifts in India's social, cultural, political and cinematic histories. It examines how a 1959 Bengali novel by Tarashankar Bandyopadhyay and its cinematic adaptation, *Saptapadi* (dir. Ajoy Kar, 1961), or 'The seven steps of marriage', a Tamil film, *Ratha Thilagam* (dir. Dada Mirasi, 1963), or 'The blood-mark on the forehead', influenced by the Bengali film, and a Hindi Bollywood movie, *Hamraaz* (dir. B. R. Chopra, 1967), or 'Confidant', all made in the 1960s, cite the climactic murder scene from *Othello* to articulate ideas of transgressive love, couple-hood, marriage and conflicts between religions and communities and to question how these may be negotiated within the modern vision of the post-colonial nation. The imaginary of the emerging nation is sited on the construction of Desdemona's character and draws from as well as frames notions of normative Indian femininity as this emerges through a dialectic of tradition and modernity. Finally, the chapter will explore the film, *Hrid Majharey* (dir. Ranjan Ghosh, 2014), or 'Within the heart', which intertextually alludes to the film adaptation of *Saptapadi* fifty-three years after it was made and deploys *Othello* in narrating a private story of heartbreak, jealousy and unreason to articulate a conception of neoliberal modernity.

Elokeshi and Desdemona: The colonial companionate marriage

But first a quick flash back to the nineteenth century. In 1873, a sensational murder case came up before the Hooghly sessions court in Srerampore, Bengal. The powerful priest of Tarakeshwar temple, *mohunt* (head priest) Madhav Chandra Giri, was accused of seducing and raping Elokeshi, the young wife of Nobin Chandra Bannerjee. When confronted, the repentant wife confessed and Nobin forgave her. When they were leaving, the *mohunt*'s goons stopped them. In a fit of passion, Nobin slit Elokeshi's throat with a fish knife. Horrified at his own deed, he surrendered to the police. An Indian jury acquitted him on grounds of insanity, but the European judge sentenced him to life imprisonment. In 1875, following public petitions, he was pardoned. The *mohunt* was sentenced to three years of rigorous imprisonment and a fine of Rs 3,000.

This scandal triggered public debate around questions of Hindu marriage, conjugal codes and the role of the *sati* (ideal wife) – her duties, chastity and fidelity. Plays and farces were written about the scandal, and satirical images appeared in *patas* (folk paintings) and woodcuts. Questions were asked. Who was the good woman? What was to be made of Elokeshi? Was she a wicked seductress or a victim? Despite the nationalists' condemnation of her as a fallen woman, there was also a growing sympathy for Elokeshi. Her adultery was blamed on her conniving parents, on a panderess and the villainous *mohunt*. She was portrayed as a woman controlled by patriarchy who had little agency. Some representations showed her as being drugged before being raped. *Bengalee* (8 November 1873), a reformist newspaper, commented: 'In sympathizing with the unfortunate Nobin people forget that the victim was not the man that he and all Bengal believe to be a vile seducer, nor the still worse scoundrel who bartered his daughter's virtue ... but a tender girl of 16 years ... what had she done to forfeit her young life?' (Sarkar 2001: 93).

Nobin's touching love for her mitigated Elokeshi's guilt and made her murder appear less as a punishment for immorality and more of a *crime passionnel*. According to a newspaper, *Friend of India* (5 June 1873), Nobin was supposed to have said when surrendering to the police: 'Hang me quick. This world is a wilderness to me. I am impatient to join my wife in the next' (Sarkar 2001: 981). This statement, quoted in newspapers, songs and stories, was not the Hindu husband's *dharma* speaking – this was the voice of the new companionate conjugality and affective marriage which had colonial sources. During the trial the courtrooms were so crowded that the authorities charged people money. Newspapers, such as *Bengalee* (22 August 1873), commented on the Shakespearean histrionics of the trial, stating 'people flock to the sessions court as they would flock to the Lewis theatre to watch *Othello* being performed' (Sarkar 2001: 74). Did the enormous popularity of Shakespeare's play, which was running at the same time on the Kolkata stage, influence the reception of Nobin's murder of his wife and shape the discourse on Elokeshi, Hindu femininity and conjugality? Did the unexpected sympathy for Elokeshi derive partly from the impact that Desdemona's innocent death had on a Bengali audience? And how, if at all, could the Elokeshi scandal have influenced the reception of *Othello*?

Desdemona and the nineteenth-century new woman

Shakespeare's Desdemona was a popular icon in Bengal, shaping the discursive constructions of Hindu womanhood and colonial modernity since the early nineteenth century. She was the foremost Shakespearean heroine to provide a model for the new urban gentlewoman or *bhadramahila*, who was not only educated, intelligent and independent but also dutiful and subservient to her husband. These sometimes contradictory ideals of the Bengali housewife emanated from the larger debate between tradition and modernity, of which the New Woman or *Nabina* becomes the focus. Colonial paradigms of the modern woman and Victorian companionate marriage triggered re-evaluations of Indian, Hindu womanhood, caught between the imperatives of an indigenous tradition and the needs of a modern world. Fashioning the New Woman becomes a central concern in the natives' complicated negotiations with colonial modernity.

In the nineteenth-century Shakespeare translations, the heroines are indigenized to become amalgams of Western modernity and Hindu tradition – while the intelligence, efficiency and domestic skills of the Portias and the innocence of the Mirandas and Juliets are praised, their independence is toned down to make them ideal *bhadramahilas*. In colonial translations of *Othello*, the Desdemona character combines the spiritedness of a European heroine with the submissiveness of the ideal Hindu bride.

In Tarini Charan Pal's 1875 Bengali translation of *Othello* (*Bhimsingha*), and in Debendranath Basu's 1919 adaptation of *Othello*, Desdemona is the New Woman who defies her father to marry the man of her choice, but she is subservient to her husband and dies unprotestingly when accused wrongly of adultery. Thus, she is a modern *sati* (chaste wife) who dies to protect her husband's honour. In *Bhimsingha*, Chandranath (Cassio) describes her as a '*pativrata* (loyal to her husband) like Savitri, pious like Damayanti and compassionate like Sita' (Pal 1875: 18).[1]

In his essay, 'Shakuntala, Miranda and Desdemona', first published in 1873, Bankim Chandra Chattopadhyay compares Shakespeare's heroines to Kalidasa's Shakuntala and finds the former to be better *satis*. Both Desdemona and Shakuntala defy guardians to choose their husbands, but, unlike Shakuntala, Desdemona does not lash out at her husband even when he suspects her wrongly, thus proving to be a better *sati* (Chattopadhyay 1938: 86–7). Even in post-colonial adaptations of *Othello*, Desdemona's defiance of her father and its implications for Indian womanhood are significant. Utpal Dutt, for example, includes Desdemona with the independent heroines of Shakespeare's comedies and romances like Hermia, Jessica and Imogen who follow their impulses with elan (Dutt 1986: 11).

Dealing with marriage and love, *Othello* has generic affinities with comedy or domestic drama rather than with heroic tragedy. This is perhaps why in Indian appropriations the focus is on Desdemona's defiance of patriarchy to assert individual sexual choice as in the comedies, and the gender concerns override race issues in these adaptations.

Saptapadi: Desdemona and Rina Brown

Tarashankar Bandyopadhyay's 1959 novel, *Saptapadi*, a postcolonial novel set during the Second World War in colonial India, explores the romance between a Bengali man, Krishnendu (the dark moon), and an 'English' (later revealed to be Anglo-Indian) woman, Rina Brown. Structured around Shakespeare's *Othello*, the novel uses its cultural capital to validate, frame and enable this inter-racial and intercommunity relationship. The climactic murder scene is enacted three times – first with Rina as Desdemona and her English fiancé Clayton as Othello at a college social and then with Krishnendu as the Moor opposite Rina in an impromptu domestic performance and later on the public stage. The scene acts as a mnemonic and synecdoche for Rina and Krishnendu's fraught affair in a text alternating between the present and the past, as recalled in flashbacks marked by the memory of the play.

In Rina Brown, Tarashankar produced a singular and iconic heroine of modern Bengali fiction – a beautiful and troubled Anglo-Indian woman, audacious, almost reckless, a devout Christian turned defiant atheist, darkly haunted by her past and capable of loving passionately. *Saptapadi* opens with a drunk Rina being carried by an American army officer into a clinic run by Krishnendu, who is a doctor and a Christian priest in a Bengal village. Described as 'possessing a strange, seductive and brazen beauty which evokes a greedy lust' (Bandyopadhyay 2015: XVI, 314). Rina cannot speak, vomits and collapses in a stupor on her first appearance. The officer accompanying her calls her a 'bitch', abusing her wildness while acknowledging her beauty and appetite for life. This Desdemona is far from the demure *sati* that Bankim Chandra Chattopadhyay praised. However, the association with Shakespeare's heroine is made consistently – even when Krishnendu medically examines Rina he quotes *Othello*, 'Peace, and be still' (5.2.46), and grieves because it appears that 'these unforgettable words from *Othello* enter her ear but do not open any doors of her memory' (Bandyopadhyay 2015: XVI, 318). But, in fact, she does remember.

Disallowed from kissing his Desdemona because of the racial segregation in the colonial India of the 1940s, Krishnendu weeps passionate tears when they enact the murder scene. Rina, too, recollects, crying: 'When you said "think of thy sins", I said "they are loves I bear you"; at that moment, tears welled into my eyes' (Bandyopadhyay 2015: XVI, 336). By the end of the performance, both awaken to an awareness of their unspoken and unspeakable love rendered impossible by social norms. Later, when Clayton calls off his engagement with Rina, Krishnendu proposes marriage to her and converts to Christianity on her father's insistence. Rina is shocked at the alacrity with which Krishnendu renounces his religion for her. Echoing Brabantio's warning to Othello that Desdemona would betray him as she had betrayed her father, Rina states that if Krishnendu could so easily abandon his religion for her he could just as easily desert her for another woman. There appears to be a role reversal here as it is Othello rather than Desdemona who gives up his religion and family (his father disowns him) for love. Also, the psychological turmoil of Othello seems to be displaced on to Rina/Desdemona.

Unlike *Othello*, religion in *Saptapadi* is more important than race. Rina leaves Krishnendu for renouncing Hinduism. However, she soon finds out that her mother was their domestic help, an *adivasi* (tribal person), and that she is herself a half-caste bastard child who had never been baptized. Rina's much vaunted Christian identity is revealed to be a sham. Filled with self-loathing, she turns into a disillusioned atheist and leaves home, becoming a camp follower to the American soldiers of the Allied forces in India, having flings with them, drinking and smoking, trying to forget her past. Krishnendu, on the other hand, comes to be known as Krishnaswamy – a Christian priest who is also a Hindu *sanyasi*, promoting a syncretic religion of Man. A trained doctor, he serves poor villagers who consider him God. As Rina moves from being a devout Christian to a godless non-believer, Krishnendu's initial atheism leads him to an inclusive humanist religion. When they meet after many years, the two argue over their still-divergent religious positions, only to realize that the only link still connecting them is Shakespeare's poetry. In Rina's faithless world, the only anchor of belief is her memory of Othello.[2] Blaming herself for what she considers a waste of Krishnendu's life, she leaves him again to continue her self-destructive journey across the war front where she meets Clayton, who takes her back to Krishnendu. Meeting Krishnendu, who has since contracted leprosy, Rina calls him a saint and says that she felt unworthy of his love, while he admits that as a man of god his journey was alone.

Their parting of ways seems inevitable given their irreconcilable positions on religion. Unlike *Othello*, love ends tragically in *Saptapadi* not because of inter-personal and psychological issues such as jealousy and mistrust but because of religious differences. The intensity of the personal psycho-drama of the lovers is projected onto the *Othello* scene, its performances as well as its repeated recalling, while the interactions between Rina and Krishnendu take on a public and polemical form. While in Shakespeare's play the movement is centripetal where the issues of gender and race, of militaristic masculinity and honour codes, gravitate inward into a vortex of private, domestic drama leading to the tragedy, in *Saptapadi*, there is a centrifugal tendency where the tensions of the personal relationship radiate outwards into the space of the new nation. The debate on faith and faithlessness that divides the lovers inflects the vision of modern India which provides the context for the love story. Krishnendu's rural clinic, bearing images of Christ, Ramakrishna and Vivekananda, appears to embody the secularism of the new polity which manifests itself in a syncretic union of religions rather than through a nonreligious worldview characterized by Rina. Despite the loving delineation of Rina's character in all its tempestuousness and brooding melancholy, she is accorded no space in the post-colonial social imaginary. A relic of the empire, her destiny is with her compatriot, Clayton, while it is Krishnendu, the *sanyasi* priest, who engages alone in the work of Gandhian nation building through developing the villages of India. Rina, despite her identification with Desdemona, is not allowed her transgressive love and must return to the fold of her own people – although she is part Indian *adivasi*. She fails to be the *sati* who sacrifices her family and society for her lover. Although she remains an iconic figure in modern Bengali fiction, like many other Anglo-Indian characters, she cannot be integrated into the idea of the modern Indian nation.[3]

Cinematic Rina Brown: The Anglo-Indian *sati*

In the 1961 popular Bengali film, *Saptapadi*, based on Tarashankar's novel, Rina Brown's character is toned down, yet it remains one of the most unconventional roles played by Suchitra Sen, the star of the Bengali screen of the 1950s–60s. Associated with upper-class and upper-caste educated *bhadramahila* roles in traditional saris and long hair, Sen's portrayal of Rina Brown in billowy skirts and fitted blouses with bobbed hair stands out visually as a symbol of Western modernity. The sympathetic portrayal of a feisty and passionate Anglo-Indian woman also challenges the social and cinematic stereotypes of a community which contributed many artists to early Indian cinema.

The social prejudice against middle-class 'respectable' Indian women joining the theatre and cinema led often to Eurasian, Jewish and Anglo-Indian women being recruited to play female roles between 1920 and 1940 (language was not a barrier because most films were silent). Some took Indian screen names. Ruby Myers (Sulochana), Mary Ann Evans (Nadia) and Esther Victoria Abraham (Pramila) were celebrated Anglo-Indian stars of the Indian screen.[4] When the talkies arrived and actors had to speak Indian languages, 'foreign' artists had to make way for Indians. Some Anglo-Indian women continued in Bollywood as cabaret dancers, like Helen. As Western, liberal, professional women who often smoked, drank, danced and pursued film careers, Anglo-Indians were stigmatized. In the film, *Mahanagar* (dir. Satyajit Ray, 1963), the Anglo-Indian secretary is fired because the boss refuses to believe she was ill and assumes that she was out with her boyfriend since 'they are like that'. Rina Brown's affirmative portrayal is thus both refreshing and radical.

However, some concessions had to be made for popular cinema – unlike the novel, the film provides a happy ending by reuniting

Rina and Krishnendu (Uttam Kumar) and suggesting a marriage rather than the tragic collapse of an inter-racial relationship. It also revives the legacy of indigenizing Desdemona as the New Indian woman, an amalgam of tradition and modernity, defying her father to marry her lover yet submissive to her husband, a modern *sati*. While Tarashankar underlines Rina's wild promiscuity and her indifference to social norms, the cinematic Rina is much more conforming. She accedes to Krishnendu's orthodox Hindu father's request to leave his son and save him from religious conversion and social ostracization – an event absent in the novel. The couple in the film is thus separated not because of incompatibilities of religious faith, as in the novel, but because of Rina's *sati*-like sacrifice of her own happiness to preserve harmony between father and son. The two are united only when the father acknowledges Rina's magnanimity and his mistake in separating them. The film also invents a scene in which Rina appears in a traditional *sari* after hearing of Krishnendu's mother's death and dutifully packs his suitcase for his journey to his native village. The more unsavoury aspects of Rina's life at the war front are whitewashed in the film in which she is not a flamboyantly dressed camp follower, with multiple liaisons with the soldiers, but a uniformed nurse engaged in noble service. In another extrapolated event in the film, Rina heroically saves her dead friend's mother, a woman who, like her own mother, was raped by an English plantation owner and had a daughter by him. Stigmatized by neighbours, she was left behind when the village was evacuated anticipating bombing. Rina drives to the village to rescue the old woman and gets injured on her way back. Fortuitously, Krishnendu is at hand to perform a surgery and save Rina's life. The film ends with Krishnendu carrying Rina towards a church as bells toll. Eliminating the religious differences which divide Rina and Krishnendu in the novel, the film provides a vision of a modern India where marriages are celebrated across community and race and Anglo-Indians, Hindus and Christians can be integrated into a common destiny. The end of the film is suffused with the hope and romance of the emerging nation, which is different both from the jealousy-riven domestic claustrophobia of Shakespeare's play or the sad exclusion of Rina and Clayton from Krishnendu's new India.

Saptapadi represents the new genre of romantic melodrama which emerged in the 1950s following the long domination in

Bengali cinema of the 'socials' – narratives of traditional extended families and feudal social relations, usually in rural settings. Influenced by the Hollywood romantic comedies of the 1950s, these new Bengali films focused on heterosexual couple-formation, marking a transition from the extended family to a new nuclear domesticity. Often starring Uttam Kumar and Suchitra Sen, they portrayed stories of young urban couples and their aspirations for modernity. In these movies, romance becomes a site around which emerge new modes of intimacy and belonging, individuation and community life, family organization and gender roles. Promoting 'love marriages' rather than 'arranged' ones, prioritizing romantic love in choosing a partner over the dictates of a patriarchal family or the affiliations of religion, race or caste, the protagonists of these films embody ideas of autonomous personhood and secular citizenship of a modern nation. Central to these concerns is the conception of the New Woman who is educated, professional, mobile, urban, makes her own romantic choices and is framed not by domestic but by public city spaces like offices, hospitals or colleges.

India's newly introduced co-educational system allows Rina and Krishnendu, who are from very different backgrounds, to meet in the Medical College. The college social and the staging of the murder scene in *Othello* initiate their cross-racial romance, which would otherwise have been socially impossible. A character remarks about the *Othello* performance, 'good lord, are men and women going to act together then?'. Both Shakespeare and the institutions of the new nation forge a modernity where *Othello* is appropriated not as a domestic tragedy but as an enabling trope of transgressive conjugality in a democratic civic society. By bringing a private bedroom scene onto the public stage, performances of *Othello* help to create a space of sexual freedom. The shock of witnessing a consummation-like murder of a white woman by a black man challenges traditional bourgeois morality. However problematic the implications of the murder are, *Saptapadi* manages to find in it possibilities to challenge middle-class conservatism both in 'real life' and as seen on the stage and the screen, wresting from the play an image of modern social and sexual mores.[5]

Significantly, the three *Othello* performances in the novel are telescoped into a single performance in the film, with Krishnendu replacing Clayton as Othello when the latter fails to show up.

The unrehearsed unpreparedness of the scene intensifies the sexual frisson. Edited to limit the exchange between the two main protagonists, the scene excises the roles of Emilia, Iago, Montano, Graziano, Lodovico and Cassio. This makes the performance intensely private, rendering Othello's 'one that loved not wisely, but too well' (5.2.342) speech a personal testimony delivered exclusively to Desdemona's inert body. This intimate exchange leading to a wordless communication between the two actors ironically unfolds on a public stage, framed by the gaze of an audience. Yet none of the later meetings of Rina and Krishnendu has this degree of closeness, although there are visual reminders of the scene which evoke its intensity – such as Krishnendu bending over Rina on a hospital bed after surgery to examine her. Even the poster for the film features an image from the *Othello* performance.

But, beyond the *Othello* scene, the concerns in the relationship are much more public. Rina and Krishnendu fall out not because of personal jealousy or suspicion but incompatibilities based on religious faith, racial divide and the purpose of life. And, unlike the novel, the film finds a way of resolving these differences and accommodating Rina, despite her atheism and her non-normative lifestyle, into a vision of the modern India.

Ratha Thilagam and *Hamraaz* – Nationalist and post-colonial modernities

The nation figures even more centrally in *Ratha Thilagam*, a Tamil-language film released two years after *Saptapadi* and inspired by it. It recreates the *Othello* scene enacted by two college students, Kumar (Shivaji Ganesan) and Kamala (Savithri), who later fall in love. The costumes, set and even the dubbing artists in the scene, Utpal Dutt and Jennifer Kendal, are the same as in *Saptapadi*. Even the last-minute substitution of the Othello actor is followed in the Tamil film as are other details. Also set against the backdrop of a war, the Chinese aggression of 1962, *Ratha Thilagam* unfolds in the new post-colonial nation. Racial differences are replaced by differences of nationalist identities – Kumar/Othello is a patriot who joins the Indian army when war breaks out, while Kamala, whose family is settled in China, goes to visit her father, stays on and marries a Chinese army officer, calling into question her loyalties towards both Kumar and India. It is later revealed that Kamala's marriage was a ploy to glean military secrets from her husband and pass them on to Indian officials. Trying to escape after she is found out, she meets Kumar, who attempts to save her. But she is killed by her husband, and Kumar is martyred while planting the Indian flag in Chinese territory. As A. Mangai points out, in *Ratha Thilagam* private concerns of romance are subordinated to those of patriotism: the film 'complicates the importance of loyalty in personal relationships by extending it to the public sphere – in this case the nation' (Mangai 2019: 247). Unlike *Othello* where the tensions of the public sphere, racial conflicts and professional jealousies entangle intimate relationships, *Saptapadi* and *Ratha Thilagam* demonstrate a movement outwards. Kamala/Desdemona in *Ratha Thilagam* is framed not by domestic concerns – she emerges as a nationalist rather than a *sati*. Her decision to marry a Chinese army officer and to betray his trust is judged not by traditional norms of sexual morality because she undertakes these actions to serve her country.

The modernization of the Indian cinematic Desdemona continues in the B. R. Chopra-directed 1967 Hindi film, *Hamraaz*, which is also set against the Indo-China war and deploys the murder scene from *Othello*. Combining the genres of the woman's melodrama and the urban thriller, *Hamraaz* narrates a complex story of triangulated love between Meena (Vimi) and her two husbands, Rajesh (Raj Kumar) and Kumar (Sunil Dutt).[6] While the melodramatic form imposes a moral pattern on the narrative, it is complicated by the generic needs of the thriller to tell a fast-paced story of crime and intrigue. Although stylistically different, the film has elements of *noir*, particularly in its morally ambivalent heroine who is nothing like the devoted *satis* of Hindi film melodrama. *Hamraaz* suggests the possibilities of reading *Othello* as a *noir* drama. It could be seen as a speculative reflection on what would have happened if Desdemona had indeed loved another man, albeit believing Othello was dead.

Hamraaz opens with Meena and Rajesh, an Indian army captain, marrying secretly since Meena's father does not approve of a soldier for a son-in-law. Meanwhile the Sino-Indian war breaks out and Rajesh leaves for the front. Soon the news of his death arrives even as Meena realizes that she is pregnant. After she gives birth, her father informs her that the child has died. After a period of inconsolable grief, Meena meets and falls in love with Kumar. They marry and leave for Bombay and spend several happy years together. On his deathbed, Meena's father reveals that Meena's child is alive and being brought up in a local orphanage. Meena tries but fails to convince Kumar to adopt the child. Soon Rajesh turns up, announcing that the news of his death was false. Meena lies to Kumar about him, thus sowing seeds of suspicion in his mind. At this juncture, Kumar, a professional actor, enacts two scenes from *Othello*, a performance that Meena misses because she secretly goes to meet Rajesh.

While the murder scene in *Saptapadi* and *Ratha Thilagam* is intense and modern, done in stark black and white, using an imposing set reminiscent of Orson Welles' *noir*-inspired *Othello* (1951), the excerpt in *Hamraaz* evokes the Parsi theatre in all its colour, variety and spectacle, using an indigenized Hindustani translation of the play where Desdemona is referred to as '*Begum* Othello' and Iago as 'Aiyago'. The acting is melodramatic, punctuated with the hero's agitated screams and the villain's loud laughter. With little respect for textual integrity, the events of the play surrounding the handkerchief are considerably altered, while Othello uses Hamlet's 'Frailty, thy name is Woman' (Q2, 1.2.146) accusation to characterize his wife. When Iago suggests that Desdemona was out visiting her lover, Othello storms into their bedroom, to be informed by Emilia that her mistress was not in. This replicates Kumar's own experience of calling in at his house and being informed by the maid that his wife is out, which surprises him since she had skipped his play, pleading a headache. Spurred by his own jealousy, Kumar gives a frenzied performance in the murder scene and almost strangles the stage Desdemona to death. The director has to pull him away and urge him to be less 'naturalistic' in his acting, which is ironic, given the exaggerated histrionics. However, the Hindustani Desdemona shows much more spirit than Shakespeare's heroine. When Othello shows her the handkerchief given to him by Iago, she refuses to respond to his questions about whether she had left it at her lover's house: 'If Iago has given you the handkerchief I would consider it an indignity to answer that question'.

When Kumar returns home, a near-identical scene unfolds but without the expostulations, accusations and tragic killing. There is a seamless transition from the elaborate stage set to a similarly curtained bed in Kumar's house, where Meena lies in her nightdress. She wakes up to be confronted with Kumar's question about where she had gone, to which she responds that she had been to the doctor. Quietly and civilly, Kumar leaves the room and phones the family doctor, only to discover that she had not visited him. Convinced that she had been on a secret assignment, he starts following her. But, before he can discover Rajesh's identity, Meena is found mysteriously murdered. Thereafter, the thriller genre takes over, as a police officer steps in to investigate and Kumar, a suspect in Meena's murder, is on the run.

The conventions of the thriller temper the melodramatic expectations of popular Hindi cinema, which requires deference to traditional values. Despite remarrying and being an absent mother, Meena is not framed as a failed *sati*. Meena's dressing to meet Rajesh – widow-like in white and with the traditional '*ghungat*' (veil) – is less about modesty and more about avoiding attention and hiding her face. When she touches Rajesh's feet and begs forgiveness, he does not blame her for loving another man. He feels their clandestine marriage was in fact illicit because it lacked social validation. Kumar never confronts Meena, even when he knows she is lying. There are no accusations or jealous attacks which are exorcised through the savage performance of *Othello*, in which Kumar almost kills his co-star. Shakespeare's play helps Kumar achieve a catharsis of violent jealousy to attain a civility and restraint more appropriate for modern, urban life. The murder scene, through its exaggerated style and language, is identified with a savage masculinity, which is repressed in the main narrative. Thus, Kumar does not challenge Rajesh, his rival in love. Overcoming the natural urge to mistrust and be jealous of each other, Rajesh and Kumar, both suspects in Meena's murder and both innocent, become allies and together find Meena's killer, who has also kidnapped Rajesh's and Meena's child. The child is rescued, and the murderer handed over to the police, but Rajesh dies, leaving his daughter with Kumar. The film ends with Kumar blaming himself for Meena's death by suspecting her, keeping secrets from her and by failing to become her '*hamraaz*', literally 'secret-sharer'. Instead of accusing her of concealing her past from him, he finds his own jealousy unacceptable in a modern companionate marriage. The *Othello* scene, adumbrating the tragic consequences of lies, secrets and mistrust, functions almost as a negative example in *Hamraaz*, which makes a plea for trust and transparency in conjugal relationships. The film ends with a disavowal of the thriller genre associated with covert activities and a reassertion of the melodramatic ending with the reunited and happy, albeit slightly unconventional, family constituted of Kumar's co-actor and the child of his former wife. Also, the *dénouement* takes place not in the usual domestic space but in the public forum of the theatre. The film narrative moves outwards, away from the prison of mendacity, jealousy and crime that *Othello* represents, towards an honest acknowledgement of 'reality'. Here, less an enabler of modernity, Shakespeare's play stands for pre-modern urges that must be overcome in the modern, law-bound civic society. Full-length Indian cinematic adaptations of *Othello*, the best-known being *Kaliyattam* (dir. Jayaraj, 1997) and *Omkara* (dir. Vishal Bhardwaj, 2006), use a pre-modern setting. *Kaliyattam*, subtitled '*The Play of God*', uses the context of traditional ritualistic *theyyam* dance, while *Omkara* unfolds in the caste-ridden bad-lands of Uttar Pradesh, which seem to lie outside the purview of law. The 2014 Bengali film, *Hrid Majharey*, seems to be an exception in this regard.

In the heart

Set in contemporary globalizing Kolkata, *Hrid Majharey* features characters who are middle-class urban professionals – Abhi / Othello is a mathematics teacher in a college, and Desdemona/ Debjani is a cardiologist. Both are orphans, and there are no familial or social impediments to their relationship. In the genre of the dialogue heavy, bourgeois drawing-room dramas popularized by Rituparno Ghosh and Aparna Sen in the 1990s, *Hrid Majharey* exemplifies the 'cinema of confinement' (Chowdhury 2016: 104–22). Recreating the intimacy of the television format in cinema, Ranjan Ghosh's frames and characters remind us of Rituparno's 'visual chamber drama ... stagey in its management of space ... private in scope, deeply middle class in concern', with elements of 'heightened interiority, protracted conversations, endless close ups and fade ins, and measured twists of narrative' (Chowdhury 2016: 110). A function of neoliberal individualism, this interiority intensifies as Abhi is sucked into a vortex of adversities, which isolates and challenges his middle-class security. After a student wrongly accuses him of sexual harassment, he is arrested, humiliated by his boss and colleagues, and loses his job. To add to these tribulations, the file of the academic book he was writing is damaged because his laptop crashes when Debjani, his girlfriend, tries to copy *Saptapadi*, the film, onto her pen drive. This intertextual reference draws our attention to the relationship of these two imaginings of *Othello* in Bengali cinema. As the couple watch *Saptapadi* on the laptop, the audience hears only the audio track, with Utpal Dutt reciting the 'It is the cause' (5.2.1) speech. The word 'cause' has a different resonance in *Hrid Majharey* since mathematician Abhi, inspired by the classic concepts of Western Enlightenment, delivers lectures on causality, refusing to believe that, to instance Hamlet, 'There are more things in heaven and earth, Horatio, / Than are dreamt of in your philosophy' (Q2, 1.5.165–6).[7] Yet the reversals of Abhi's fortune initiated by the crashing of the laptop become linked with *Saptapadi* and its associations with Othello's tragic destiny. The connection is underlined by the extra-diegetic fact that Debjani/Desdemona is played by Raima Sen, granddaughter of Suchitra, who played Rina Brown in *Saptapadi*.

The second half of the film moves to the Andaman Islands, a setting which suggests Cyprus. Debjani takes a job there so that Abhi may make a fresh start. But, as in Shakespeare's play, the island represents a tragic space where the couple is further insulated and caught up in a claustrophobic circle of psychological conflict. This is conveyed through the insistently domestic frames. Although there are some spectacular exterior shots of limpid seas and white beaches as also of the Cellular Jail, the dreaded colonial prison that housed nationalists, the gaze is detached and touristy. The title *Hrid Majharey*, alluding to a song, expresses a lover's resolve to preserve the lover in her heart forever, but it could also refer to the film's inward journey into a psychological space. Abhi starts suspecting Debjani of having an affair and descends into a spiral of jealousy and madness, convincing himself that somehow she is to blame for all his reversals. He remembers a Chinese soothsayer he had met in Kolkata, who had asked him to be wary of love. He hallucinates images of Debjani as an idol of the goddess, Durga, being immersed into the sea. Doubting his previous faith in science and logic, he tells his students to challenge these paradigms of reason and causality. Abhi loses his job and decides to leave Debjani, the source of all his troubles. When she tries to stop him, he accidentally injures and kills her with her hairpin. An alternative closure is also provided in the film with a happy ending where the lovers discover that Debjani is pregnant and Abhi decides to stay on.

While Abhi's descent into madness and an atavistic faith in the supernatural, fatalism and irrational jealousy can be seen as a turn towards the premodern, Debjani, by contrast, provides the image of a modern, professional woman who defends her right to have her own friends without arousing Abhi's suspicions. Reversing traditional gender roles, it is Desdemona/Debjani who undertakes the journey to the Andamans/Cyprus for her work while Abhi follows her. In *Hrid Majharey*, Abhi and Debjani are not divided by race, class or caste – they are separated by their different affiliations to and distance from modernity. The two perspectives provide us with two versions of the events which lead to the two different endings the film provides – Debjani's expansive worldview leads to a comic resolution, while Abhi's fatalism leads to tragedy.[8]

While Bankim Chandra Chattopadhyay's influential essay framed Desdemona as a combination of tradition and colonial modernity, in subsequent cinematic adaptations she has been associated with post-colonial nationalist and global modernities. Shakespeare's plays provide endless possibilities for self-fashioning for Indian women – even as his heroines articulate the codes of propriety, *sati*-hood and indigenized modernity for the *bhadramahila*, they also create spaces of romance, sexual self-assertion, choice and autonomy outside prescriptive femininities. Thus, they help not only in forging a template of Indian womanhood but also in disrupting many of its assumptions.

Notes

1   The references are to Hindu heroines from the *Puranas* known for their chastity.
2   For a discussion of how Shakespeare became an alternative religion, a non-denominational spirituality, and the new '*mantra* in [the] fight against obscurantism and traditionalism', see Bagchi 1991: 151.

3   This brings to mind the Anglo-Indian Shakespeare teacher, Miss Stoneham, in Aparna Sen's *36 Chowringhee Lane* (1981), who is shut out of the Christmas party thrown by the Bengali couple she had befriended.
4   For a comparable discussion, see Poonam Trivedi's chapter in this volume.
5   For a related discussion, see Chatterjee 2010: 15–25.
6   On the 'urban thriller', see Mukherjee 2016: 116–36. On the 'melodrama', see Prasad 1998: 79–87. Prasad analyses the genre as a 'melodrama' from a woman's perspective that uses narratives of love, betrayal, sacrifice and reunion and that often deploys triangulated love stories. A relevant example is *Sangam* (dir. Raj Kapoor, 1964), which is also set against the Sino-Indian war, with the war hero claiming the heroine because of his nationalist credentials.
7   The line is quoted by the soothsayer in the film.
8   On these generic polarities, see the discussion in Bamber 1982.

References

Bagchi, J. (1991), 'Shakespeare in Loin Cloths: English Literature and the Early Nationalist Consciousness in Bengal', in S. Joshi (ed.), *Rethinking English: Essays in Literature, Language, History*, 146–59, New Delhi: Trianka.

Bamber, L. (1982), *Comic Women, Tragic Men: Gender and Genre in Shakespeare*, Stanford: Stanford University Press.

Bandyopadhyay, T. (2015), *Tarashankar Bandyopadhyay Rachanabali*, ed. G. Mitra, 25 vols, Calcutta: Mitra & Ghosh Publishers.

Chatterjee, S. (2010), 'Bengali Popular Melodrama in the 50s', *South Asian Journal*, 29 (July–September): 15–25.

Chattopadhyay, B. C. (1938), 'Shakuntala, Miranda and Desdemona', in B. Bandyopadhyay and S. Das (eds), *Bijnan-rahasya, Samya, Vividha Prabandha*, 80–8, Calcutta: Bangiya Sahitya Parishad.

Chowdhury, S. (2016), 'The Endangered City in Rituparno Ghosh's Early Cinema of Confinement', in S. Datta, K. Bakshi and R. K. Dasgupta (eds), *Rituparno Ghosh: Cinema, Gender and Art*, 104–22, London and New York: Routledge.

Dutt, U. (1986), *Shakespeare er Samaj Chetana*, Calcutta: M. C. Sarkar.

Hamraaz (1967), [Film] Dir. B. R. Chopra, India: N. H. Studios/All-India Film Corporation.

Hrid Majharey (2014), [Film] Dir. Ranjan Ghosh, India: A. P. Films/Piyali Films.

Kaliyattam (1997), [Film] Dir. Jayaraj, India: Jayalakshmi Films.
Mahanagar (1963), [Film] Dir. Satyajit Ray, India: R. D. Banshal & Co.
Mangai, A. (2019), 'Not the Play but the Playing: Citation of Performing Shakespeare as a Trope in Tamil Cinema', in P. Trivedi and P. Chakravarti (eds), *Shakespeare and Indian Cinemas: 'Local Habitations'*, 238–50, London and New York: Routledge.
Mukherjee, M. (2016), 'That Figure in the Dark: Of Melodrama, Noir and Multiplicity during the 1950s', in G. Kaul (ed.), *Indian Film Culture/Indian Cinema*, 116–36, Kolkata: Federation of Film Societies of India.
Omkara (2006), [Film] Dir. Vishal Bhardwaj, India: Shemaroo Video, Big Screen Entertainment, Panorama Studios.
Othello (1951), [Film] Dir. Orson Welles, USA: Marceau Films/United Artists.
Pal, T. C. (1875), *Bhimsingha*, Calcutta: People's Friend.
Prasad, M. (1998), *The Ideology of the Hindi Film*, New Delhi: Oxford University Press.
Ratha Thilagam (1963), [Film] Dir. Dada Mirasi, India: National Movies.
Saptapadi (1961), [Film] Dir. Ajoy Kar, India: Alochhaya Productions.
Sangam (1964), [Film] Dir. Raj Kapoor, India: Mehboob Studio/Filmistan.
Sarkar, T. (2001), *Hindu Wife, Hindu Nation*, Delhi: Permanent Black.
36 Chowringhee Lane (1981), [Film] Dir. Aparna Sen, India: Film-Valas.

PART TWO

Translations

3

Indian Shakespeares in the British Library collections: Translation, indigeneity and representation

*Priyanka Basu and
Arani Ilankuberan*

The British Library holds over 500,000 South Asian printed books and more than 80,000 South Asian manuscripts. The British Library's Indian collections, which form a part of the wider South Asia collections, hold a fascinating collection of Shakespeare translations dating from the nineteenth century, the period when printing and the book trade commenced in the Indian subcontinent.[1] The makeup of the British Library's Indian collections stems from the formation of the British Library in 1973. The passing of the British Library Act of 1972 ensured that in 1973 the British Library became the UK's national library, which comprised material from several libraries that had merged to form the new British Library's resources. Two such libraries were the India Office Library and Records (1600–1947) that moved to the British Library in 1982, and the British Museum Library, founded in 1753, that contributed to the British Library's historical South Asian collection items. This rearrangement is in addition to postcolonial acquisitions across the South Asian languages, which make up the current South Asia holdings of the British Library.

'Two Centuries of Indian Print' at the British Library is an ongoing research and digitization project in collaboration with the School of Cultural Texts and Records (SCTR) at Jadavpur University; Srishti Institute of Art, Design and Technology in Bangalore; and the SOAS Library in London.[2] The project specializes in bringing to light an extensive and rich repository of rare Bengali, Assamese and Sylheti books (printed between 1714 and 1914), of which approximately 1,800 titles have now been digitized and made available online. This chapter looks first at some of these early Bengali Shakespeare works, and then explores some of the Tamil translations in the South Indian collections, in order to understand how 'Indianized' translations of Shakespeare's plays catered to local sentiments and also acted as pedagogical and instructive tools in the English language education curriculum. More importantly, it explores the Indian colonial, local socio-historical and political attitudes towards women in the nineteenth and early twentieth centuries that these translations underline.

TABLE 3.1 *Table of Manuscripts and Proscribed Publications in North Indian Collections by Language*

Language	Manuscripts	Proscribed Publications	Total
Assamese	19	5	24
Bengali	222	106	328
Gujarati	138	58	196
Hindi	286	679	965
Marathi	258	75	333
Oriya	91	9	100
Punjabi	19	87	106
Nepali and Newari	27		
Total	1060	1019	2079

Source: Priyanka Basu, compiled using British Library catalogues.

Early Shakespeare translations in Bengali

Writing in 1926 for the Shakespeare Association, C. J. Sisson of University College, London, produced a pamphlet titled 'Shakespeare in India: Popular Adaptations on the Bombay Stage', in which he affirmatively states:

> There is but one country in the world to the best of my knowledge, except possibly Germany, where the plays of Shakespeare have of recent times formed the safest and surest of attraction to the indiscriminate masses who attend popular theatre, where the proprietor of a theatre could count on a profit on a Shakespeare production. That country is India, and the theatres in question are a group of theatres in the city of Bombay, clustered together in the heart of a poor Indian population.
>
> (1926: 7)

Despite the essay's subject matter, hinting at Sisson's perusal of Shakespearean theatre in Bombay, he moves occasionally into the subject of Shakespeare's popularity in Bengal, at one point comparing Shakespeare with Rabindranath Tagore and eventually dismissing Tagore's plays as unfit both in terms of 'hope of success or even of a patient hearing' (1926: 7) at the public theatres.

South Asia's tryst with Shakespeare has been the subject of numerous scholarly interventions, critical responses as well as continuous archival explorations.[3] Of these, the scholarship on Bengali Shakespeare both from the literary and performative points of view has encompassed the text, its translations, its adaptations for the stage and a range of other media, and the socio-historical responses that the Shakespearean oeuvre has elicited both from litterateurs and artists. This section of the chapter follows the existing literary historical trends of reading Shakespearean translations and adaptations in late nineteenth- and early twentieth-century Bengal to analyse the socio-political attitudes towards women that are refracted in these works. It does so by taking account of the rare and unique texts that have been recently digitized and made available online by the ongoing 'Two Centuries of Indian Print' project. Some of these Bengali translations and adaptations include: *Tales from Shakespeare* by Charles and Mary Lamb (**Figure 3.1**), translated into Bengali by Muktaram Bidyabagish and others (1852); *Sushila-Birsingha*, a translation of *Cymbeline* by Satyendranath Thakur (1867); *Sushila-Chandraketu*, an adaptation of *Twelfth Night* by Kantichandra Bidyaratna (1872); *Jhanjha*, a translation of *The Tempest* by Nagendra Prasad Sarbbadhikari (1913); and *Rani Tamalini*, a translation of *The Winter's Tale* by Dhanadacharan Mitra (1914).

Translations of Shakespearean drama in Bengal date back to the mid-nineteenth century, with *The Merchant of Venice* translated by Harachandra Ghosh as *Bhanumati Chittabilas* (1853). The introduction of Shakespeare into the educational curriculum of English-medium institutions like the Hindu College, however, began much earlier, with students at the College performing the 'Court Scene' from *The Merchant of Venice* at the Governor's House in 1837 (Bhattacharya 1964: 29). Bidyabagish's translation of the *Tales* clearly states in the 'Preface' to the edition that it is meant for educational purposes and for an appreciation of the English literature canon.[4]

In translations/adaptations with Bengali titles – especially those from the mid-nineteenth century onwards – the translators specify their use of what Poonam Trivedi terms the 'indigenization' or

FIGURE 3.1 *Image of* Tales from Shakespeare *by Charles and Mary Lamb (1852), British Library VT 1623(b)*

'Indianization' of Shakespeare (2005: 15, 23). These translated plays have South Asian settings – North India, the Malay Peninsula, Sri Lanka and so on – and underline the need for adapting Shakespeare according to the manners and customs of the colonies.

This section of the chapter is divided into two parts. The first is a careful reading of the translators' notes and prefaces from the digitized plays mentioned above in order to explore how 'Indianization' or 'indigenization' works in the context of Shakespeare translations. The second tries to understand a play-text within the framework of gender and the representation of women in literature, with a particular focus on ideas of chastity, honour and the duties of the *kshatriya* (warrior class).

Shakespeare as a pedagogic tool in nineteenth-century Bengal

Bengali studies of and around Shakespeare in the nineteenth century are synonymous with the sphere of learning, connoting knowledge, humanity, modernity and exceptional linguistic ability. Such varied areas of engagement emphasize pedagogy, entertainment and the combative stances occupied by colonial subjects. Scholars have shown how Shakespeare was used as a strategy to check insurgency in the colonized space, for the Bible as a pedagogical tool might offend, but not the inclusion of Shakespeare (Banerji 2016: 30). Hema Dahiya has argued how the practice of Bardolatry was prominent both in Europe and in India in the eighteenth and nineteenth centuries, positioning Shakespeare above 'religions and races, known for embodying universal, not religious, racial, or nationalist values' (2014: 71). Almost all the prefaces and translators' notes from the Bengali Shakespeares under discussion here testify to this universality in advocating the need for reading, and specifically internalizing, Shakespeare. Bidyabagish (1852: i–ii) writes in the 'Preface' to his translations of the Lambs' *Tales from Shakespeare* how, despite the simplification of the propositions of the Great Bard in the form of novels, his ideas nonetheless inspire a deep satisfaction in the soul, instigate moral value and judgement in the imagination, provide inspiration towards works of dignity, teach perseverance in experiencing entertainment and help one refrain from selfish and base acts/instincts. Muktaram also underlines the fact that, while the translations are meant for youth (perhaps the young schoolboys and students of the erstwhile Hindu College), the literary and entertainment value of Shakespeare is capable of transcending barriers of age and appealing to the elderly as well.

That the early years of Shakespeare translations in Bengal marked primarily a pedagogical intention following the introduction of English education in Calcutta is attested to further by Harachandra Ghosh in his 'Preface' to *Bhanumati Chittabilaash* (1853), a translation of *The Merchant of Venice*. The *bhumika* (here, the introduction, preface or the translator's note) in the Bangla language and the 'Preface' in English to this translation, though by the same author, offer interesting differences that might be useful in thinking about circulation and reception. However, while such an in-depth study is beyond the purview of this chapter, it is sufficient to take into account how Ghosh points out that the translation was meant for encouraging the quest for knowledge of the young boys of his country. Written nearly twenty years after the English Education Act of 1835 and the publication of T. B. Macaulay's *Minutes on Education* (1862), these notes and prefaces were possibly following the trend set by the Christian missionaries in the 1820s in relation to the running of schools for young boys.[5]

Indigenizing Shakespeare translations and the representation of women

By the early twentieth century, following the first partition of Bengal in 1905 and the ongoing *Swadeshi* (self-sufficiency) movement, nationalist sentiments manifested themselves in literature, plays, songs and propaganda in general. A look at the Bengali Shakespeare translations, especially through the voices of the translators during this period, clarifies the insurgent socio-political feelings of the times. Nagendra Prasad Sarbbadhikari, in his translation of *The Tempest* (**Figure 3.2**) titled *Jhanjha* (1913), mentions that the translation deviated from the original metre

TRANSLATION, INDIGENEITY AND REPRESENTATION 71

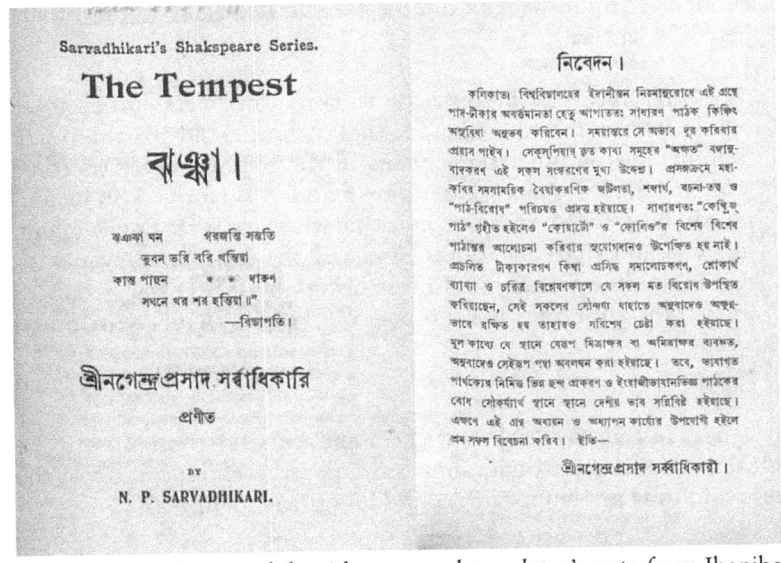

FIGURE 3.2 *Image of the title page and translator's note from* Jhanjha *(1913), a translation of* The Tempest *by Nagendra Prasad Sarbbadhikari, British Library VT 3285(b)*

and imparted 'a familiarity with the indigenous' (*deshiya bhaab*) for those not experienced in the English language (1913: i). More interesting, perhaps, is the title page of the translation that includes two couplets in Brajabhasha (the Braj or Western Hindi language) by the Maithili poet, Vidyapati.

The couplets appear strategically below the Bengali translation of the title, capturing the essence of tempests as natural calamities for the reader. The play was published in 1913, the year marking the first Nobel Prize in literature for Bengal won by Rabindranath Tagore, this celebratory event imaginatively finding expression in Vidyapati's couplets that Tagore had set to music earlier in 1884 in his *Bhanusingher Padabali* (or 'The Songs of Bhanusingho').

While this Bengali counterpart to *The Tempest* retains the original setting of the play, a translation of *Cymbeline* from 1914 by Dhanadacharan Mitra shifts it to the Malay Peninsula. Both translations speak of indigenizing the text; however, Mitra offers a rationale behind the act of translation that clearly takes into account the Hindu Bengali middle-class in its social and domestic sphere. He writes:

> It is advisable to adhere strictly to Hindu manners and customs while attempting to make an English household liveable for a Hindu. Just as the arrangements of the Hindu prayer room or congregational spaces are more mandatory for a Hindu and mark his Hindu identity in comparison to the English ball, billiard and smoking rooms, similarly the translator (even with his limited understanding) must bring about necessary changes in a translation of a foreign poem in keeping with the national duty.
>
> (1914: ii)[6]

It is here in this 'Preface' that Mitra alludes more than once to the ideal of the chaste woman in ascertaining the Hinduization of the text and thus pre-empts a Bengali Hindu readership:

> We are easily mesmerised on hearing the descriptions of a woman whose hair is as dark as the bee or whose eyes are like those of a deer. The imagination of the glare of a cat-eyed foreign woman instils nothing but aversion/disgust in our souls.
>
> (1914: ii)

Here, Mitra further includes moral prescriptions, justifying why a public display of man-woman affinities in the 'original' text are impermissible in the translation, and even the liberties that the translator has taken to retain a female character as a celibate widow conforming to her duties rather than remarrying.

Such prescriptions about women's roles and behaviours help us look at a trajectory of these translated texts where each in its own way upholds the duties of the woman. Partha Chatterjee (1986; 1988; 1989) has shown how the home in this period was projected as the inner spiritualized space of the nationalist male, where women preserved the age-old Indian *dharma*. This brings us to an interesting adaptation of one of Shakespeare's romantic comedies, Bidyaratna's *Sushila-Chandraketu* (1872), set in the erstwhile Sinhala region or present-day Sri Lanka (**Figure 3.3**).

The characters Sushila and Chandraketu in the title of the play correspond to the characters of Viola and Duke Orsino in the

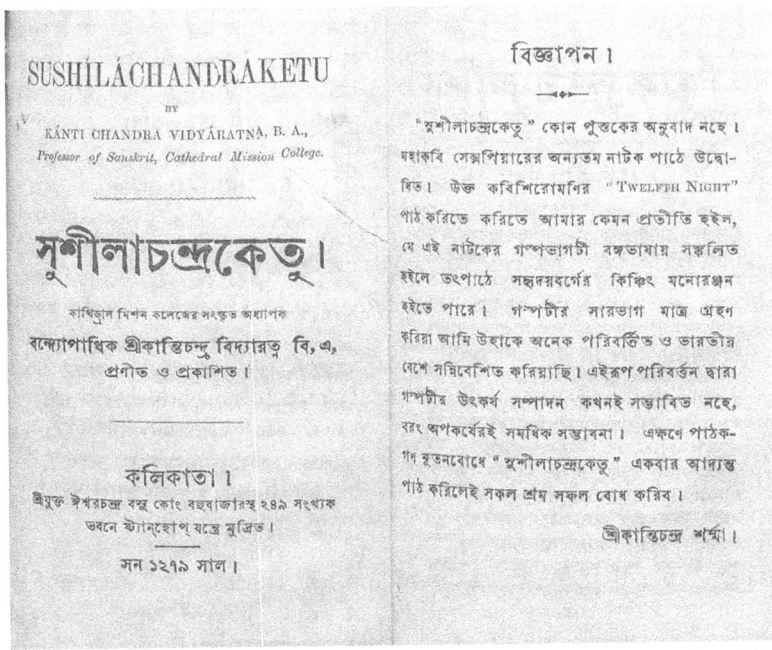

FIGURE 3.3 *Image from* Sushila-Chandraketu *(a translation of* Twelfth Night*) by Kantichandra Bidyaratna, British Library VT 963(l)*

original play, *Twelfth Night*. The narrative, however, has only a slight relation to the 'original', thus relying mostly on the idea of identical twins and the incidents that are propelled by mistaken identities. *Sushila-Chandraketu* is written in the format of a novella. It is divided into five sections or chapters, probably following the five-act structure of *Twelfth Night*; however, it bears little or no resemblance to the sequence of the 'original'. Instead, a close reading of the first two-and-a-half to three chapters reveals that they seem to borrow from Barnabe Rich's *Apolonius and Silla* (1581), the latter being one of the sources for *Twelfth Night* itself. More intriguing perhaps is the name 'Sushila' for Viola, since it refers to the translation of the play in the Bengali version of Charles and Mary Lamb's *Tales from Shakespeare* (1852: 304) where the Sea Captain, who rescues Viola, refers to Olivia as *Sushila* (indicating her noble birth and character). The epithet's interchangeable use for women characters in Bengali Shakespeare translations signals the prevalent and permissible portraitures of women in the mainstream literary traditions/translations of the times. Bidyabagish adds at one point in his translation of the *Tales* that it is rather polluting for a woman of good character (he actually uses the Bengali word 'Sushila') to cross-dress as a man and appear before a king (1852: 305).[7] Interestingly, one can find an echo of the translator's sentiments in later debates (especially in nineteenth-century Bengali newspapers like *Madhyastha*) about whether women actresses should be employed to perform female roles on the Bengali stage at all.

Sushila-Chandraketu is largely about the various tests and obstacles that a woman of good moral character faces as she ventures out of the domestic sphere. There are no counterparts of characters from the play, such as Feste, or Sir Andrew Aguecheek or even Sir Toby Belch. Orsino and Sebastian (here, Chandraketu and Sushil, respectively) uphold *kshatriya* (or warrior) values and prowess, and at several points in the narrative the qualities of a dutiful *kshatriya* are stated explicitly. Following the Indian epic traditions, the narrative includes battles among the southern Indian kingdoms, while Sushila/Viola is cast in the tradition of female figures such as Savitri, Sita, Damayanti and Durga.[8] The closer resemblance to Sanskrit dramatic traditions is clearer in the inclusion of the trope of forgetfulness, an element that scholars like Wendy Doniger (2017) have explored in the histories of Sanskrit literary traditions. There are constant references to deaths (an actual murder takes place in the narrative), including a brief allusion to the dagger scene in *Macbeth*, employed in the manner of a woman's fear of losing her chastity and the consequent urge to commit suicide in order to save *kshatriya* pride.

In conclusion to this discussion on Bengali Shakespeare translations, we include a reference to gender roles and cross-dressing in the text that might offer some comparison between the Bengali adaptation and the English 'original'. As Sushila/Viola is sent to court Olivia/Chandrakumari by Duke Orsino/Chandraketu, Sushila is introduced as a eunuch. In fact, the reference to a eunuch's identity is boldly held against prescriptive *kshatriya* qualities in the narrative. Androgynous identity in Renaissance England suggests prosthetic attempts to fix gender on the one hand, as Anne Rosalind Jones and Peter Stallybrass (2000) have argued, and, on the other, points to the ways in which 'androgyny is recuperated into a masculine ethos that supports patriarchal gender hierarchy' (Casey 1997: 125). The absence of same-sex erotic affinities and possibilities in the Bengali adaptation foregrounds a man–woman, public–private, binary, as the milieu grappled with issues of women's institutional education *and* the arrival of the public woman as a public actress on the Bengali proscenium stage. Similar attitudes towards women can be located in South Indian Shakespeare translations as well, discussed in detail in the following section in an overview of the Tamil-, Telugu-, Kannada- and Malayalam-language Shakespeare translations in the British Library collections.

South Indian Shakespeare translations in the British Library

This section of the chapter seeks to illuminate the rich holdings of Shakespeare translations in the South Indian languages at the British Library. It also explores the ways in which South Indian translators have portrayed Shakespeare's female characters, using examples of Shakespeare translations from the Tamil language collections. The first part of this section serves as an introduction to the British Library's South Indian collections, which is a significant subset of the larger South Asia collections. Having contextualized the South Indian collections, it then provides an overview of Shakespeare translations in the four main South Indian languages: Kannada, Malayalam, Tamil and Telugu. Here, the South Indian Shakespeare translations' collections history is explored by highlighting the earliest examples of Shakespeare translations in each of the South Indian languages and by providing a measure of the breadth of the early nineteenth- to twentieth-century printed translations that are represented in the British Library's South Indian collections. The second part of this section focuses on the Tamil collections and analyses two Tamil plays across two genres: tragedy and comedy. The Tamil translations of the plays *Othello* and *The Comedy of Errors* are studied, with a focus on the translators' interpretations of the tragic heroine, Desdemona, in A. Madhaviah's 1902 *Otello enra Venis Moriyan*, and of the comic heroine, Adriana, in A. Venkatacharyar's 1905–6 *Viprama Vihasam*. Thus, this part of the chapter explores the early twentieth-century translators' uses of Tamil sensibilities and literary traditions in relation to the 'indigenization' or 'Indianization' (Trivedi 2005: 15, 23) of women in Shakespeare.

The South Indian collections at the British Library, currently numbering a total of over 124,000 printed books and manuscripts, are a subsection of the South Asia collections and constitute items in the four major Dravidian languages of Kannada, Malayalam, Tamil and Telugu, in addition to collections from Sri Lanka in Sinhalese and Sri Lankan Tamil. Besides the items in the table below, the collection also houses items in several minor South Indian language collections that are either linguistically Dravidian or geographically located in the South of India.

The largest of the South Indian collections are the Tamil language collections with over 50,000 collection items, followed by the Telugu language collections that are around half the size of the Tamil collections. The final two South Indian language collections of Kannada and Malayalam are similarly sized, with around 20,000 collection items each. Naturally, the number of the South Indian Shakespeare translations across all four South Indian languages also follows the size of the collections, as there are: fifty-seven Tamil language Shakespeare translations; twenty-two Telugu language Shakespeare translations; thirteen Malayalam language Shakespeare translations and twelve Kannada language Shakespeare translations. Therefore, across the four major South Indian languages in the British Library, there are a total of 104 Shakespeare translations.

TABLE 3.2 *Table of South Indian Collections by Language*

Language	Manuscripts	Printed Books	Total
Kannada	82	19,480	19,562
Malayalam	65	18,275	18,340
Tamil	204	54,460	54,664
Telugu	80	26,620	26,700
Sinhalese	2,464	2,100	4,564
Total	2,895	120,935	123,830

Source: Arani Ilankuberan, compiled using British Library catalogues.

Tamil

The fifty-seven Tamil language Shakespeare translations are made up of twenty-three translations from the India Office collections and thirty-four from the British Museum collections. In the 1909 British Museum catalogue, there are nine Shakespeare translations, the earliest being S. M. Natesa Sastri's 1892 translation of *Twelfth Night*, and from the India Office collections, there are twenty-three translations of Shakespeare, the earliest of which is an 1874 translation of *Othello*. There are also another twenty Shakespeare translations from the 1931 British Museum catalogue, and, from the 1980 catalogue of the British Museum collections, there are a further five Shakespeare translations ranging from the 1920s to the 1950s.

Telugu

The British Museum collections hold thirteen Telugu translations of Shakespeare, dating from 1894 to 1910. The oldest translation in this collection is *Othello* (1894) by V. Padmanabha Razu, and, from the India Office collections, there are a further nine translations of Shakespeare dating from the late 1920s to the mid-1930s. The most popularly translated work in the collection is *Othello*, with four translations, closely followed by *King Lear* and *The Tempest*, with three translations each.

Malayalam

In the British Museum collections, there are eleven translations of Shakespeare and a further two translations of Shakespeare from the India Office collections.[9] The most popularly translated work is *Othello* with five translations, followed by two translations of *The Merchant of Venice*. Other plays here include: *The Comedy of Errors*, *The Winter's Tale*, *Pericles* and *The Taming of the Shrew*.

Kannada

There are twelve Kannada translations of Shakespeare in total, published between 1876 and 1925 from both the India Office and British Museum collections. The earliest translation in the Kannada language collections is an 1876 publication of *The Comedy of Errors*, alongside two other translations of this play. Other plays here include *The Merchant of Venice*, *The Taming of the Shrew*, *A Midsummer Night's Dream* and multiple translations of *Macbeth*. **Figure 3.4** shows a scene from a Kannada stage production of *A Midsummer Night's Dream* in which a male actor (first from left) can be seen sporting a stern and accusatory pose and representing a woman through wearing a sari, being adorned in jewellery and having jasmine garlands in the hair.

It is clear from the actor's *Tripundra*, a signifier of a follower of Saivaism comprising three lines of sacred ash on the forehead complete with central dot, that this is also a localized production,

FIGURE 3.4 *Image of a scene from a production of* A Midsummer Night's Dream, *from S. A. Hirematha,* Vasantayamini Svapnacamatkara Natakavu *(1925), British Library 14176.e.28(7)*

in which the royal courts and fairy magic of the play have been transposed along cultural and religious lines in keeping with the predominantly Hindu Kannada audience's sensibilities. The following section on Tamil Shakespearean women also looks at such 'Indianization' of Shakespeare but focuses more on the textual and para-textual levels by examining the South Indian translators' modes of adapting Shakespeare's women to Tamil cultural contexts.

Tamilized Shakespearean women

As Poonam Trivedi and Dennis Bartholomeusz's seminal study, *India's Shakespeare: Translation, Interpretation and Performance* (2005), demonstrates, it is clear that *Othello* and *The Comedy of Errors* are among the most widely translated plays, not only in South Indian Shakespeares but across all the Indian languages. The fact that both plays are popularly adapted, though they belong to the different genres of tragedy and comedy, reveals the broad appeal of Shakespeare in India, with K. R. Srinivasa Iyengar noting that:

> Besides the Comedies are as a general rule more popular with the 'common reader' in India than the Histories or the Tragedies. After all, since Kalidasa is our great exemplar in drama, it is not surprising that we should feel particularly attracted to what is Kalidasian in Shakespeare.
>
> (1964: 2)

To this, K. Subramanyam adds that, for Tamil audiences, 'The first of Shakespeare's own plays to be adapted for the Tamil stage was characteristically enough *The Taming of the Shrew* with its boisterous comedy which was dear to the Tamil public' (1964: 121).[10]

However, it is not just Shakespeare's comedies that took root in an India that was already primed by Kalidasian drama to be receptive to the comedies; Shakespearean tragedy too found fertile ground in the Indian poetic tradition represented by its own tragic women and men. Specifically in relation to the Tamil context, K. Muruganandan credits Shakespeare as an important influence, which worked together with existing tragic narratives in Tamil Hindu and literary epics, for the birth of tragedy as a genre in the western sense in early modern Tamil literature. He writes:

> Tamil identity and colonial modernity shaped the emergence and establishment of tragedy in Tamil. In turn, absence of this genre was conceived to be a lacuna for the Tamil language, and its birth was received with a great amount of reverence. Thus, Tragedy also shaped the process of constructing Tamil identity and colonial modernity.
>
> There were at least three trends most visible in the birth of tragedy as a genre in Tamil drama:
>
> 1. Creative Experimentations in the urban theatre,
> 2. Shakespeare adaptations, and
> 3. Plays centred on the tragic Puranic and folk characters.
>
> (2019: 210)

Therefore, the two plays identified here demonstrate the ways in which translators have engaged with realizing Shakespeare's female characters in Tamil by suiting the conventions of the genre and by indigenizing and Tamilizing the characters with varying degrees of proximity to the 'original' Shakespearean women to whom they are related.

Othello

Desdemona's connection in temperament to the revered figures of the wronged and chaste Indian wives like Kannaki and Sita has not gone unnoticed among scholars studying parallels between the Tamil epics, Hindu *purana*s (ancient legends) and Shakespeare's works (Gokhale 2009; Lakshmanan and Nagarathinam 2015). However, Desdemona's pleading and acceptance of her death at Othello's hands stand in stark contrast to the equivalent actions of her Indian counterparts – to Sita and Kannaki's displays of righteous anger at their respective predicaments symbolized in the use of fire. Sita's trial by fire to prove her purity and Kannaki's dramatic and fiery retribution towards the city of Madurai in response to an unjust ruling show two women who speak out against the injustices levelled at them by authority.

Considering this difference, this section explores, then, how Tamil translators understand and relay Desdemona's character to their audiences. In Madhaviah's critically acclaimed faithful translation of *Othello* (**Figure 3.5**), Shakespeare's words are reproduced with

FIGURE 3.5 *Title page of A. Madhaviah's Tamil translation of* Othello *(1902), British Library 14171.i.1.(1.)*

care and accuracy, ensuring the translator, through word choices, is also reflecting the same zeal as expressed in the 'original'. Yet, however closely he replicates Shakespeare in his translation, his own analysis of the character, paratextually perhaps, better reflects his internalized process of reproducing and envisioning Desdemona as a tragic Tamil heroine.

Madhaviah's contemporary, Pammal Sambanda Mudaliar, openly changed Shakespeare's portrayal of more morally ambiguous and complex female characters like Lady Macbeth and Gertrude, for his translation ran counter to his own views of women and he felt it would offend the sensibilities of his female audience (Muruganandan 2019). However, Madhaviah opts here for a different approach, keeping the translation as closely bound to the 'original' as possible whilst bookending it with his own views of women and Shakespeare's women.

It is telling (an indication of just how important the translator thought Desdemona) that, though Madhaviah translates *Othello*, it is not its eponymous hero who gets the first mention. Instead, it is his teacher, and in particular Dr Miller's criticism levelled at Desdemona's character, which leaves a lasting impact on the writer, also hinting perhaps at his motives in translating the play. Madhaviah's sentiments are expressed in the English foreword to his translation, where he states of his teacher that:

> his regretful words at the close of our study of this play can never be forgotten. Said he, commenting on the heroine's character: "The worst defect in Desdemona's character is *thoughtlessness*. In this world
> 'Evil is wrought by want of thought,
> As well as by want of heart.'
> And now, my boys, the best of you are only so many Desdemonas." How sad! And yet, how true to the life we live!
>
> (Madhaviah 1902: 6)

The translator was a well-known staunch supporter of women's education; years later, when his own daughter challenged this very notion of Desdemona's thoughtlessness, Madhaviah 'wrote to the principal with some pride about his daughter's spirited defence of Desdemona's actions' (Madhaviah 2005: xiii). Madhaviah's response here reveals both the translator's own progressive vision for the future of modern, liberated Tamil women as well as his affection for Desdemona, the Shakespearean woman who is unblemished and innocent and who embodies much of the spirit of Sita in her 'guiltless death' (*Othello*, 5.2.121).

The Comedy of Errors

While it was noted earlier that *The Taming of the Shrew* was a more popular comedy than *The Comedy of Errors* among Tamil audiences, the popularity of both plays could be attributed to the relationship strife endured by the witty, headstrong and therefore considered 'shrewish' female leads of the plays. Additionally, the comedy that ensues through the relationships between the various sisters and their significant others in each of these plays appeals culturally to the audiences.

In this illustrated translation of *The Comedy of Errors* (**Figure 3.6**), by A. Venkatacharyar (1905-6), the scene is one of only a handful of illustrations across the serialized play, released in the periodical *Sri Vani Vilasini* (the home in which Goddess Saraswati resides). The character of Adriana here is shown to be wild, with her hair flowing behind her, as she raises her hand towards a cowering Dromio, while standing next to her is her demure sister, Luciana, who, in contrast, has her hair in its proper place and further wraps her sari around her in a show of humility.

In Venkatacharyar's translation, the scene where Adriana threatens violence is given a cultural makeover, with humour specific to the Tamil context. In the 'original', Adriana states, 'Back, slave, or I will break thy pate across' (*The Comedy of Errors*, 2.1.77), while here, she becomes Kanjanamalai, who says, '*Ni pokavitil un mantaiyaip panankay kiruvatu pola netukappilantu vitukiren par*', which translates as 'If you do not go, watch! I will split your head open the way a palmyra fruit is repeatedly cut into!' Though a direct translation would have also been possible, through the 'Indianization' (Trivedi 2005: 15) employed, with the inclusion of the fruit of the palm tree native to the Indian subcontinent, the Tamil audiences are better able to recognize and connect to the anger of Kanjanamalai and can picture the violence she threatens towards her husband's servant.

FIGURE 3.6 *Image of Adriana threatening Dromio with violence in* Viprama Vihasam *(1905–6), A. Venkatacharyar's Tamil translation of* The Comedy of Errors, *British Library, 14172.m.1. (vols 1–2)*

In general, Venkatacharyar adheres to the play's format, structure and characterization; unlike Madhaviah's *Othello*, in which he seeks to imitate Shakespeare verbatim, the translation here is looser in places, revealing how when translating a comedy, in particular, the writer's expressions not only have the spirit of the 'original' text that is used as inspiration but also have the freedom to find Tamil humour to entertain readers. Conclusively, from mythologizing the heroines to localizing their humour, the work of Tamil translators demonstrates that, as in the 'original', it is in the women of Shakespeare where the heart of the plays lies.

Conclusion

The centrality of Shakespeare to the relationship between print and performance is vital not only to performance cultures in early modern England but also to those in its erstwhile colonies. Especially in Bengal, with the introduction of the English-styled Bengali theatre in the mid-nineteenth century, original and translated versions of Shakespeare's plays began to be regularly printed and performed. Illustrations from the South Indian translations amply testify to this intrinsic linkage between print and performance. This chapter has engaged in surveying some of the printed and digitized Shakespeare translations in Bengali and across the Kannada, Malayalam, Tamil and Telugu language collections of the British Library. Through a discussion concentrating on Bengali and Tamil translations of plays, including *Twelfth Night*, *Othello* and *The Comedy of Errors*, we have explored the ways in which translators Indianized and Tamilized Shakespearean comedies and tragedies, making connections with and at the same time reimagining women in the plays. In a sense, these translations prompt us to think about the complexities of the colonial roots of Shakespearean translations that eventually found expression in 'our post-colonial diversities' (Loomba and Orkin 1998: 19) and of their varied local/cultural receptions in South Asia. And, as this exploration has suggested, the 'woman question' still remains integral to postcolonial approaches, as multiple instances of translation reveal.

Notes

1   See the Appendix to this collection for a selection of Shakespeare translations/adaptations from the nineteenth century onwards in the British Library collections (in Assamese, Oriya, Rajasthani, Hindi, Punjabi, Gujarati, Sindhi, Marathi, Konkani Urdu, Bengali and Hindustani languages). For further details, see 'British Museum

Catalogs in PDF Form' 2013. For the printing and book trade, see Derrick 2017.
2. For the project, see 'Two Centuries of Indian Print' 2020.
3. See, for example, Nagarajan and Viswanathan 1987; Shankar 1999; Trivedi and Bartholomeusz 2005; Kennedy and Yong 2010; Panja and Saraf 2016; Trivedi and Chakravarti 2019; Sen 2021; Thakur 2020; Trivedi, Chakravarti and Motohashi 2021, among others.
4. For a comparable discussion, see Thea Buckley's chapter in this volume.
5. For example, see the instructions of missionary Pearson 1827.
6. Translation by Priyanka Basu.
7. See Poonam Trivedi's discussion of the 'whore' and 'actress' conflation in her chapter in this volume.
8. See Taarini Mookherjee's discussion of mythical female figures in her chapter in this volume.
9. There are only ten translations attributed to Shakespeare in the 1972 British Museum catalogue of Malayalam printed books; recently, Thea Buckley has identified one more: V. T. Sankunni Menon's 1929 translation of Shakespeare's *All's Well That Ends Well*.
10. This can be seen as an indication of the South Indian preoccupation with the ideal of a conformist wife supported by a largely patriarchal India; for further information, see Taarini Mookherjee's chapter in this collection, which focuses on the virtues of the ideal Indian wife as read through a Bengali context.

References

Ahmed, S. (1988), *Bangadeshe Sheskspiyar [Shakespeare in Bengal]*, Dhaka: Bangla Academy.

Banerji, R. (2016), '"Every college student knows by heart": The Uses of Shakespeare in Colonial Bengal', *The Shakespearean International Yearbook*, 12: 29–42.

Barnett, L. D. (1910), *A Catalogue of the Kannada, Badaga, and Kurg Books in the Library of the British Museum*, London: British Museum.

Barnett, L. D. (1912), *A Catalogue of the Telugu Books in the Library of the British Museum*, London: British Museum.

Barnett, L. D. (1931), *A Supplementary Catalogue of the Tamil Books in the Library of the British Museum*, London: British Museum.

Barnett, L. D. and G. U. Pope (1909), *A Catalogue of the Tamil Books in the Library of the British Museum*, London: British Museum.

Bhattacharya, S. K. (1964), 'Shakespeare and Bengali Theatre', *Indian Literature*, 7 (1): 27–40.
Bidyabagish, M. (1852), *Tales from Shakespeare by Mr. and Miss Lamb*, Calcutta: Sambad Purnachandroday Press.
Bidyaratna, K. (1872), *Sushila-Chandraketu*, Calcutta: Stanhope Press.
British Library India Office Collections (1998a), *A Catalogue of Kannada Books of the India Office Library, 1972–1983*, London: British Library.
British Library India Office Collections (1998b), *A Catalogue of Telugu Books in the Joint Collections of the India Office Library and the Oriental Collections 1910–1983*, London: British Library.
'British Museum Catalogs in PDF Form' (2013). Available online: https://dsal.uchicago.edu/bibliographic/bmcatalogs (accessed 5 April 2021).
British Museum Department of Oriental Printed Books and Manuscripts (1999), *Second (supplementary) Catalogue of Telugu Books: 1912–1939, vol. 1, A–L*, London: British Library.
Casey, C. (1997), 'Gender Trouble in *Twelfth Night*', *Theatre Journal*, 49 (2): 121–41.
Chatterjee, P. (1988), *The Nationalist Resolution of the Women's Question*, Calcutta: Centre for Studies in Social Sciences.
Chatterjee, P. (1989), 'The Nationalist Resolution of the Women's Question', in K. Sangari and S. Vaid (eds), *Recasting Women: Essays in Colonial History*, 233–53, New Delhi: Kali for Women.
Chatterjee, P. (1986), *Nationalist Thought and the Colonial World*, London: Zed Books.
Dahiya, H. (2014), *Shakespeare Studies in Colonial Bengal: The Early Phase*, Newcastle-upon-Tyne: Cambridge Scholars Publishing.
Derrick, T. (2017), 'Quarterly Lists: Digitally Researching Catalogues of Indian Books'. Available online: https://www.bl.uk/early-indian-printed-books/articles/quarterly-lists-digitally-researching-catalogues-of-indian-books (accessed 28 December 2020).
Doniger, W. (2017), *The Ring of Truth and other Myths of Sex and Jewellery*, Oxford: Oxford University Press.
Gaur, A. (1972), *Catalogue of Malayalam Books in the British Museum: With an Appendix Listing the Books in Brahui, Gondi, Kui, Malto, Oraon (Kurukh), Toda and Tulu*, London: British Museum.
Gaur, A. (1980), *Second Supplementary Catalogue of Tamil Books in the British Library Department of Oriental Manuscripts and Printed Books*, London: British Library.
Gaur, A. and S. K. Havanur (1985), *Supplementary Catalogue of Kannada Books in the British Library*, London: British Library.
Ghosh, H. (1853), *Bhanumati Chittabilash*, Calcutta: Sambad Purnachandroday Press.

Gokhale, N. (2009), *In Search of Sita: Revisiting Mythology*, New Delhi: Penguin.

Hirematha, S. A. (1925), '*Vasantayamini Svapnacamatkara Natakavu*' *[A Midsummer Night's Dream]*, Bangalore: Bangalore Press.

India Office Library Records (1979a), *Catalogue of Malayalam Books: Pre-1950*, London: India Office Library and Records.

India Office Library Records (1979b), *Catalogue of Tamil Books: Pre-1950*, London: India Office Library and Records.

India Office Library Records (1979c), *Catalogue of Telugu Books*, 5 vols, London: India Office Library and Records.

India Office Library Records (1982), *Catalogue of Tamil Books: 1950–1971*, London: India Office Library and Records.

Jones, A. R. and P. Stallybrass (2000), *Renaissance Clothing and the Materials of Memory*, Cambridge: Cambridge University Press.

Kennedy, D. and L. L. Yong, eds (2010), *Shakespeare in Asia: Contemporary Performance*, Cambridge: Cambridge University Press.

Lakshmanan, L. and D. Nagarathinam (2015), 'Kannagi and Desdemona – A Comparative Study', *Language in India*, 15 (11): 275–90.

Loomba, A. and M. Orkin, eds (1998), *Post-colonial Shakespeares*, London and New York: Routledge.

Macaulay, T. B. (1862), *Minutes on Education in India*, Calcutta: Baptist Mission Press.

Madhaviah, A. ([1915] 2005), *Clarinda: A Historical Novel*, New Delhi: Sahitya Akademi.

Madhaviah, A. (1902), *Otello enra Venis Moriyan. Shakespeare for Tamil Homes. 1. Othello. A Translation, with a Life of the Poet and Notes*, Madras: Srinivasa Varadachari & Co.

Mitra, D. (1914), *Rani Tamalini*, Calcutta: Dhanadacharan Mitra.

Muruganandan, K. (2019), 'Birth of the Tragedy in Tamil: Colonial Compulsions and Cultural Negotiations', *Language in India*, 19 (6): 203–11.

Nagarajan, S. and S. Viswanathan, eds (1987), *Shakespeare in India*, Oxford: Oxford University Press.

Panja, S. and B. M. Saraf, eds (2016), *Performing Shakespeare in India: Exploring Indianness, Literatures and Cultures*, New Delhi and London: SAGE.

Pearson, J. D. (1827), *Instructions for Modelling and Conducting Schools*, Calcutta: The School-Book Society.

Sarbbadhikari, N. P. (1913), *Jhanjha*, Calcutta: Kuntalin Press.

Sen, S. (2021), *Shakespeare in the World: Cross-Cultural Adaptation in Europe and Colonial India, 1850–1900*, London and New York: Routledge.

Shankar, D. A., ed. (1999), *Shakespeare in Indian Languages*, Shimla: Indian Institute of Advanced Study.

Sisson, C. J. (1926), *Shakespeare in India: Popular Adaptations on the Bombay Stage*, London: The Shakespeare Association.
Srinivasa Iyengar, K. R. (1964), 'Shakespeare in India', *Indian Literature*, 7 (1): 1–11.
Subramanyam, K. (1964), 'Shakespeare in Tamil', *Indian Literature*, 7 (1): 120–6.
Thakur, S. (1867), *Sushila-Birsingha Natak*, Calcutta: New Sanskrit Press.
Thakur, V. S. (2020), *Shakespeare and Indian Theatre: The Politics of Performance*, London and New York: Bloomsbury.
Trivedi, P. (2005), 'Introduction', in P. Trivedi and D. Bartholomeusz (eds), *India's Shakespeare: Translation, Interpretation and Performance*, 13–43, Newark: University of Delaware Press.
Trivedi, P. and D. Bartholomeusz, eds (2005), *India's Shakespeare: Translation, Interpretation and Performance*, Newark: University of Delaware Press.
Trivedi, P. and P. Chakravarti, eds (2019), *Shakespeare and Indian Cinemas: 'Local Habitations'*, London and New York: Routledge.
Trivedi, P., P. Chakravarti and T. Motohashi, eds (2021), *Asian Interventions in Global Shakespeare: 'All the World's His Stage'*, London and New York: Routledge.
'Two Centuries of Indian Print' (2020). Available online: https://www.bl.uk/projects/two-centuries-of-indian-print (accessed 5 April 2021).
Venkatacharyar, A. (1905), '*Viprama Vihasam* (Shakespeare's *Comedy of Errors*)', *Sri Vani Vilasini*, 1 (3): 245–53.

4

Women translating Shakespeare in South India: *Hemanta Katha* or *The Winter's Tale*

Thea Buckley

This chapter offers a case study of *Hemanta Katha* [*The Winter's Tale*], an 1892 translation of Shakespeare's late play into the Malayalam language by O. M. Lakshmy Amma. Her book is a rarity, for female-authored works represent only a handful of the existing Indian-language translations of Shakespeare made before India's 1947 Independence, with hers the only such recorded work in Malayalam. In documenting such early works, the researcher's task is rendered more complex by their paucity, emblematic of the interlocking obstacles facing the pre-Independence-era female Indian translator of Shakespeare. Feminist critic and translator Pilar Godayol writes of the theory and practice of 'translating as/like a woman, being a political and social discourse that criticises and subverts the patriarchal practices which render women invisible' (2005: 11). Certainly, Lakshmy Amma's preface locates her work in a patriarchal world at the outset, ascribing its publication to the 'desire' of her 'affectionate father', even while stating the intention to empower women (1892: n.p.). Indeed, her own work has remained relatively invisible. The British Library copy that this chapter discusses had been lost in storage until late 2020.[1] An internet search turns up a single mention of her text, on a reprinted 1913 Malayalam-language curriculum (Frohnmeyer 2004: viii). Nor is *Hemanta Katha* listed in scholarly works with Malayalam Shakespeare translations appendices, published as recently as 2020.[2]

Through examining Lakshmy Amma's recovered work, this chapter aims to illuminate the position of a female translator amid intersections of feminism, casteism, colonialism and Marxism in the author's region of today's Kerala. Kerala's Shakespeares are rooted in its identity as a state in the culturally and linguistically distinct Dravidian region of South India. I look at Lakshmy Amma's work as exemplifying several features of the local translation of Shakespeare – translation from Charles and Mary Lamb's prose *Tales of Shakespeare* rather than the verse originals, fidelity to the source text and the tactic of localization or 'domestication', these latter two representing general strategies 'of the translator translating into Malayalam' (Chandran 2015: 98, 100). Discussing Kerala's assertive regionalization of the non-local, K. G. Paulose points out that 'localization, as a form of resistance, itself is a progressive step' (2016: 4). While Lakshmy Amma's work represents an entirely faithful, if localized, translation, Beatrice Lei alerts us to ways in which we can recognize a translator's individuality: 'word choice … and even omissions are all interpretive acts. Appended materials (Shakespeare's biography … an introduction, etc.) can also reveal a translator's position' (2016: 10). Accordingly, through examining these parts of Lakshmy Amma's translation, including her English and Malayalam prefaces and her Malayalam introduction incorporating a Shakespearean mini-biography, we can discern traces of the translator herself.

Hemanta Katha's prefatory material links the act of translation to female agency at a time of growing anti-colonial activism, providing a rare, gendered perspective of the colonial subject interpreting and translating Shakespeare in an age of rapid socio-political evolution. Lakshmy Amma's English preface alerts us at the outset to her intent, stating that to better inform her Malayali readership, 'I have given a short life of the author' and that her publication is meant 'to offer some encouragement to female education in Malabar' (in today's Kerala) (1892: n.p.). Significantly, she also selected a

Shakespearean play where 'restorations are achieved by the rich presence and compelling actions of its women' (Neely 1988: 171), and to work from a version prepared by another female writer (Mary Lamb condensed most of *Tales*' twenty plays, although co-credited only after multiple reprints).

In exploring these angles, this chapter first summarizes *Hemanta Katha*'s Shakespearean storyline, with a close reading of the localized names in her 1892 translation. Next, it looks at the work as an example of intercultural translation, including its adaptive strategies and resonances with India's epics. It then sets *Hemanta Katha* in its wider political context of local matrilineal traditions, intersectional caste and gender rights issues, and educational reforms. Finally, I situate Lakshmy Amma's work among other Malayalam versions of Shakespeare, examining linguistic strategies and investigating whether its particularities typify or problematize colonial-era hierarchies and shed light on her outlook as a South Indian female translator.

Strategies of localization

Hemanta Katha mirrors Mary Lamb's prose version of *The Winter's Tale*, Shakespeare's late 'romance' play dating to 1610–11. Lamb faithfully retains the core plot of Shakespeare's tragicomedy, while excising the comic subplot of peddler clown Autolycus and the framing device of narrator Gower. Lamb's version likewise opens in Sicilia, where King Leontes imprisons pregnant Queen Hermione upon his erroneous conviction that she carries the child of his visiting friend Polixenes, King of Bohemia. When Leontes orders his servant Camillo to poison Polixenes, they escape to Bohemia. Leontes submits Hermione's fate to the Oracle of Delphi; meanwhile, the imprisoned queen gives birth, and the king commands her waiting-woman Paulina's husband Antigones to cast away the infant. The verdict arrives: '*Hermione is chaste, Polixenes blameless, Camillo a true subject, Leontes a jealous tyrant, his innocent babe truly begotten, and the king shall live without an heir if that which is lost be not found*' (3.2.130-3). Heedless, Leontes sentences Hermione to death, whereupon young Prince Mamillius dies of grief; Hermione collapses; Leontes realizes his error; Paulina declares the queen's death. Abandoning the infant Perdita in the Bohemian wilds, Antigonus is slain by a bear; shepherds adopt the baby. Sixteen years pass; in Bohemia, King Polixenes' son Florizel conducts a secret love affair with 'shepherdess' Perdita. Upon discovery, the couple elope to Sicilia, where the missing princess is identified. Reconciled, Polixenes and Leontes bless the couple; Paulina unveils a statue of the late queen, revealed as the living Hermione herself. Leontes rewards Paulina by wedding her to Camillo. The tragicomedy concludes with unions and reunions in the comic tradition, even if Mamillius' and Antigonus' deaths cast a lingering shadow.

In Lakshmy Amma's faithful prose translation of Lamb's Shakespeare, localizations and mythical Hindu allusions illuminate the translator's cultural perspective. While Sicily and Bohemia retain their Anglicized appellations, characters take on alliterative flowery Malayalam names: Perdita becomes Prakashadeepam, or 'shining light'; Florizel is Pushpagandhan, or 'flower-fragrant man', and his alias Doricles becomes Doshajnan, or 'evil-knower'; Leontes becomes Loondakan, or 'thief', and Hermione is renamed Hemagatra, or 'beautiful-bodied lady'. Mamillius is Mamayan, the 'auspicious one', and Antigonus is Anthakapadan, the 'ultimate cheater' in Shakespeare's tale of jealousy, loss and redemption. Other names assume Hindu mythical and metonymical connotations hinting at their intertwined futures: Paulina becomes Palazhi, or 'ocean of milk'; Camillo, Kamalam or 'lotus'; and Polixenes, Patmalaya or 'lotus-abode', a name synonymous with goddess Lakshmy, who dwells on the milk-ocean with her lotus-navelled consort, Vishnu.

Localization is a strategy commonly employed by Indian translators of Shakespeare. Jayashree Ramakrishnan Nair notes that in an 1893 Malayalam translation of *The Taming of the Shrew*, for character and location names a 'sincere effort has been made to achieve a phonetic similarity with the originals' (1999: 128). Another contemporary translation, P. Velu's 1891 Malayalam-language translation *Paraklesarajavinte Katha* (*The Story of King Pericles*) nativizes European names alliteratively (my translation): Thaisa becomes Dayesha, or the 'kind lady'; Marina is Samudrika, or 'maiden of the sea'; and Tyre alters to Tharapuram, or 'city of the stars' (1891: 2). While Velu's prefatory remarks claim that he pioneered this method to accommodate the Malayalam language, this is debatable. Yet like Lakshmy Amma, he chooses to translate and localize Shakespeare, via the Lambs' *Tales*, written in an 'ordinary prose manner', to better render the text intelligible to his Malayali readership (1891: 2).

In its localization, Lakshmy Amma's translation reflects not only contemporary local trends but also intercultural dynamics. Susan Bassnett highlights the importance of culture to translation, terming language 'the heart within the body of culture' (2014: 25). The translation of Shakespeare into Indian languages can be viewed as not merely linguistic transfer but as an equation of intercultural power dynamics; D. A. Shankar maintains that *'translations and adaptations are major attempts on the part of one culture to come to terms with another'* especially with a 'dominant culture' like the British in India (1999: 15–16). Several critics see Shakespeare's plays as especially interculturally facilitative; H. H. Anniah Gowda remarks that Shakespeare's late plays can facilitate East-West exchange of 'dramatic poetry' and exhibit 'many significant features of the drama of the East', with their 'fate', 'oracles', 'visionary spirituality', 'more idealism and less realism', 'essentially poetic quality', centrality of 'family relations' and representation of a 'felicitous, imaginary universe into which suffering is indeed admitted ... yet there in the end all is happily resolved' (1999: 80–2). These tropes recur throughout India's epics and folklore, particularly the *Ramayana* and *Mahabharata*, India's central Hindu epics that narrate adventures of warring gods, humans and demons. Their chaste female protagonists undergo tribulations – slander, forced marriage, elopement, spousal separation – not unlike those of Shakespearean heroines.

For Lakshmy Amma's readership, the trials of the central female figures of *The Winter's Tale* would present familiar mythical correspondences. The court trial scene of Queen Hermione, hurried from childbed, aligns with the attempted public humiliation of *Mahabharata* queen Draupadi, whose five husbands allow their cousins to drag her to court from her menstrual seclusion in the women's quarters; divine intervention saves her, similarly. Hermione's public purity test also evokes the trial of the *Ramayana*'s central heroine, Sita, who walks unsinged through fire. Despite thus proving her fidelity to King Rama, he banishes Queen Sita to the forest, where she gives birth to their twin sons; their rural upbringing and repatriation as teenage heirs mirror Perdita's journey. Even

Shakespeare's statue scene finds a parallel in the story of beautiful Ahalya, seduced by lascivious God Indra in her husband's guise. As penance, Ahalya becomes rock until purified by Rama's divine touch, much as Paulina promises to revive the statue after requiring spectators to 'awake your faith' (5.3.95). The *Ramayana* remains relevant across Kerala, where Hindu households read it aloud daily during the chilly month of *Karkkitakam*, a custom evocative of the 'winter's tale' which, Lakshmy Amma's preface explains, functioned to help people pass the coldest months together by the fireside.

The gendered translator under colonialism

It is necessary to locate Lakshmy Amma's work in the context of the gendered colonial-era subject and attendant pressures. Ania Loomba's observation is relevant here, that patriarchal domination provided a model for establishing colonial domination (Loomba 2002: 7). Lakshmy Amma's preface makes clear that it is only due to her father's encouragement that she published her 'home exercise', hoping to further the cause of female education (1892: n.p.) at a time when 'few in Kerala thought about the need of women's education' (Pillai 1988: 82). Yet her work is also an act of feminine agency. As both the women's rights and freedom movements gained traction, translation became simultaneously literary enrichment and political subversion. India's Shakespeare translations helped native speakers both to prepare for the English Civil Services Exam, and to gain insight into the colonial mind.

A decade before *Hemanta Katha*'s 1892 publication, local royals had spearheaded the ongoing drive to publish Malayalam-language translations of English works. Translators included royal Kerala Varma, a 'strong advocate of women's education' (Pillai 1988: 82). In the 1880s, Travancore ruler Vishakham Thirunal Maharajah had 'asked Kerala Varma to translate English books to facilitate education', endowing Rs 5,000 (roughly £117,000 or Rs 1.17 crore today) for English-to-Malayalam translations and requesting Chidambara Vadyar personally to translate *The Winter's Tale* 'from Lamb's *Tales of Shakespeare*' (Devi 1978: 13–14). Varma maintained that 'God endowed man and woman with a power to grasp and retain knowledge in equal measure' and argued that 'if women imbibe knowledge through education, they can command much better respect from men than at present' (Pillai 1988: 82). It is no coincidence that the earliest extant Malayalam Shakespeare translation by a woman dates to this period.

For additional socio-political context, Lakshmy Amma's 1892 work can be examined in conjunction with one of the earliest Malayalam novels, O. Chandu Menon's 1889 *Indulekha*. Both *Indulekha* and *Hemanta Katha* belong to the wave of local reforms in which 'Westernization served to purge Hinduism of outmoded customs and superstitions, to raise the status of women, discredit caste and polygamy' (George 1972: 58). Malayali translators worked in a twin sense, P. P. Raveendran posits: 'translation of the values of modernity ... connected with reform as well as the translation of literary works' (2017: 179–80). Lakshmy Amma's preface indicates that not only was its student translator likely a young, unmarried girl living at home, but also that it was clearly intended to empower a similar readership in a time where most women were not English-educated. These women might not only use the Malayalam work in reverse to understand its English original, but also through it read a tale of independence where the young female protagonist stands up to authority and selects her own marital partner.

Hemanta Katha's young female heroine Prakashadeepam weds for love, as does Indulekha, Menon's titular heroine and a mashup of Western literary characters that likely include Shakespeare's Innogen.[3] Adapter and descendant Chaithanya Unni identifies Menon's novel as 'critical of caste divisions, feudalism, oppression of women and lack of proper education' (M. 2018: n.p.). Menon's novel advocates free marital choice, centring on Indulekha and her beloved Madhavan, whose extended family feud inspires misunderstandings and temporarily disrupts their betrothed happiness. Menon's prefatory letter to his English translator, W. Dumergue, then British Government translator and Malabar Collector, outlines the author's motives and indicates reforms that local translators were attempting to bring about through infusing local-language literature with Western language and ideas. Menon declares that 'one of my objects in writing this book is to illustrate how a young Malayalee woman, possessing, in addition to her natural personal charms and intellectual culture, a knowledge of the English language, would conduct herself in matters of supreme interest to her, such as the choosing of a partner in life' and expresses his intent 'to show to the young ladies of Malabar how happy they can be if they have the freedom to choose their partners' (Menon and Dumergue 1980: 10–11). In a culture of patriarchally arranged marriage, Shakespearean heroines were thus co-opted as modern models of free feminine choice.

What is notable is that Lakshmy Amma did not seize the opportunity to adapt Shakespeare more extensively than in creative name choices, preferring to translate. Sherry Simon observes that colonialism exacerbates 'gendered aspects' of linguistic exchange with its 'heritage of inequality', and that for a female writer long 'excluded from the privileges of authorship', translation may prove a more 'permissible form of public expression' then adaptation or composition (1996: 2). Yet even early female Malayali translators remained rare, likely due to gendered educational and socioeconomic disparities that still affect many of their countrywomen. Clearly, the translator of *Hemanta Katha* was from a family that both valued and had the means for English-language education.

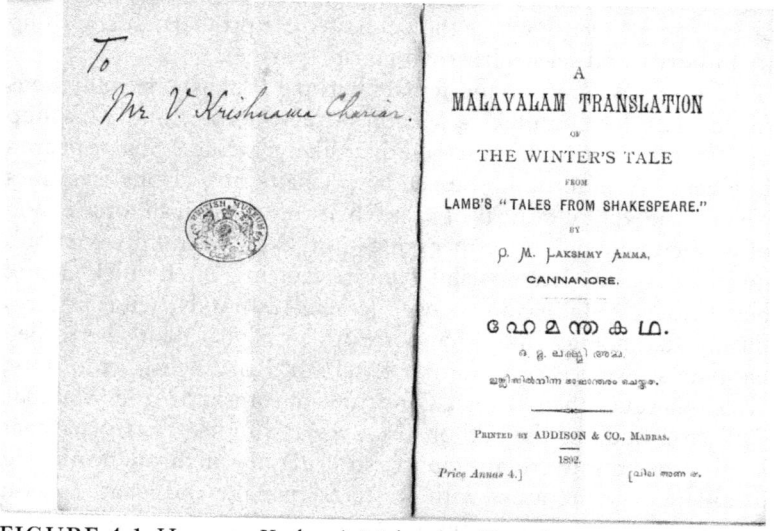

FIGURE 4.1 Hemanta Katha: A Malayalam Translation of The Winter's Tale, *trans. O. M. Lakshmy Amma (1892), flyleaf dedication, British Library 14178.aa.34*

Lakshmy Amma's Malayalam-language preface locates us in the writer's socio-political geography, stating that she is of Cannanore (now Kannur), North Malabar. The region's early Shakespeare reflects his colonial imposition. While the majority of Kerala was 'never directly ruled by any colonial power ... Kerala's Malabar region ... [became] part of the Madras Presidency until Indian independence' (Lowthorp 2015: 174–5). In 1892, the year that Lakshmy Amma's edition was published in Madras (now Chennai), Kannur was still under direct British rule. After India's Independence, when new states were constituted among linguistic lines, the Malayalam language 'served as an important factor in the emotional and cultural integration of the people of the three areas of Malabar, Travancore and Cochin' (Menon 2008: 87). The Malayalam language is spoken exclusively in Kerala or by the Malayali diaspora. While the majority of existing pre-Independence Malayalam-language Shakespeares were published locally within the Malabar and Travancore regions, during the colonial era, translations of Shakespeare were also published in Madras in multiple South Indian languages – Tamil, Malayalam and Telugu. These testify to the stranglehold of colonial rule on contemporary printed texts that fell within the geographical remit of British print laws requiring a mandatory government copy. Significantly, the British Library copy of *Hemanta Katha* bears a handwritten dedication on its flyleaf: 'To Mr. V. Krishnama Chariar', the name of the Madras official curator of government books, raising the possibility that Lakshmy Amma herself provided the official copy (1892: n.p.). It is increasingly evident that South India's Shakespeare straddles greater linguistic, artistic, socioeconomic and political intersections than formerly documented. The linguistic variety of Shakespearean translations also suggests the fluid regional circulation of texts enabling intracultural and interlinguistic exchange.

Shakespeare in Malayalam translation

Among the documented nineteenth-century Malayalam-language translations of Shakespeare, *Hemanta Katha* is the sole female-translated work, but it shares similarities with others. For example, Lambs' *Tales* was a popular source text for translators in the four main regional languages of Malayalam, Kannada, Telugu and Tamil, and these both pre- and postdate Lakshmy Amma's work. This section looks specifically at Malayalam; Sangeeta Mohanty lists eighteen extant Malayalam-language Shakespeare translations, all male-prepared, largely by English-educated academics or playwrights (2010: 59). The earliest work is *Almarattam (Substitution)* (1866), Kalloor Oommen Philippose's translation of *The Comedy of Errors* (Thomas 2016: 106).[4] Around the time of Lakshmy Amma's 1892 publication there is a cluster of early Malayalam-language literary translations, including K. Chidambara Vadyar's *Kamakshee Charitham*, 1880–5 (from *Tales from Shakespeare: As You Like It* by Mary Lamb, 1807) and *Varshakala Katha*, 1880–5 (*The Winter's Tale*, also from the Lambs' collection), among his reported several others (George 1972: 150).[5] P. Velu adapted *Pericles* from Lamb in 1891. *The Merchant of Venice* was adapted twice, as *Porsya Svayamvaram (Portia's Wedding-Choice)* (1888) and *Venisile Vyapari (The Merchant of Venice)* (1902); in 1893, Kandathil Varghese Mappilai authored a 'colloquial free rendering' of *The Taming of the Shrew* as *Kalahinidamanakam* and K. Gangadhara Sastri translated *The Comedy of Errors* as *Sambhrantisancayam* or *Manorama Sukumaram* (Valentine 2001: 121). And in 1898, royal A. R. Rajaraja Varma translated the Lambs' *Othello* into simple Sanskrit prose as *Uddalacharitham* (George 1972: 48, 58). While there is no evidence that Lakshmy Amma read any of these works, her prefatory intents resemble those expressed by other early Malayali Shakespeare translators, who state the dual intention of enriching their own local literature through translation, and of aiding native students of Shakespeare's English works.

Translator A. J. Varkki testifies to the popularity of the Lambs' *Tales* in the Malayalam preface to his *Hamlet*, a 'word for word' 1923 prose translation of the Henry Irving and Frank A. Marshall edition. Varkki remarks that most non-English-educated Malayalis still know many of Shakespeare's dramas; the translator attributes this familiarity to the Lambs' *Tales* and to English-educated college students' plays on special occasions (1923: vii).[6] For university students and those attempting the mandatory Shakespearean section of the Indian Civil Services Exam under the colonial British, the Lambs' family-friendly collection was already widely used nationwide as a study guide. Presumably, Lakshmy Amma's household was English-educated enough to have both its own *Tales* copy and a young woman with the ability to translate its entirety.

Lakshmy Amma's translation adheres faithfully to Mary Lamb's abridged version of *The Winter's Tale*, and her plain literary prose reflects its simple, everyday English. Her prose translation is entirely different from the theatrical version translated by C. P. Sadasivan into Malayalam as *Shaityakala Katha* [*The Winter's Tale*] (2000). Sadasivan's performance-ready version uses more formal vocabulary and contains stage directions, including entrances and exits, while each speech is prefaced with the appropriate Shakespearean character name. By translating *The Winter's Tale* as *Hemanta Katha*, Lakshmy Amma's work is also distinctly suggestive in its title. While both *hemanta* (snowy season) and *shaityakala* (chilly/frosty season) translate to winter, the South Indian region sees no snow; Kerala is largely tropical. However, the Himalaya Mountains feature heavily in India's epics, and Hema (daughter of eponymous mountain-lord Himavan) is a local appellation of the popular Hindu goddess Parvathi. Lakshmy Amma's Malayalam preface explains that she alters the characters' Shakespearean names as otherwise, these might prove too difficult for her compatriots to understand. Yet in renaming Hermione 'Hemagatra', the heroine is consciously aligned alliteratively with the title, and her name further evokes the regenerative connotations of Parvathi/Hema, the earth-born goddess who was reborn after giving up her first body, and who insisted that her son Ganesha be restored to life after her consort Shiva slew him in a quarrel.

In very few places does *Hemanta Katha* depart substantially from Mary Lamb's version of *The Winter's Tale*. When examining translations and adaptations of Shakespeare, D. A. Shankar tells us, 'what ought to interest us in our study is *not the fidelity to but the departures from* the original texts' (1999: 16). For example, Lakshmy Amma departs from Lamb in translating Bohemia's 'desert coast' as '*kattil*' (a lonely/forested area), retaining the sense of 'deserted' while excluding aridity, a natural localization for those familiar with the lushly verdant Malabar coastal region (1892: 9). Lakshmy Amma also makes full use of Malayalam's colourful, onomatopoeic possibilities. In her retelling, the brief Shakespearean stage direction, '*Exit, pursued by a bear*' (3.3.57 SD), mediated through Mary Lamb's interpolation of karmic justice – 'a bear came out of the woods, and tore him to pieces; a just punishment on him for obeying the wicked order of Leontes' (n.d.: 284, 286) – becomes satisfyingly alliterative and elaborate: '*oru karadi chadi vannu avane chhinnabhinnamakki kalannju*' (A bear came leaping and, having rent him hither and thither in pieces, dispensed with him) (1892: 12–13). Lakshmy Amma's translation also mirrors places where Mary Lamb incorporates passages of dialogue. For Paulina's exchange with the maid, she employs formal conversational Malayalam and includes speech prefixes: '*Palazhi. __ Hey Amale!*' (Paulina: Here, Amala/Emilia!), etc. She places other utterances within quotation marks. For example, where Shakespeare's Hermione tells her infant, 'My poor prisoner, / I am as innocent as you' (2.2.27-8) – Lamb adds 'are' – Lakshmy Amma translates this sentence as '*Ente sadhuvayabandhaputhree ... njan ninne pole nirddoshiyakunnu*' ('My wretched, imprisoned daughter, like you, I am blameless') (1892: 6). Her chosen Malayalam term, '*sadhu*' or 'poor wretch', also connotes 'innocent' and 'saint', and the translator takes advantage of these multiple meanings. She uses rhyme for Shakespeare's Oracular prophecy: '*Hermione is chaste, Polixenes blameless, Camillo a true subject, Leontes a jealous tyrant, his innocent babe truly begotten, and the king shall live without an heir if that which is lost be not found*' (3.2.130-3) becomes '*Hemagatra nirddoshi, Patmalayan niraparadhi, Kamalam paramarthi, Luntakan dusshankayotukootiya krooran, nashtamayatinu kandu kittiyillenkil rajavu avakashirahitanaya bhavikkum!*' (Hemagatra is innocent, Patmalayan blameless, Kamalam true, Luntakan an unreasonably suspicious, cruel man, and if that which was lost be not recovered, the king will surely become one without heir!').[7]

Throughout, Lakshmy Amma demonstrates her grasp of linguistic and rhythmic subtleties. For the old shepherd's metaphorical 'not half a kiss to choose' (4.4.177), she translates 'kiss' accurately in the metaphor as *sookshmattil* (to a minute degree), while retaining the word's literal sense in the case of Leontes': 'Let no man mock me ... I will kiss her' (5.3.79-80) – *Njan nirllajjanayi itine chumbikkatte* (Let me kiss this, unabashed). In another similar scene, the translator even redistributes lines of dialogue, giving one character a greater say while adding alliterative emphasis. Where Shakespeare's (and Lamb's) Florizel remarks, 'Mark our contract' and Polixenes retorts, 'Mark your divorce, young sir' (4.4.421), the translator merges both into Polixenes' response: '*Ninte vivahamalla, vivahamochanam sakshippetuttum*' (It's not your wedding, but your divorce that I will witness) (1892: 19). At other times, she waxes poetic to underscore scenes of intense emotion – 'Leontes could scarcely support the excess of his own happiness' (Lamb n.d.: 293) becomes '*Luntakarajavu modasagarattil munngi*' (King Luntaka plunged into the ocean of joy) (1892: 30) – and she renders 'the long-suffering Hermione' (Lamb n.d.: 294) as '*Kleshapashattal deerghakalam bandhitayaya*' (She who for so long had been bound by the rope of sorrow) (1892: 32).

Occasionally, where Lakshmy Amma's choice of vocabulary alters shades of meaning that in turn enhance shades of character, her translation borders on an act of interpretation. This effect can be seen in 4.4. Where Prakashadeepam/Perdita remarks that their shepherds' huts are lit by the same sun that lights Polixenes' palace, Lakshmy Amma heightens the tone of egalitarianism subtly, replacing Mary Lamb's 'Though we are all undone' (n.d.: 289) with the bolder '*namukku ashvasthatabhavicchenkilum*' (Though we have been unsettled) (1892: 20). Lakshmy Amma builds up this tension in translating the earlier passage 'This is the prettiest low-born lass I ever saw' (Lamb n.d.: 288, adapted from Shakespeare 4.4.156) as '*Heena kula jatamaraya kanyakamaril ivale poleyulla sundariye nam kandittila*' (Among those maidens born to low-caste families, we have never seen such a beauty) (1892: 16–17). Crucially, this rewording not only substitutes the royal 'We' for 'I', increasing the king's perception of his own higher status as ruler, but it also locates the lovers in the South Indian Hindu caste system, where marital alliances are traditionally arranged by parents from families of equal social standing. Now illegal but still widely practised, the caste system fixed one's social status at birth; royals belonged to the second-tier martial *kshatriya* caste, below the *brahmin* or priest and above the *vaishya* or merchant, while shepherds belonged to the fourth *shudra* or labourer caste (the still lower 'untouchable' castes were excluded from polite society entirely). Where Camillo rejoins that she is indeed the 'queen of curds and cream' (4.4.161; Lamb n.d.: 288), in *Hemanta Katha* he remarks, '*Yuvatimanikalilveccha ival shiromani tanne*' (Among young female gems, she is indeed the crown jewel) (1892: 17). This substitution hints further at Prakashadeepam's royal birth and exalted character; exalted or royal personages are often termed poetically the 'crest-jewel' of their clan. Taking Shakespeare's phrase 'curds and cream', Lakshmy Amma translates it in the sense of 'cream of', or '*crème-de-la-crème*'.

Curds and cream are closely associated with the boyhood of avatar Krishna, the *Mahabharata* prince raised incognito by cowherds and milkmaids before his restoration as adolescent royal heir. The neatness of this mythical parallel is hard to ignore, suggesting a conscious substitution that fits both with Lakshmy Amma's strategy of localization and her feminist portrayal of egalitarianism.

Gender and caste equality and matriliny

Finally, it is vital to note that, given Lakshmy Amma's choice to translate a tale involving a recalibration of relationships of both gender and power, *Hemanta Katha* can be said to reflect the local budding equal rights movement. This populist movement predates India's Independence, the subsequent legal abolition of caste discrimination, and the local Marxist reform movement of the 1950s that emphasized anti-casteism, equal gender rights and universal education. If the Marxist drive advocated ideals of literacy and equality via staging Shakespeare and other dramatists in translation, Kerala's indigenous rulers had already propagated these via prose translations of Western authors, of whom Shakespeare was arguably merely one of the most accessible. By 1936, Travancore had become the first kingdom to open temples to all lower castes through royal proclamation, a decade before Independence. Arguably, female literacy was a potent weapon against the colonizer, allowing not only the spread of indigenous information but also the understanding, translation and reverse-engineering of colonial icons such as Shakespeare.

Certainly, the rarity of female writers among Lakshmy Amma's contemporaries can be connected directly to their relative lack of educational opportunities at the time, despite Kerala's longstanding tradition of female empowerment through matriliny. *Hemanta Katha*'s local readers would understand that the caste system operated with a difference in the case of Nair caste families, including royals. Many of these practised *marumakkatayam*, or matriliny, whereby both royal bloodline and caste passed through the female line; a senior female's brother sat on the throne, and his nephew succeeded. Malayali readers would likely accept unquestioningly where Stephen Orgel enquires cogently, 'why (is) the death of Mamillius – only son and heir – so much less of an issue dramatically than the death of his wife and the loss of his daughter?' (1996: 6). Seen through the lens of *marumakkatayam*, here a prince's death (or unsuitable marriage) pales in comparison to the catastrophic destruction of a royal female line with the simultaneous loss of queen and infant princess. Lakshmy Amma's 1892 translation of *The Winter's Tale* was published two years after the British appointment of the Malabar Marriage Commission to investigate the viability of *marumakkatayam*, an instance that recalls Loomba's aforementioned contention that patriarchal and colonial control are closely linked (2002: 7). In 1891, committee member and *Indulekha* author O. Chandu Menon opposed proposed reforms, advocating legalizing the practice (Kodoth 2001: 379), another indication that contemporary Malayalam-language translations and adaptations of Shakespearean literature promoting free feminine marital choice were intertwined with ideas of political and social reform.

Furthermore, Lakshmy Amma's navigation of intercultural tensions in translation arguably privileges female freedom. Her inclusion of Leontes' kiss proves that, unlike some South Indian translators, she was prepared to retain unredacted the Western custom of public affection, often linked to female emancipation from patriarchal strictures. Another early translation of Shakespeare published in Madras, S. V. Srinivasiar's 1908 Tamil-language *Ramyanum Jolitaiyum* [*Romeo and Juliet*], sheds light on the contemporary cultural disjunction between the conduct of a free-spirited Shakespearean heroine and conventional public behaviour expected of the 'good Indian girl'. In his English preface, Srinivasiar clarifies that throughout, 'the reference to kissing has been omitted to suit the Indian taste' (1908: xiii), even while meditating on the difficulties faced by the local translator:

> To render into this language the spirit of a Shakespearean play is not an easy task. For instance the pre-matrimonial love and courtship, the brides' freedom of choice, the free intercourse of men and women in public feasts and dances, the greeting of women by men with kisses in public, the liberty of the fair sex and the equality of the sexes are strange and perhaps in some cases repulsive to the Hindu mind ...
>
> (1908: xi)

Clearly, Lakshmy Amma held no such qualms. Vijaya Guttal enumerates these gendered expectations as 'the traditional Hindu notions of chastity, domestic passivity, and an asexual motherhood' (2015: 43) that persist even in twenty-first-century India, where patriarchally arranged marriage remains the norm. Lakshmy Amma omits any mention of gender in outlining the story's moral, in her Malayalam preface: 'in sum, what needs to be grasped from this story is that if a mistake is made, rather than committing revenge one should forgive, prevent harm, and, to those who accuse one of wrongdoing, allow them sympathy and remission in one's own time' (1892: x). Yet Guttal argues convincingly that the 'representation of female sexuality and an alternative perception of purity' form 'part of the gender politics of translation' (2015: 43). It is notable that Lakshmy Amma retains Lamb's emphasis on Hermione's happiness as the karmic fruit of her own wifely fidelity: '*Hemagatrayute pativratya kshamakalal a rajni sukhanubhogiyay bhavicchatu nam kantuvallo*' (Due to Hemagatra's chastity and clemency, we have seen that queen become an enjoyer of happiness indeed), rather than portraying this as the natural reward of her individual integrity (1892: 32).

Conclusion

Over a century since *Hemanta Katha*'s publication, Kerala is the only Indian state with a greater female–male population ratio, and an official 90–100 per cent literacy rate for both sexes, both legacies of the state's emphasis on equal rights. In this movement, Lakshmy Amma's work played its own small part by shifting Shakespeare from colonial icon to vehicle for promoting regional, egalitarian concerns. The nexus of socioeconomic inequalities that makes up the Gordian knot left by the British colonization of India is one complicated by so many factors that it seems specious to pick out gender as a social category that still suffers the brunt of this injustice. Yet as late as 2019, male priests still bar women of childbearing age from universal temple entry, for which Kerala's women have petitioned the High Court. Swapna Mukhopadhyay argues that viewing Kerala's social reforms from a feminist perspective suggests that 'the proposed "emancipation" of women has invariably been looked upon as an instrument that is to be used for the benefits of the family and society, not for the benefit of the woman as an individual' (2007: 15). She posits that Kerala's literacy drive 'may even have been an instrument facilitating the process of internalization of that message', pointing out that Malayali society remains conservative on public, gendered issues (Mukhopadhyay 2007: 15). Since the 1950s, however, female translators of Shakespeare have become the norm alongside men, and they have work; translations account for 15–20 per cent total of the books published in Malayalam, showing their continued popularity (Chandran 2015: 95). Two generations after her ground-breaking effort, Malayali women have achieved the educational opportunities that Lakshmy Amma wished *Hemanta Katha*'s publication to promote, using Shakespeare as a tool for female literacy; surely the next generation of literate women will only continue to reap the rewards.

Notes

1 I am exceedingly grateful to Arani Ilankuberan for unearthing this book.
2 The latest table of Malayalam-language Shakespeare translations lists thirty-three male-authored works, none including *The Winter's Tale*; see Thakur 2020: 222–5.
3 See Irumbayam 1981, indicating that the earliest novels draw on *Cymbeline*, which was then on the local B.A. curriculum.
4 English spellings for Malayali names vary; also see Kalloor Umman Philipose, and K. Chidambara Vadhyar/Wadhyar.
5 The Lambs' *Tales* were popular with both colonizers and native translators across Asia; see Dai 2019.
6 This is my own translation from the original.
7 The Lambs' version bowdlerizes Shakespeare, changing 'chaste' to 'innocent', and removing the phrase about the babe entirely (n.d.: 285).

References

Bassnett, S. (2014), *Translation Studies*, 4th edn, London and New York: Routledge.
Chandran, M. (2015), 'In the Marketplace: Publication of Translations in Regional Indian Languages', in M. Chandran and S. Mathur (eds),

Textual Travels: Theory and Practice of Translation in India, 92–111, London and New York: Routledge.

Dai, Y. (2019), '"I should like to have my name talked of in China": Charles Lamb, China, and Shakespeare', *Multicultural Shakespeare*, 20 (1): 83–97.

Devi, R. L. (1978), *Influence of English on Malayalam Novels*, Trivandrum: College Book House.

Frohnmeyer, L. J. (2004), *A Progressive Grammar of the Malayalam Language*, 2nd edn, New Delhi and Chennai: Asian Educational Services.

George, K. M. (1972), *Western Influence on Malayalam Language and Literature*, New Delhi: Sahitya Akademi.

Godayol, P. (2005), 'Frontera Spaces: Translating as/like a Woman', in José Santaemilia (ed.), *Gender, Sex and Translation*, 9–14, Manchester and Northampton: St Jerome Publishing.

Gowda, H. H. A. (1999), 'Shakespeare's Last Plays', in D. A. Shankar (ed.), *Shakespeare in Indian Languages*, 178–85, Shimla: Indian Institute of Advanced Study.

Guttal, V. (2015), '*Singarevva and the Palace*: Translation across Genre', in M. Chandran and S. Mathur (eds), *Textual Travels: Theory and Practice of Translation in India*, 35–47, London and New York: Routledge.

Irumbayam, G. (1981), 'Treasures of Malayalam Literature from Europe', *Indian Literature*, 24 (4): 95–102.

Kodoth, P. (2001), 'Courting Legitimacy or Delegitimizing Custom? Sexuality, Sambandham, and Marriage Reform in Late Nineteenth-Century Malabar', *Modern Asian Studies*, 35 (2): 349–84.

Lei, B. (2016), 'Shakespeare's Asian Journeys: An Introduction', in B. Lei, P. Trivedi and J. C. Ick (eds), *Shakespeare's Asian Journeys: Critical Encounters, Cultural Travels, and the Politics of Geography*, 1–15, London and New York: Routledge.

Loomba, A. (2002), *Shakespeare, Race and Colonialism*, Oxford: Oxford University Press.

Lowthorp, L. (2015), 'Voices on the Ground: Kutiyattam, UNESCO, and the Heritage of Humanity', *Journal of Folklore Research*, 52 (2–3): 157–80. Available online: https://www.jstor.org/stable/pdf/10.2979/jfolkrese.52.2-3.157.pdf (accessed 15 May 2015).

M., A. (2018), 'Chandu Menon's Descendant Adapts *Indulekha* into a Musical', *The Hindu*, 18 January. Available online: https://www.thehindu.com/entertainment/dance/chaithanya-unnis-theatre-musical-based-on-o-chandu-menons-indulekha/article22464030.ece (accessed 14 November 2020).

Menon, A. S. (2008), *Political History of Modern Kerala*, Kottayam: D. C. Books.

Menon, O. C. and W. Dumergue (1980), '*INDULEKHA*: Selections', *Journal of South Asian Literature*, 15 (1): 7–15. Available online: https://www.jstor.org/stable/40872307 (accessed 14 November 2020).

Mohanty, S. (2010), 'The Indian Response to *Hamlet*: Shakespeare's Reception in India and a Study of *Hamlet* in Sanskrit Poetics', PhD diss., University of Basel, Basel. Available online: http://edoc.unibas.ch/diss/DissB_8931 (accessed 22 August 2012).

Mukhopadhyay, S. (2007), 'Understanding the Enigma of Women's Status in Kerala: Does High Literacy Necessarily Translate into High Status?', in S. Mukhopadhyay (ed.), *The Enigma of the Kerala Woman: A Failed Promise of Literacy*, 3–31, New Delhi: Berghahn Books.

Nair, J. R. (1999), 'Towards a Malayalee Shakespeare: The Search for an Ideal Form of Expression', in D. A. Shankar (ed.), *Shakespeare in Indian Languages*, 127–40, Shimla: Indian Institute of Advance Study.

Neely, C. T. (1988), '*The Winter's Tale*: Women and Issue', in W. Shakespeare, *The Winter's Tale*, ed. F. Kermode, 171–83, London: Signet Classic (Penguin).

Orgel, S. (1996), 'Introduction', in W. Shakespeare, *The Winter's Tale*, ed. S. Orgel, 1–83, Oxford: Oxford University Press.

Paulose, K. G. (2016), 'Theatre: Classical and Popular', *Dr. K. G. Paulose*, 7 May. Available online: http://kgpaulose.info/index.php/12-articles/41-theatre-classical-and-popular (accessed 14 July 2020).

Pillai, P. K. N. (1988), *Kerala Varma*, New Delhi: Sahitya Akademi.

Raveendran, P. P. (2017), 'Introduction', in P. P. Raveendran and G. S. Jayasree (eds), *The Oxford India Anthology of Modern Malayalam Literature*, 2 vols, I, 170–93, New Delhi: Oxford University Press.

Shakespeare, W. (1923), *Hamlet*, trans. A. J. Varkki, Kottayam: C. M. S. Press.

Shakespeare, W. (1892), *Hemanta Katha: A Malayalam Translation of The Winter's Tale, from Lamb's 'Tales from Shakespeare'*, trans. O. M. Lakshmy Amma, Madras: Addison & Co.

Shakespeare, W. (1891) *Paraklesarajavinte Katha (A Malayalam Translation of 'Pericles, Prince of Tyre', from Lamb's 'Tales From Shakespeare')*, trans. P. Velu, Calicut: Dakshina Murthy Iyer and Sons.

Shakespeare, W. (1908), *Ramyanum Jolitaiyum* [*Romeo and Juliet*], trans. S. V. Srinivasiar, Madras: Srinivasa Varadachari and Co.

Shakespeare, W. (2000), *Shaityakala Katha* [*The Winter's Tale*], trans. C. P. Sadasivan, in K. Ayyappapanicker (ed.), *Shekspiyar Sampoorna Kathakal* [*The Complete Works of Shakespeare*], 4 vols, IV, 209–310, Kottayam: D. C. Books.

Shakespeare, W. (n. d.), '*The Winter's Tale*', in C. [and M.] Lamb, *Tales From Shakespeare*, 281–94, Broadway, Ludgate Hill, Glasgow and New York: George Routledge and Sons.

Shankar, D. A. (1999), 'On Translating Shakespeare', in D. A. Shankar (ed.), *Shakespeare in Indian Languages*, 15–28, Shimla: Indian Institute of Advanced Study.

Simon, S. (1996), *Gender in Translation: Cultural Identity and the Politics of Transmission*, London and New York: Routledge.

Thakur, V. S. (2020), *Shakespeare and Indian Theatre: The Politics of Performance*, London and New York: Bloomsbury.

Thomas, S. (2016), 'The Moor for the Malayali Masses: A Study of *Othello* in *Kathaprasangam*', *Multicultural Shakespeare*, 13 (1): 105–16.

Valentine, T. M. (2001), 'Nativizing Shakespeare: Shakespearean Speech and Indian Vernaculars', *The Upstart Crow*, 21: 117–26.

PART THREE

Representations

5

'I dare do all that may become a man': Martial desires and women as warriors in *Veeram*, a film adaptation of *Macbeth*

Mark Thornton Burnett and Jyotsna G. Singh

Veeram (2016), which translates as 'courage', completes a trilogy of Shakespeare films by acclaimed Malayalam director, Jayaraj, his previous adaptations being *Kaliyattam* (1997) and *Kannaki* (2002), reworkings of *Othello* and *Antony and Cleopatra*, respectively. What kinds of intercultural, aesthetic and affective engagement does *Veeram*, an adaptation of *Macbeth*, offer local and global audiences? In asking this question, we want to point to a new 'turn' in approaches to Global Shakespeares which emphasizes intercultural and intracultural productions and interpretations that aim to be global in reach yet 'native' to distinctive cultures and affects. That 'turn' is made manifest in *Veeram*, an adaptation set in the medieval world of Northern Malabar (now Kerala) amidst the *kalarippayattu* or martial arts clans. Distinctively, the film is a double adaptation that brings together Shakespeare's *Macbeth* and stories and characters from the *Vadakkan Pattukal* or 'Northern Ballads'. There have been, of course, previous film adaptations in Malayalam of the 'Northern Ballads', but *Veeram* is the first to introduce Shakespeare's tragedy as a constituent component (Rajadhyaksha and Willemen 1999: 136, 371, 491).[1] Working in this doubled capacity, the film dramatizes *Macbeth* in ways that go beyond Western coordinates derived from Holinshed's chronicles and Jacobean political contexts. As Craig Dionne and Parmita Kapadia note, 'there is in Shakespeare's writing the capacity to release voices and agents that exceed the canonical uses to which he is traditionally put' (Dionne and Kapadia 2008: 2). *Veeram* is a case in point, Jayaraj working closely with the language of *Macbeth* but inside settings, vocabularies and cultural idioms at considerable distance from the 'original'. On processes of adaptation that cross Western canonical boundaries, Martin Orkin notes how the combination of 'Shakespeare's texts' and 'non-metropolitan knowledges' disrupts 'existent epistemological certainties' (Orkin 2005: 1, 3, 4). Yet it is also important to register that these are enriching processes: film adaptations reinforce and illuminate the materials out of which they emerge. In boldly drawing on Shakespeare's play via cultural idioms that may seem distant and even alienating, especially to Western audiences, *Veeram* offers a radical appropriation rather than a reverential adaptation. The rugged world of the Scottish play, with its preoccupations with masculinity, both martial and sexual, is in *Veeram* pulled apart in spectacles of sensuality and ritualized violence.

An essential part of its doubling strategy is *Veeram*'s deployment of the 'Northern Ballads' as if they were Holinshed's chronicles. A canonical source text, then, is replaced with a South Indian source text – and in ways that play up their consanguinity. The chronicles draw on a sprawl of lives and histories, many of oral origin; similarly, the 'Northern Ballads', circulating in the sixteenth century but centred on the exploits of heroic figures from the twelfth to the fourteenth centuries, can be traced to earlier traditions. The film's explanatory opening voiceover situates the story inside these oral cultures:

> The ballads of North Malabar are songs praising heroic fighters ... *Paanan*, like a bard of the medieval and British culture, a poet

and singer ... brings the most celebrated story of all ... the tale of Chandu, that is starkly similar to Shakespeare's *Macbeth*, but [which] took place even before Shakespeare's time.

In this formulation, the ballads are conjured in terms of a story which, uncannily resembling *Macbeth*, simultaneously predates the play. The narrative *Veeram* 'brings' is a poetic precursor to Shakespeare, a historical positioning that affirms *Macbeth*'s local/ global purchase. Playing up the originality of the ballads while, at the same time, suggesting they should be read through the Scottish play also attests to the cultural power of Shakespeare: the voiceover mobilizes a two-way movement. Or, to put the point in another way, for the story of Chandu fully to be told, *Macbeth* and the 'Northern Ballads' must work in concert, an adaptive strategy *Veeram* pursues and celebrates. The significance of the ballads, and their formative contribution, is foregrounded via the *paanan*, who functions throughout as a type of chorus. Wearing a ceremonial shawl and bearing a bell-encrusted staff of office that proclaims his musical role, he is continually present as messenger or audience member; he sings the stories as they happen, always on hand to relay shifts and developments. Affirming newsworthy contemporaneity, and dutifully supplying suitable honorifics and titles, the *paanan* is both supporter of the *kalarippayattu* system he narrates and a contributor to how it is received and interpreted. Meanwhile, *Macbeth* is apprehended in the film through scenic structure and plot, the lineaments and language of Shakespeare's tragedy infusing the story of Chandu with resonant complexity and complementing the characteristics of an earlier oral idiom.

Crucially, *Veeram*'s local/global dialectic is seen not just in content but also in the sphere of its reception. The film was shown at the BRICS film festival, Delhi, and at the IFFI, Goa, and was self-evidently intended to reach audiences beyond a regional base, being shot simultaneously in Malayalam, Hindi and English and backed by a Rs 350,000,000 investment. (This chapter concentrates on the Malayalam version of the film with English subtitles.) In addition, in terms of personnel, Jayaraj recruited Hollywood veterans Allan Poppleton (choreography), Trefor Proud (make-up) and Jeff Rona (music), lending the film a range of expertise. In this way, a narrative familiar from one of India's regional film industries hopes for a global appeal and legitimacy. This chapter argues that, as a double adaptation, *Veeram* opens new gendered perspectives.

By harnessing a martial history from South Indian culture, the film introduces innovative interpretive possibilities within the language, meaning and context of Shakespeare's play. Particularly important is the radically different direction taken by *Veeram* as it prioritizes intersecting martial and sexual desires and practices far removed from early modern constructions of femininity. Lady Macbeth's goading speeches about manhood ('then you were a man ... you would / Be so much more the man' [1.7.49, 50-1]), and Macbeth's defences of his masculinity ('I dare do all that may become a man' [1.7.46]), mutate in *Veeram* inside a three-way triangle. As the film understands *Macbeth*, Chandu/Macbeth (Kunal Kapoor), a brilliant and charismatic *chekavar* or warrior, is brought down by two women, Kuttimani/Lady Macbeth (Divinaa Thakur), who contributes to his fall, and Unniyarcha (Himarsha Venkatsamy), who engineers his death. Shakespeare's poetic palette in *Macbeth* takes on in *Veeram* fresh emotional, sexual and martial contours via vivid cinematic settings, epic landscapes and stunningly choreographed battle scenes that evoke distinctive and affective sensory structures of feeling and response. This chapter first examines those settings, and then explores the interpretive importance of, and meanings conveyed through, *kalarippayattu* as preconditions for an extended discussion of the film's doubly gendered imagination.

Settings/ceremonies

In keeping with its ambitious undertaking to meld Shakespeare's *Macbeth* and the folklore of northern Malabar, and in the interests of aesthetic impact, *Veeram* looks to a variety of spectacular locales. The topographies of Kerala are exploited, as in Chandu/Macbeth's encounter with a sorceress (Seema) and a virgin (Martina), the witches: they are discovered in a cave beyond a waterfall, the scene trading on the lush waterways and verdant forests for which Kerala is popularly known. More frequently, however, *Veeram* visually cultivates a fantasy medieval Malabar landscape, not least in its use as setting of the Ajanta and Ellora Caves, Maharashtra, and Fatehpur Sikri, Uttar Pradesh, both in Northern India. The ancient caves, rocky edifices carved into volcanic lava and basalt cliffs, comprise a series of (Buddhist, Brahmin and Jainist) temples and monasteries and feature an extraordinary array of reliefs and sculptures – statues of deities, lions and elephants and soaring colonnaded architecture (*The World's Heritage* 2015: 156, 160, 247). These are patently not palaces nor are they 'accurately' rendered *kalarippayattu* compounds; rather, they represent affectively extravagant and exaggerated environments that, even in ruined splendour, signal histories of epic proportions in play. Accordingly, the *mise-en-scène* in *Veeram* focuses repeatedly on outcrops and drops, upper and lower levels, dizzying stairwells, lofty arches and *kalarippayattu* practitioners speaking in and around columns in varying degrees of conspiratorial conversation. The gigantic stone structures may be regionally and culturally awry, but they are perfectly at one with the scale and magnitude of the clan rivalries at the adaptation's heart. Thanks to vertiginous cinematography, and liberal recourse to aerial shots, a powerful impression of a Shakespeare before Shakespeare is afforded. This is also a self-consciously wrought environment. In the same way that the *paanan* alerts us to the process of the story being told, so are we sensitized to the ways in which the Ajanta and Ellora complexes furnish the action with rows of (judging) viewers and onlookers (sometimes assisted by CGI). For example, when Chandu/Macbeth announces, in response to the passing of Aaromal/Duncan (Shivajith Padmanabhan), 'Now it feels as if there is no meaning to life' (the film's version of Macbeth's 'There's nothing serious in mortality' [2.3.93]), the camera swings to specify how he is looked down upon by effigies of Hindu deities: it is as if they silently reprimand him for his dissimulating performance.

Matching its extravagantly realized setting, *Veeram* takes an equivalent care to detail the colours and costumes of the *chekavars*. Arguably, inspiration for the appearances of the main players comes from early modern woodcuts, older film adaptations of the *Vadakkan Pattukal*, and passages in the ballads themselves (Zarrilli 1998: 36). Hence, the ballad description of an in-preparation-for-combat Aaromal/Duncan singles out how he is 'adorned with ... decorations', including 'bracelets with left-hand and right-hand twists' (Raghavan 1932: 74). Yet, just as often, cinematic invention is evident, as suggested in the fighters' shaved hairstyles, pigtailed look, voluminous trousers and cropped tops that accentuate honed male and female physiques. Piercings and jewellery of all kinds – such as coiled necklaces and conch-shaped earrings – are congruent with the evocation of a culture in which the body is, at one and the same time, a spectacular instrument and a work of art. Invariably, those selected for combat are painted in variations of orange, red and vermilion, much like the multi-coloured cockerels that are trained to fight in archetypal expressions of masculinity. A human/non-human association is continually emphasized in accoutrements and design. Snake patterns adorn the foreheads of the *chekavars*, while cobra shapes loom large on shields. Animal statues in the Ajanta and Ellora Caves are reiterated in weapon imagery, underscoring an intricately inter-related martial milieu. More generally, forehead markings – including suns, crescents and *shakti* (power) symbols – suggest a world observant of natural processes, dutifully dependent on potential sources of divine energy and attuned to the cosmos.

Where *Macbeth* accentuates practices of hospitality, *Veeram* prioritizes the rhythms of ritual. In an early 'snake ceremony', therefore, staged to honour the successes of the Puthooram clan, ecstatic singing voices, glimpses of offerings of fruit and areca nut and a focus on the ranked members of the family suggest the affirmative powers of *puja*. Typically, the establishing shot is of a *kalam* or floor design in coloured powders of cobras, their intertwined forms connoting internecine clan conflict. Suresh Kumar writes that, in Keralan *naga* (snake) worship, the *kalam* comprises 'geometrical representations of idols … abstract shapes of the absolute' (Kumar 2008: 106), but, in a registration of his distance from the deities, Chandu/Macbeth in this scene is asleep in his chamber, having absented himself from communing with the divine. By contrast, when rituals are observed later in the film, the accent is on group activity and identifications. Just before the final duel, the Puthooram clan, now joined by the Kotha Baidya clan, worship in the rain: each member of the assembled army touches the sacred flame, simultaneously seeking blessing and bowing at the feet of elders. This is a ceremony, the sequence of action implies, with all due observances done and the forces of right in the ascendant.

Textual practices/martial arts

If, at one level, *Veeram* is a visual spectacle, it operates at another as a creative fusion of the language of Shakespeare and the 'Northern Ballads'. The ballads depict a feudal – and agrarian – world and occupy themselves with a range of medieval matters, embracing inheritance laws, land tenure, legal praxes and, of course, *kalarippayattu* combat (Kunhikrishnan 1999: 1159). Composed by a *paanan*, the ballads are written in a lively and muscular metre, the idea being that singing songs, as K. V. Ramakrishnan notes, 'would bring forth general welfare to the society' (Ramakrishnan 1987: I, 347). *Veeram* takes many dialogic cues from the *Vadakkan Pattukal* while simultaneously cleaving to pared-down approximations of *Macbeth*'s poetry. For example, often interlaced with colloquial slang terms, the film's dialogue strips back the protagonist's self-reflection in keeping with a visceral and masculine ethos. Chandu/Macbeth soliloquises, but moments of interiority are invariably delivered in voiceover and animated by accompanying expressions of physical dexterity. Illustrative is the scene in which he prepares for the final duel: while his words sound ('The kind of life I have led, I am left with no one', the film's realization of 5.3.22–8), the camera concentrates on Chandu/Macbeth's swipes of the sword, twirls of the body and leaps in the air, on the choreographed perfection of technique. Acts of training take precedence over, even as they compensate for, philosophical exploration. Elsewhere in *Veeram*, while the action is punctuated by a series of duels, the *paanan*'s songs report the same, dovetailing the conventions of balladry with *Macbeth*'s war-torn universe.

According to Keralan mythology, the art of *kalarippayattu* dates from the origins of Malabar itself when Parashurama, an avatar of Vishnu, wielded his axe to create the region and subsequently instituted *kalari* schools (Raghavan 1929: 137). Certainly, there are sixth-century records of martial arts, with *kalarippayattu* also being described in sixteenth-century travel narratives. As the Portuguese scrivener, Duarte Barbosa, recounts in *c*. 1516, '*nairs* are ... sent to school to learn all manner of feats of ... gymnastics for the use of their weapons ... after they have exercised in this, they teach them to manage ... the sword and buckler ... there is much agility and science' (Barbosa 2010: 128). *Kalarippayattu* depends on a mastery of footwork (*chuvattu*) and stances (*vadivu*) which are combined with ten postures (*ashta vadivukal*) based on animal movements (the elephant, lion, horse, boar, snake, cat, cockerel and peacock). So it is that the ideal *kalarippayattu* practitioner jumps, flies, fixes an opponent with a steely gaze and attacks, recalling both the physical power of a particular animal and the patterns of the *kalam* or floor design (Zarrilli 1998: 100–1; Pati 2010: 185). Crucially, the trained fighter is proficient in the use of the sword (*val*), shield (*paricha*) and flexible sword (*urumi*), the last reserved only for those who have achieved the greatest skill and experience. As *chekavars*, *kalarippayattu* practitioners were often selected as proxies to right a wrong or resolve a conflict between high-caste families. Thus identified, they fought a formal duel (*ankam*) on a raised platform (*ankathattu*), exploiting opportunities for the acquisition of honour and displays of valour. In fact, the *ankam* was akin to a performance; conceived of as a spectacular and public event, it represented a quintessentially theatrical occasion. As much is indicated in one ballad's account of 'fencing feats and practices' with accompanying 'triumphal archways, / The golden litter or palanquin, / Processions with great pomp, / The five kinds of music and firing of salutes … Shouts and acclamations of triumph / And great bustle and noise' (Raghavan 1932: 114, 115, 207). The description, we suggest, is the prompt for the film's opening scene in which Chandu/Macbeth fights and defeats Malayan/Macdonwald (Monachan) – crouching and clashing, and interlocking arms and bodies, the *chekavars* are cheered on by a spear-wielding and banner-bearing crowd until the *ankam* culminates in a fatal decapitating blow.

In one of the few critical discussions of *Veeram*, C. S. Venkiteswaran states that Chandu/Macbeth is 'courageous and erotically charged on the one hand but gullible and fearful on the other' (Venkiteswaran 2019: 91). This is fine as far as it goes but neglects to reflect on Chandu/Macbeth's vexed and contradictory status as a *chekavar* – from the Malayalam *sevakam*, connoting service or servant. As lieutenant to the Puthooram clan, Chandu/Macbeth is both a hired professional taken on by the family and a cousin to Aaromal/Duncan, who earlier stood in the way of the *chekavar*'s plan to marry Unniyarcha, leading to bitterness on all sides. In this sense, Chandu/Macbeth is a multifaceted creation, indebted to Shakespeare in terms of resolve and ambition and rooted in the ballad tradition in his association with service and treachery. Throughout, indeed, Chandu/Macbeth is haunted by what he terms an 'embarrassing past'. Alternating between its two 'sources', *Veeram* elaborates Chandu/Macbeth in a radical redevelopment of how the Shakespearean protagonist is usually imagined. In that two women desire and provoke Chandu, *Veeram* complicates the singular, monogamous relationship of *Macbeth*, replacing it with a series of encounters that point up praxes of gender destabilization and realignment, compromised manhood and empowered female warriorhood.

Gendered triangulations

Overlaying the opening credits to *Veeram* is a song, 'We Will Rise', featuring Kari Kimmel as vocalist: 'We will fight ... this is the path we chose ... we will stay strong and never give up'. At one level, the English lyrics declare the film's aim to circulate globally; at another, and without specifying any of *Veeram*'s women characters, they put into play notions of valour and heroism that are marked as female. This 'power ballad' furnishes a context for the two equally powerful women in *Veeram*, both fierce in action and determination. In one instance, Kuttimani/Lady Macbeth asserts her desire for the supremacy of her Aringodar family clan, only to self-implode; in the other, Unniyarcha leads the forces against Chandu/Macbeth so that the Puthooram dynasty may triumph. Privileging women in this way, *Veeram* bucks the trend of some popular Malayalam cinemas which is to install, in Meena T. Pillai's words, 'a "patrifocal" ideology ... pegging down with vigour the contours of a normative femininity' (Pillai 2010: 5). By contrast, *Veeram* takes energy from traditions of matrilineage associated with the Malabar *chekavar* castes. At the same time, it raids the resources of Keralan folklore (in which Unniyarcha was extolled for taking on exploitative landlords and bandits) and the 'Northern Ballads' which praised the 'martial prowess and war tactics' of *kalarippayattu*-practising 'heroines' (Ulamparambath 2014: 393). Distinctively, *kalarippayattu* in medieval Malabar was pursued across gendered boundaries.

Veeram makes visible the significance of its heroines in parallel scenes, the effect of which is to shift the parameters of conventional womanhood and situate Chandu/Macbeth in a debilitating triangulated arrangement. It is in the gendering of relationships that a radically distinct and different direction is taken in *Veeram*. What are simply in Shakespeare's play Lady Macbeth's goading speeches mutate in the film into a three-way love triangle in which the women *become* the warriors. Exemplary is the scene in which Unniyarcha leaves the 'snake ceremony' to visit Chandu/Macbeth in his quarters. Here, Unniyarcha is paradoxically motivated both to be revenged on the *chekavar* who earlier spurned her and to secure his promise that, as Aaromal/Duncan's lieutenant, he will protect her brother in a forthcoming duel. In contrast to the ballads which discover the encounter coyly and quickly ('I shall cheer you up and make you happy' [Raghavan 1932: 153], Unniyarcha states), *Veeram* extends the episode into a seduction bordering on a violent assault, old resentments jostling with erotic attraction. Hence, the *mise-en-scène* focuses on her putting out the sacred candles (darkness and illicit desires are equated), her seductive appearance (the hair is lightly coiled up and the girdle worn loosely) and the diaphanous veils fluttering about the bed (the bodies beyond are suggestively half-concealed, half-revealed). The knotty nature of Unniyarcha's motivations is most obviously indicated when she lets down her hair, only to show that the pins that have held it in place are daggers. And they are clarified at the point where, biting and allowing herself to be disrobed, she simultaneously instructs Chandu/Macbeth. 'If you find an opponent using a false sword, come to his right and push it away', she warns in a sharing of technical confidences and *kalarippayattu* stratagems. The priority is to assume the dominant position. Accordingly, Unniyarcha resists being wholly won over, twice forces Chandu/Macbeth beneath her and cuts short the moment of consummation. As a result, Chandu/Macbeth is forced into tearing off her pearl necklace (a metaphor for climax) and seizing his sword in masochistic frustration. 'She is once again seducing and overpowering you', he intones, as he self-mutilates in thwarted desire, his realization aptly summing up a reversal in power and the robbing of his martial spirit.

The parallel scene takes place when Chandu/Macbeth visits Kuttimani/Lady Macbeth, niece to Aringodar of the rival *kalarippayattu* clan. Prompted by the pressures of self-preservation, Kuttimani/Lady Macbeth plots to persuade Chandu/Macbeth to 'cheat' Aaromal/Duncan in the forthcoming duel, substituting bamboo nails for iron nails in his weapons, so that he is the more easily vanquished. Brilliantly synthesizing its sources, this state-room episode operates according to a performative logic of vulnerability ('I only ... have ... an uncle and you', Kuttimani/Lady Macbeth confesses) and availability ('Co-operate with me, and I will always be there for you', she promises). Unlike the play, in which the couple are married, Chandu/Macbeth and Kuttimani/Lady Macbeth in

Veeram barely know each other, and their relationship begins at the point where he succumbs to her advances. As in the parallel scene with Unniyarcha, Kuttimani/Lady Macbeth engineers a dominant position, in part via insult: as a Puthooram *chekavar*, Chandu/Macbeth is a 'scavenger', she insists, tainting him with the slur of an inferior creature. Consummation assured – the hapless warrior falls to his knees as he is undressed – Chandu/Macbeth and Kuttimani/Lady Macbeth, the episode implies, are bound to a destructive path. The accelerating tempo of drumbeats, and the smearing of the floor's ceremonial powder on their bodies, suggest cosmic disruption or, at least, an undoing of human-divine harmonies. The animation of the scene has a precise precedent in the ballads in which Kuttimani/Lady Macbeth's preparations are detailed: she 'takes out her jewels, / And looking in the mirror puts on the *pottu* [*bindi*] ... Wears the necklace, which heightens her charms ... rings on her fingers ... She proceeds flirting / Towards the gatehouse' (Raghavan 1932: 205–6). *Veeram* dramatizes this ordering of events, showing Kuttimani/Lady Macbeth slipping on bracelets and head decorations before a mirror and touching herself lovingly, an arch-exponent of strategy and narcissism. However, Shakespearean lines are simultaneously interlaced, as when Kuttimani/Lady Macbeth counsels, 'look like the innocent flower but be the serpent underneath it'. The introduction of 1.5.63–4 into a new context points up both the film's easy exchange between different textual cultures and the martial codes of the environment (snakes are privileged in *kalarippayattu* rituals and symbols). That Kuttimani/Lady Macbeth's instruction is successful is indicated not only in the two-shot of the now lovers' clasped bodies but also in the close-up on Chandu/Macbeth's clenched hand which, in contrast to the previous scene, relaxes in satisfaction, releasing to the floor sacred *kalam* powder.

What brings Unniyarcha and Kuttimani/Lady Macbeth together is the common denominator of courage. Already in the opening voiceover Unniyarcha is introduced as a 'valiant daughter' (the same descriptor is omitted in relation to Chandu/Macbeth), while, later, Kuttimani/Lady Macbeth claims the virtue for herself, reflecting on her lover-to-be, 'courage ... that I shall give you'. The heroines are tied, too, at the level of martial prowess, an alliance that again is instanced in scenic parallelism. In the first of these scenes, Kuttimani/Lady Macbeth prays in the clan shrine before a vast effigy of the goddess, Kali; distinctively, she is dressed in red, suggesting bloodshed, passion and fire. Medieval *kalarippayattu* compounds were presided over by images of deities of 'arms and war' which, as George Pati observes, required that 'lamps be lit' and 'acts of devotion performed' (Pati 2010: 178). The film's iteration of the 'letter scene', therefore, finds its rationale in martial cultures of worship even as it makes visible the invisible forces that Lady Macbeth invokes in Shakespeare's play. Furthermore, because Kuttimani/Lady Macbeth writes back to Chandu/Macbeth before the effigy ('you should change this kind action of yours', she reflects), her words become infused with the goddess' energies and import. In one manifestation, Kali, as Alain Daniélou writes, signifies 'the supreme night ... the field of battle ... [and] the power of destruction' (Daniélou 1991: 271–2). Certainly, the effigy in *Veeram* suggests a ferocious divinity who, with exposed breasts, bears a trident and sword and wears a crown of horns. In this connection, Kuttimani/Lady Macbeth's plea – 'O Goddess, let all the evil and murderous spirits enter my body and make me less of a woman, and more of a man' – could not be better directed. In fact, Kuttimani/Lady Macbeth and Kali appear almost as one. As well as the phonetic similarity in their names, the goddess and Kuttimani/Lady Macbeth are identically adorned (sporting upper-arm bracelets), decorated (with bells) and armed (swords). More specifically, Kuttimani/Lady Macbeth becomes Kali; in the wake of the failure of her propitiatory *puja* and the success of Aaromal in the duel, she decapitates in a whirl of fury the six statues (or avatars) of the goddess that surround the shrine, wielding the coiling *urumi* with consummate ease. The wordless sequence highlights Kuttimani/Lady Macbeth's martial accomplishments in the same moment as it blurs gender distinctions. 'To see tomorrow's sunrise ... Aaromal won't be alive', Kuttimani reflects, this statement embodying in one utterance the Macbeth/Lady Macbeth dialogue from the play ('Tomorrow ... never/Shall sun that morrow see' [1.5.58–9]). If only intertextually, the realignment of lines repurposes Kuttimani/Lady Macbeth with male and female identities, focusing the thoughts and emotions of the Shakespearean protagonist and his wife into a single, threatening declaration.

In the second of the scenes centred on female courage, Unniyarcha demonstrates her own *kalarippayattu* abilities in a training exercise. *Veeram* quickly uses up the Macduff subplot of *Macbeth* and, having done so, proceeds to establish Unniyarcha as the narrative's revenger but with a gendered twist. With Chandu/Macbeth's treachery brought to light (his having engineered the murder of Kelu/Banquo [Sreeraj]), Unniyarcha declares herself her fighting family's moral and martial representative. Unless Chandu/Macbeth is defeated, the 'honour of the Puthooram clan is in jeopardy', she announces (even though there is the underlying suggestion that she still smarts from her historical rejection at his hands). Revealingly, while the half-trousered, battle-attired Unniyarcha shows off her aggressive athleticism (jewellery is now at a minimum), the camera alights on elephants and deities behind her: she gains strength, it is suggested, from a range of natural and mythological supporters. Additionally, a viewer's eye is directed to rows of swords and shields: the whole community, it seems, is willing her enterprise. Clarifying her new role, Unniyarcha takes on Kannappa (Ashraf Curukkal), her father and head of the clan, eventually, through a series of magnificent pirouettes with her *val*, throwing him to the ground; she thus assumes his mantle and emerges as her clan's leading *chekavar*. (Earlier, Unniyarcha had talked about tactics; now, she executes them in a fully realized demonstration of her experience.) The training scene continues in the film's version of 4.3, the meeting between the Puthooram and Kotha Baidya clans that, together, work to bring about Chandu/Macbeth's downfall. Here, immersed in the waters of a river, and dodging gnarled trees, a monsoon-soaked Unniyarcha fends off her opponents, leading one grizzled warrior to approve: 'He who stands firmly on slippery ground resembles ... the wind that blows fiercely'. The proverbial saying is revealing for its identification of courageous virtues and, with reference to Unniyarcha, its ascription of maleness ('he'). Alongside the shift of Kannappa to a spectatorial role only, and the emphasis placed on her tactical foresight, Unniyarcha's transformation into warrior woman is complete.

The contrast with Chandu/Macbeth is telling. While the clans gather against him, Chandu/Macbeth remains supine on an upper lodge in the complex of caves, a study in disengagement. Indeed, in the ways in which masculinity is tested in *Veeram*, there is frequent recourse to such structural and visual comparisons, the effect of which is to recalibrate more familiar Shakespearean conceptions of manhood. While the opening duel establishes the *chekavar*, in the *paanan*'s 'heroic tale', as a 'brave ... Lion', the emphasis is more often on guilt and conflicted desire. For example, picking up on details from the ballads, one episode shows us Chandu/Macbeth cradling Aaromal/Duncan after the duel ('He is resting peacefully on my lap'), the position of the bodies suggesting a male tenderness of care linked to a guilty knowledge of his treachery. Fusing ballads and play, and atmospherically embellished by a soundscape of screeches, wails and the flap of wings, the murder scene discovers Chandu/Macbeth sapped of force ('I dare do all only what is proper for a man to do') and pressured into killing by Kuttimani/Lady Macbeth's persuasions. Because she appears here disguised as an old woman, reminding Chandu/Macbeth of 'every word the sorceress said', the suggestion is that the *chekavar* is demonically manipulated. Indeed, it is Kuttimani/Lady Macbeth who supplies Chandu/Macbeth with the *kutthu vilakku* (brass lamp) with which he dispatches Aaromal/Duncan: hers is the agency and the *chekavar* is her agent. And the distance Chandu/Macbeth has travelled from 'unmatched' warriorhood is clarified in the ways in which motifs of seduction combine with *kalarippayattu* footwork (the *chekavar* advances on his quarry as if in a duel) to point up a fall from martial grace. More generally, Chandu/Macbeth's decline is illustrated in gloomily lit confessions ('I fear ... I am scared even to remember') that testify to a loss of courage, his black silhouette throwing into relief the colourful fighter of before. Typically, echoes of Chandu/Macbeth's glories on the platform sound at set-piece moments. Mourning over Kuttimani/Lady Macbeth's body (she has stabbed herself in the shrine), Chandu/Macbeth laments, 'I wish she had died after the duel. Tomorrow and tomorrow and tomorrow ... life is ... like a poor actor who struts and worries his hour on stage'. The close but reduced realization of the famous soliloquy goes hand in hand with Chandu/Macbeth's appalled actions (he kicks at a decapitated avatar head and throws another at the shrine's bells): suiting the film's representational idioms, grief is articulated not so much in language as in a combative stand-off with his clan's presiding deity and an angry attempt to resurrect masculine energy. Drawn in contrary directions and caught between the demands of 'desire' (1.7.41) and the effects of 'deed' (2.2.15), Chandu/Macbeth is ultimately compromised as *chekavar*, challenged in his possession of the virtue of *Veeram*, and overcome by the consequences of his derelictions.

Humiliation keeps company with reductionism as Chandu/Macbeth declines. This is suggested not least in the *chekavar* trajectory from high to low but also in reminders of the triangulated relationship that proves his undoing. Hence, the murder of Aaromal/Duncan is cut across by a *theyyam* performance. In this South Indian religious practice, an elaborately dressed dancer takes on the role of a deity, eventually being possessed by and becoming the godhead. Because three whirling, screeching and laughing *theyyam* performers collide in the sequence in *Veeram*, we are reminded of Chandu/Macbeth, Kuttimani/Lady Macbeth and Unniyarcha and their conflicted dynamics. One figure is that of the *Kundora Chamundi* or 'Terrible Mother' who acts out Kali's vanquishing of an evil spirit; another is that of the *Pottan Daivam* or low-caste 'loafer' or 'idiot' who criticizes elders and authorities (Pallath 1995: 70, 74, 99). Both the mythic narratives, and masks and costumes that reveal lolling tongues, red breasts and ecstatic eyes, reflect pejoratively on Chandu/Macbeth, playing a variation on social and cosmic struggles and tensions. In addition, the gender destabilization implied in the *Kundora Chamundi* (a male dancer impersonating a goddess), and the mocking attitudes embodied in the *Pottan Daivam*, work to foreground Chandu/Macbeth's vexed connection with women warriors and the critical belittling of his martial pride. If *theyyam* speaks to Chandu/Macbeth's predicament, so, too, do the scenes with the film's 'witches'. These are seamlessly integrated into the medieval Malabar setting: the 'Northern Ballads' themselves describe 'bad omens' (Raghavan 1932: 207), while, in the film, the supernatural is rendered in ways that parody Chandu/Macbeth's exploits. The raised stage on which the sorceress and virgin announce their prophecies resembles the duelling platform on which destinies are decided, their dreadlocked and tattooed appearance is the low-caste obverse of Kuttimani/Lady Macbeth and Unniyarcha's glamour, and their cackling scattering of petals and grains represents a dark counterpoint to *kalarippayattu* ritual. Crucially, it is Chandu's 'fear' that is accentuated here, the sickly green hues of the cave reminding us of the play's stress on Macbeth's terrified 'green and pale' (1.7.37) pallor. Once again, Chandu/Macbeth is in thrall to two women, the sorceress and the virgin mirroring Kuttimani /Lady Macbeth and Unniyarcha and the two episodes of his seduction.

At the final duel, Chandu/Macbeth is pitched against Aaromalunni (Justin Antony), Unniyarcha's son. Extending the plot of *Macbeth* into the future, this deciding contest introduces versions of Fleance and Macduff's son as opponents, meaning that Chandu/Macbeth comes face to face with the next generation of *chekavars*. Painted in flames for the encounter, Chandu/Macbeth makes a last-ditch attempt to recover the stature of his former self: the body paint suggests a resurgence of, and identification with, Kali's destructive *shakti*, while his voiceover conviction ('I am not afraid ... I won't quit') hints at a clawing back of prowess. But, as the savage *ankam* in the rain reveals, this is not enough, Chandu/Macbeth being vanquished by a decapitating *urumi* move secretly taught Aaromalunni by his mother (even if she does not fight, Unniyarcha, it is implied, is victorious). In the shifting nexus of gender, desire and warrior praxes that informs and sustains this South Indian adaptation of *Macbeth*, Unniyarcha becomes the deciding focus of interest: now in black, never more forbidding-looking, and striding forwards ahead of her army, she is firmly aligned with her revenger role. But, as the duel ends, she finds her hands covered in blood, a sign of complicity which, in an echo of Lady Macbeth, suggests guilt and an acknowledgement of her part in Chandu/Macbeth's fall. The image brings full circle the local effects, and global projections, of a doubled Shakespearean adaptation that allows us the opportunity comparatively to explore varied and multiple gender positions, as they intersect with the sexual and martial world of medieval Malabar, though the cultural lens of *kalarippayattu*.

Note

1 See, for example, *Unniyarcha* (dir. Kunchako, 1961), *Aromalunni* (dir. Kunchako, 1972) and *Oru Vadakkan Veeragatha* (dir. T. Hariharan, 1989).

References

Aromalunni (1972), [Film] Dir. Kunchako, India: Excel Productions.

Barbosa, D. (2010), *A Description of the Coasts of East Africa and Malabar in the Beginning of the Sixteenth Century*, ed. H. E. J. Stanley, Farnham and Burlington: Ashgate.

Daniélou, A. (1991), *The Myths and Gods of India: The Classic Work on Hindu Polytheism*, Rochester: Inner Traditions.

Dionne, C. and P. Kapadia (2008), 'Introduction', in C. Dionne and P. Kapadia (eds), *Native Shakespeares: Indigenous Appropriation on a Global Stage*, 1–15, Aldershot and Burlington: Ashgate.

Kaliyattam (1997), [Film] Dir. Jayaraj, India: Jayalakshmi Films.

Kannaki (2002), [Film] Dir. Jayaraj, India: Neelambari Productions.

Kumar, S. (2008), 'Serpent God Worship Ritual in Kerala', *Indian Folklore Research Journal*, 5 (8): 104–22.

Kunhikrishnan, V. V. (1999), 'Historical Sense in Folk Songs – A Study of the Northern Ballads of Malabar', *Proceedings of the Indian History Congress*, 60: 1159.

Orkin, M. (2005), *Local Shakespeares: Proximations and Power*, London and New York: Routledge.

Oru Vadakkan Veeragatha (1989), [Film] Dir. T. Hariharan, India: Kalpaka Films.

Pallath, J. J. (1995), *Theyyam: An Analytical Study of the Folk Culture, Wisdom and Personality*, New Delhi: Indian Social Institute.

Pati, G. (2010), '*Kalari* and *Kalarippayattu* of Kerala, South India: Nexus of the Celestial, the Corporeal, and the Terrestrial', *Contemporary South Asia*, 18 (2): 175–89.

Pillai, M. T. (2010), 'Becoming Woman: Unwrapping Femininity in Malayalam Cinema', in M. T. Pillai (ed.), *Women in Malayalam Cinema: Naturalising Gender Hierarchies*, 3–24, New Delhi: Orient Blackswan.

Raghavan, M. D. (1932), 'A Ballad of Kerala', *The Indian Antiquary*, 61 (January–November): 9–12, 72–7, 112–16, 150–4, 205–11.

Raghavan, M. D. (1929), 'The Kalari and the Angam – Institutions of Ancient Kerala', *Man in India*, 9: 134–48.

Rajadhyaksha, A., and P. Willemen (1999), *Encyclopaedia of Indian Cinema*, Oxford: Oxford University Press.

Ramakrishnan, K. V. (1987), 'Ballad (Malayalam)', in A. Datta (ed.), *Encyclopaedia of Indian Literature*, 5 vols, I, 346–8, New Delhi: Sahitya Akademi.

Ulamparambath, S. K. (2014), 'Women in Different Characters as Depicted in the Northern Ballads of Medieval Kerala', *Proceedings of the Indian History Congress*, 75: 393–9.

Unniyarcha (1961), [Film] Dir. Kunchako, India: Udaya.

Veeram (2016), [Film] Dir. Jayaraj, India: Chandrakala Arts.

Venkiteswaran, C. S. (2019), 'Shakespeare in Malayalam Cinema: Cultural and Mythic Interface, Narrative Negotiations', in P. Trivedi and P. Chakravarti (eds), *Shakespeare and Indian Cinemas: 'Local Habitations'*, 75–92, London and New York: Routledge.

The World's Heritage (2015), 2nd edn, Glasgow: HarperCollins.
Zarrilli, P. B. (1998), *When the Body Becomes all Eyes: Paradigms, Discourses and Practices of Power in Kalarippayattu, a South Indian Martial Art*, New Delhi: Oxford University Press.

6

'You should be women': Bengali femininity and the supernatural in adaptations of *Macbeth*

Taarini Mookherjee

This chapter begins with an unconventional pairing of texts: Valmiki's *Ramayana* and Shakespeare's *Macbeth*. Both serve, I argue, as examples of two dominant archives – the ancient and the colonial – that inform and shape cultural production in India today. Both also serve more specifically as intertexts to Bharati Mukherjee's novel, *Wife* (1987); Vikram Iyengar's dance performance, *Crossings* (2004–11); and Kalyani Kalamandalam's theatrical production, *Macbeth Mirror* (2016). The unexpected overlap in the characterization of Kaikeyi and Lady Macbeth as monstrous temptresses functions as a starting point for exploring the depictions of Bengali femininity and wifehood in these three contemporary texts.

The precipitating event of the second book of the Sanskrit epic *Ramayana* is the banishment of Ram, the eldest prince of Ayodhya. Goaded by Manthara, her hunchbacked companion, Kaikeyi, one of Dasarath's queens, invokes a former promise made by her husband in order to ensure that her son, Bharata, inherits the throne instead. Kaikeyi makes her demands as her husband, torn between his love and duty to his son, and his *dharma* that prevents him from breaking his word, tries unsuccessfully to change her mind:

> The mighty king lay on the floor, a place wholly unsuited to him, like Yayati who fell from heaven when his merit ran out. But wicked Kaikeyi, the very incarnation of terror, was unmoved. 'Great king, you say that you are a man of your word, that you are firm in your resolve', she persisted fearlessly, for she had not yet been granted her boon, 'why are you trying to cancel the boons you gave me?'
>
> (Valmiki 2018: 117–18)

The easily manipulated Kaikeyi of the previous episode is transformed into this 'unmoved' figure, questioning her husband's authority and manhood in order to achieve her own goals. The *Ramayana* is one of the two major Indian epics, and though the text quoted here is from a translation of the largely accepted authoritative text, Valmiki's *Ramayana*, this is a narrative that exists in multiple vernacular, oral, performative and visual forms across the Indian subcontinent and beyond, often with striking variations in plot and characterization.[1] The protagonist, Ram, is an avatar of Vishnu, one of the central gods of Hinduism and, in many parts of India, the *Ramayana* enjoys the status of a divine text. While perhaps not as popular in Bengal, a region where the Hindu pantheon is dominated by goddesses, the *Ramayana* is nonetheless a ubiquitous narrative, familiar in literary, folk and popular forms.[2] The epic also, importantly, provides different models and interpretations of femininity, ranging from Ram's chaste consort, Sita, to the aggressive sexuality of the *rakshasa*, Surpanakha, to the scheming villainy of the wicked stepmother, Kaikeyi. Kaikeyi has, however, been alternately depicted as a tragic figure; as a pawn in a larger inevitable narrative to ensure Ram, as an avatar of Vishnu, fulfilled his purpose; and as a seductive temptress, selfishly putting forward her own son and denying Ram his birthright.

At first glance, Kaikeyi may appear to have little in common with Shakespeare's Scottish queen, Lady Macbeth. But Lady

Macbeth similarly pushes her husband to act against social codes by questioning his manhood, courage and honour:

> What beast was't then
> That made you break this enterprise to me?
> When you durst do it, then you were a man;
> And to be more than what you were, you would
> Be so much more the man.
>
> (1.7.47–51)

Lady Macbeth, in exhorting her husband to 'screw [his] courage to the sticking place', suggests that acting on his latent desires and ambitions would not only prove his manhood but propel him to the highest social position, making him 'so much more the man' (1.7.61, 51). There are, of course, a multitude of differences between Lady Macbeth and Kaikeyi: their motivations, the consequences of their actions, and, most significantly, their literary and cultural afterlives. However, in these brief intimate scenes that afford us a glimpse into their marital dynamics, the wives, described variously as an 'incarnation of terror', a 'fiend-like queen' and composed of 'undaunted mettle', emasculate their husbands who are, by comparison, prostrate, weak and cowardly (Valmiki 2018: 117; *Macbeth*, 5.9.35, 1.7.74).[3]

Like Lady Macbeth, Kaikeyi too seems to skirt the boundaries of gender conventions, accompanying her husband into the battle between the gods and the *asuras* (superhuman beings) and ultimately saving his life. The blame for the actions that precipitate the calamitous events of the epic is frequently placed on the 'malicious hunchback' Manthara, 'whose origins and birth were completely unknown' (Valmiki 2018: 114, 111). Similarly, the physically deviant and ambiguously motivated witches of *Macbeth* appear to plant the first seeds of rebellion in the minds of both Macbeths. In both texts, therefore, particularly in terms of their reception and interpretation, the actions of the king are displaced onto the machinations of an at once seductive and emasculating wife, who in turn is tempted by the prophetic pronouncements of socially aberrant figures.[4]

The purpose of this opening is not to trace a genealogy between the ancient Sanskrit epic and Shakespeare's early modern English play, but rather to use the observable parallels between these two characterizations as an opening to consider the ways in which these two cultural archives – the ancient, classical and precolonial, on the one hand, and the colonial inheritance on the other, the Sanskrit epics and the broader canon of Hindu mythology, and the Shakespearean canon – engage with and intersect in contemporary cultural production in India.

Most recent work on Shakespeare and adaptation begins with an exhortation to move beyond the fidelity paradigm, that is, an evaluation or analysis of the adaptation on the basis of its adherence to the putative 'original', ironically a Shakespeare play that is itself an adaptation. Perhaps the most prevalent among recent concepts has been Douglas Lanier's theory of the Shakespeare rhizome. Using Gilles Deleuze and Félix Guattari's theorization, Lanier makes the case for an alternative approach to the field of Shakespearean adaptations that decentres the text by considering the 'shared object of study not as Shakespeare the text but as the vast web of adaptations, allusions and (re)productions that comprises the ever-changing cultural phenomenon we call "Shakespeare"' (2014: 29). In their survey of theoretical models in the field of Shakespeare and adaptation, Sujata Iyengar and Christy Desmet term Lanier's approach in line with Franco Moretti's argument for 'distant reading', suggesting that Lanier's central point is that 'tracing the peregrinations of collective Shakespeare adaptation can reveal large patterns of production and consumption not discernible in studies of individual works or authors' (2015: 5, 3). I am particularly interested in what Lanier's model offers for scholars of Indian Shakespeare in terms of theorizing the larger field without resorting to essentialist readings of either Shakespeare or India, while still recognizing that these theatrical, filmic and literary adaptations do not take place in a vacuum.

Lanier certainly forwards a different approach and orientation to the field of Shakespearean adaptations by calling for a re-evaluation of the types of questions we as critics are asking, focusing not on evaluating whether or not the adaptation is 'really' Shakespeare but rather how these adaptations 'reshape or extend a collective conception of what constitutes' Shakespeare (2014: 33). By using the case study of the relatively obscure film *Strange Illusion* (dir. Edgar G. Ulmer, 1945) as an adaptation of *Hamlet*, Lanier 'demonstrates how these tales transform each other proleptically and retrospectively, drawing the eye to how each version creates new potentialities (and seeks to redirect or close off others) in its predecessors and in the group' (2014: 32). Despite the prominence of this theorization, it is difficult to put it into practice beyond the conventional 'original'-adaptation paradigm. Or, in other words, though Iyengar and Desmet refer to Lanier's central point as forwarding a more distant reading of the field that identifies and describes broader patterns of cultural production, it is nonetheless a theory that is invoked instead as a broad framing for a single text or performance analysis. Within the parameters of the field of Indian Shakespeares this involves asking not just different questions about how the adaptations relate to Shakespeare but also about how they relate to, represent, perform and interrogate an idea of India.

In this chapter, I focus on a range of literary and performance texts that reveal larger patterns of adaptation and intertextuality in contemporary Indian engagements with Lady Macbeth and Hindu mythological models of idealized and monstrous femininity. As Lanier does with *Strange Illusion*, I begin with a close reading of Bharati Mukherjee's novel, *Wife*, a 'barely recognizable adaptation' that I argue is part of the Shakespeare rhizome, engaged with 'an already culturally transformed' Lady Macbeth (Lanier 2014: 32; Desmet and Iyengar 2015: 3). I suggest that this text also resonates with future adaptations of the Shakespearean character via a cultural model of what I have elsewhere termed *desification*, a process of transformation that occupies the space of the everyday, the popular, and the performative. *Desification* is a term that points to a specifically Indian or *desi* mode of adaptation and is a term, I argue, that serves to encompass the continued tension between the looming dominance of homogenous nationalism and the heterogenous provocations of the local, popular and indigenous. I then move on to a reading of two performances that take a gynocentric approach to Shakespeare's Lady Macbeth, which continue to weave together her principal characteristics of wifely loyalty and aberrant motherhood with extant indigenous myths and cultural symbols. I conclude by bringing these readings to bear on the contemporary political context of West Bengal and India more broadly by briefly touching on political rhetoric as another arena where models of femininity are defined and contested.

Wifely status: Bharati Mukherjee's *Wife* and its intertexts

Bharati Mukherjee's English-language novel *Wife* follows the experiences of Dimple, a young middle-class Bengali woman, in the early days of her marriage to an ambitious Bengali engineer and their subsequent emigration to the United States. As the title suggests, the novel deals primarily with the young woman's expectations surrounding marriage. At the outset of the novel, Dimple believes that 'marriage would bring freedom ... marriage would bring her love' (Mukherjee 1987: 3), but, as she grapples with the only role she had been brought up to play, she has little perception of who she is outside of it. Ultimately, plagued by insomnia and culture shock, and struggling with trying to square her life with the glossy fictions propagated on television and in magazines, she conducts an affair and fantasizes about murdering her husband. The novel is an exploration of a single individual, focused only on her opinions, desires and frequently superficial concerns. Mukherjee provides us with access into Dimple's mind and with visceral descriptions of her physical experiences, fears, repulsions and hallucinations.

Alongside the images of wifehood that Dimple gets from family, friends and television, the element that haunts the novel from the very beginning is the culturally ingrained model of the ideal wife: *Ramayana*'s Sita, the long-suffering wife of Ram. As Dimple waits for her marriage to be arranged, for her destiny to be fulfilled, she dreams of 'Sita, the ideal wife of Hindu legends, who had walked through fire at her husband's request' (Mukherjee 1987: 6). Sita, the ideal wife who unquestioningly subjected herself to the *agnipariksha* to prove her loyalty and fidelity, becomes, for Dimple, the cultural model of ideal wifehood and the yardstick by which she measures not only her own behaviour but that of her friends. This is a model that follows her to America, as one of the first objects she glimpses at their host's home is a 'framed batik wall hanging' depicting a scene from the *Ramayana*, where 'in the background, fighting for attention with trees, mountains, monkeys and holy men, [was] a small bonfire and a short, voluptuous Sita hip-deep in pale orange flames' (Mukherjee 1987: 53). Sita is not, however, simply an ideal to strive for but becomes, in many ways, Dimple's foil, a relic of a different type of old-fashioned wife. While she has internalized this idealized model she also simultaneously questions it, for instance, when mentally rebuking her husband for his irritation at not being welcomed home with his favourite drink: 'He expected her, like Sita, to jump into fire if necessary' (Mukherjee 1987: 28).

On the one hand, Dimple associates marriage with pain and torture, yet it is simultaneously a pain that she longs to experience; she longs to play the role of the long-suffering, martyred wife. Amit and Dimple's departure for New York in Part Two of the book and their struggles with settling in and establishing a life there with the support of the diasporic community resemble in narrative structure the enforced exile of Ram and Sita. Dimple holds onto a belief that they will return to the familiar environs of Calcutta, elevated in their social circles by their experience of life in a foreign country. Yet it is in this enforced exile that she moves further and further away from the idealized Sita, and by the end of the novel she no longer even utilizes the reference as a means of critique. If there is a dominant intertext in Mukherjee's novel, then, it is the *Ramayana*, or, rather, a dominant interpretant of this narrative. It is one that, for Dimple, is constricting, unattainable and yet desirable. In his article 'Adaptation, Translation, Critique', Lawrence Venuti makes the case for the interpretant as a pertinent, yet neglected, category in adaptation studies (2007: 25–43). This category allows for a different approach to comparative analyses of intertextual relationships as it posits the possibility of a mediated relationship between the texts that supersedes, replaces or even precedes a direct one, opening up the possibility therefore of unintentional or apparent adaptation. To add to Lanier's Shakespeare rhizome then are not just versions of the Shakespeare, but also a proliferation of critical interpretants of the play that are frequently reductive yet extremely potent.

Looking more closely at the repeated imagery in Mukherjee's novel, it is clear that there is an unacknowledged and perhaps even unintentional engagement with another intertext – Shakespeare's *Macbeth*. This intertext is perhaps most obvious towards the end of the novel as an increasingly depressed, insomniac Dimple creates mental lists of the different ways she could kill herself. Dreaming of her own death – 'An after dream persisted when she woke up: someone had murdered her the night before' – she ultimately indulges in fantasies of plunging her knife into her husband, and the novel ends without clarifying whether this is a fantasy that is realized (Mukherjee 1987: 185). Unlike Lady Macbeth, Dimple's waking dreams are not a product of guilt; instead, they seem to function both as her greatest fear and as a means of wish fulfilment:

> Insomnia was what she feared most. Between two and four in the morning she thought she heard men putting keys in the front door and roaches scuttling in the closet. In those waking nightmares, the men had baby faces and hooded eyes. She lay in bed, afraid to close her eyes and miss the men treading softly on the wall-to-wall carpet, lay in bed with her eyes fixed on the ceiling and the sheet drawn up to her chin. From the next room there was only the warm noise of bodies turning in sleep; she envied them their sleep. She thought of sleeping bodies as corpses.
> (Mukherjee 1987: 87)

While this description gives us a glimpse into Dimple's mental state during a period of immense upheaval as she tries, in the cramped home of their host family, to adjust to the sounds, smells, sights and rhythms of a very different world, it also serves to reveal the resonances with Shakespeare's *Macbeth* in the very language and imagery used, of manliness and babies, of sleep and corpses, frequently linked in Lady Macbeth's speech: 'The sleeping and the dead / Are but as pictures' (2.2.54–5).

This engagement with some of the core imagery of *Macbeth*, as illustrated in dominant twentieth-century New Critical interpretations of the play, runs through Mukherjee's novel. Dimple's self-inflicted abortion in Calcutta to rid herself of unwanted baggage before beginning their new life in America – her first and most explicit rebellion against idealized wifehood – gives the novel an early secret traumatic event. This aborted baby that haunts the rest of the novel and its 'not like murder' death parallels Lady Macbeth's description of hypothetical infanticide as an instance of the negation of maternal qualities in both women (Mukherjee 1987: 42). Dimple does not neatly fit into a Lady Macbeth analogue; in many ways the fiend-like, ambitious woman is yet another version of wifehood that she tries on but does not quite fit into, and though she tries to encourage her husband's ambitions, it is apparent these are lines that she's simply parroting: 'Don't worry, you'll get the job ... I pray every night so there's no way you can fail' (Mukherjee 1987: 95–6).

However, the presence of these Shakespearean echoes offers a different mythical model for Dimple.

Though Sita is named, drawing our attention to the possible intertextual relationship with the *Ramayana*, the characterization of Dimple – shifting between ambitious partner, solicitous hostess, isolated *ingénue*, and suicidal insomniac – and the imagery of blood, sleep, nightmares and babies that runs through this diasporic novel, cannot but help bring to mind Shakespeare's fiend-like queen, especially as the novel is written by a scholar of English literature.[5] This suggestion of a possible link between Shakespeare and Mukherjee obviously raises the debate surrounding Shakespearean echoes and the questions Adam Hansen and Kevin J. Wetmore raise in their book: how do we determine what is 'really' Shakespeare and 'Is it an echo of Shakespeare if no one hears it?' (Hansen and Wetmore 2015: 17). They argue that the process of identifying these Shakespearean echoes in texts is akin to that of canonization and that, as is the case with Lanier's argument, the question of whether or not it is 'really' Shakespeare is of less importance. Unlike analyses of Shakespearean adaptations that seek to identify and evaluate the indigenous equivalences or analogues, my reading of Mukherjee's *Wife* suggests that an alternative approach is also possible, where it is the Shakespearean text that provides a point of reference in the target culture, as Dimple journeys from a middle-class neighbourhood in Calcutta to cosmopolitan New York, from naïve unmarried girl to murderous wife. The intertwining of these two intertexts, by no means the only references in the novel, requires a critical focus that does not simply locate itself within the Shakespearean rhizome but rather at the node of intersection between these two archives. If, as Lanier suggests, '[t]he tale is in fact many tales in relation with one another, an aggregate forever in flux' and 'we cannot take full analytical account of a work or its politics without being attentive to the particular historical "Shakespeare" with which it is engaged' (2014: 32), I suggest that the overlapping between Hindu mythological and Shakespearean heroines is not simply a case of searching for equivalence, but rather a persistent pattern that reveals the imbrication of both these archives in the contemporary Indian cultural consciousness. This loose rewriting or response to the character of Sita implicitly and simultaneously draws on the Lady Macbeth trope, putting into relationship 'already culturally transformed' versions of these figures (Lanier 2014: 32).

This analysis of Bharati Mukherjee's *Wife* thus works to reveal new potentialities in the contemporary *desification* of *Macbeth* in performance.

Performing femininity in Indian adaptations of *Macbeth*

Though currently dominated by the first film in Vishal Bhardwaj's trilogy, *Maqbool* (2003), *Macbeth* has a long, rich and varied performance history in India, particularly in the theatre. Many of India's most well-known theatre personalities have tried their hand at translating, adapting and performing the Scottish play: from Girish Chandra Ghosh's colonial Bengali translation (1893), to Utpal Dutt's *jatra* performance (1975), to Alyque Padamsee's glitzy *Macbeth* (2006) with a tantric flavour, to Lokendra Arambam (1997) and Ratan Thiyam's (2014) Manipuri versions, to *Maranyaka* (1998), an adaptation performed by prisoners in Karnataka, to name only a few. The ephemeral nature of theatre and the sparse archive records and linguistic barriers endemic to a multilingual country like India make a granular comparative reading of these performances especially difficult, if not impossible, as we are compelled to fall back largely on reviews in newspapers and hastily scribbled notes; if one is lucky, a recording of the performance is available. Though this section focuses on a few contemporary performances of *Macbeth*, I will first broadly sketch some of the dominant approaches to the play in Indian performance.

Broadly speaking, therefore, Indian adaptations of *Macbeth* seem to utilize two different and not necessarily mutually exclusive approaches. First, the Shakespeare play is treated as fundamentally political – whether the adaptation draws the audience's attention to contemporary Indian parallels or whether it seeks to make the case for a more abstract meditation on the essence and corrupting effects of power, the play is frequently seen in terms of the relationship or impact that Macbeth's actions have on the larger world. As is the case with Shakespeare's play, this impact may be assumed but can never be ignored: the story is important because it happens to someone in a position of authority, someone with the ability to impact the world around him, and, even if this sphere of influence contracts and diminishes, the determining dynamic is that of power. Second, these adaptations frequently map the supernatural element of the Shakespeare play onto existing folk or mythic lore, or even different performance traditions. Reviews and analyses of these performances have therefore also been largely constrained in terms of addressing the play's central themes of power and ambition as well as the success or suitability of its *desification*. These evaluations have ranged from a critique of unnecessary and superficial exoticization, to praise for a revivification or a deeper sustained engagement with local performance traditions.

However, Shakespeare's Scottish play can also be read primarily as an intimate portrait of the breakdown of a marriage, a strand of critical analysis that is frequently overshadowed in performance by the theatrics of the supernatural or the insanity of power. As Macbeth wades further in his path of blood to the throne, Lady Macbeth is no longer his co-conspirator; the couple whose responses to the witches' prophecy were almost identical at the outset of the play no longer communicate with each other. Following the fulfilment of the first of the prophecies, Macbeth provides an early access to his thoughts in an aside to the audience: 'Stars, hide your fires, / Let not light see my black and deep desires. / The eye wink at the hand; yet let that be / Which the eye fears, when it is done, to see' (1.4.50–3). Barely a hundred lines later, Lady Macbeth's response upon reading her husband's letter shares much of the same vocabulary: 'Come thick night, / And pall thee in the dunnest smoke of hell, / That my keen knife see not the wound it makes, / Nor heaven peep through the blanket of the dark / To cry, "Hold, hold"' (1.5.48–52). Despite their separation, the play sets them up as an unusually compatible and connected couple. This unusual marriage also troubles conventional gender roles, the scenes between the couple setting Lady Macbeth up as agential, forceful and confident, while Macbeth is more cautious, a reversal that has led to a strand of criticism associating Lady Macbeth with the prophetic and ambiguously gendered witches.

Over the course of 1.7, as Lady Macbeth succeeds in persuading her husband to commit regicide, he defends his reluctance as a quality of innate humanity ('I dare do all that may become a man, / Who dares do more, is none' [1.7.46–7]), while she mocks the lack of courage that makes him less than a man. Later in the play, as

Macbeth struggles with a guilty conscience, she raises the question once more: 'Are you a man?' (3.4.55). Through the rest of the scene, this ideal of manhood is repeatedly set against the supernatural – the Devil, Banquo's Ghost – or a variety of animals, women and children. To be a man, the play suggests variously, is to be mortal, to be natural, to be humane, to be courageous, to be unmoved, to be *not* a child, woman, beast or ghost. Despite the troubling of gendered roles, *Macbeth* does not conduct a similarly extended engagement with the question of what it means to *be* a woman, and despite the centrality of female characters, they are given no names or individuality except in relation to their husbands.

For the rest of this section, I want to briefly consider some Indian performances that explicitly take on this question of womanhood and the ways in which they draw on cultural and mythic models for the figure of Lady Macbeth. Most recent is a Bengali adaptation of *Macbeth* called *Macbeth Mirror* (2016) by theatre group Kalyani Kalamandalam.[6] The play is an extremely condensed adaptation that nonetheless relies on a fairly faithful colloquial translation. It is performed exclusively by three women who double up on the decreased roles, though their identical costumes make it difficult to tell which actor is taking on which character unless one is extremely familiar with the Shakespeare play. Even then, the appearance and movements of the performers suggest a re-telling of a known story rather than a realistic performance, and it is possible to read this production as foregrounding the role of the witches as puppeteers, controlling these characters for their own entertainment. As the title suggests, the women are distorted reflections of each other, just as the adaptation is a blurry mirror image of *Macbeth*; each performer shifts in and out of different characters, the boundaries never clearly demarcated, as illusion and reality repeatedly blend into each other.

The play opens with the three actors dressed in black, their backs to each other and their fingers intertwined, resembling a many-faced goddess, as persistent drumming continues in the background. With their backs to the audience, they put on red-bordered, white saris before taking their position downstage in front of three spotlit, makeshift altars that appear to comprise items necessary for ritual worship. As they move downstage, a conch shell is blown; they each light a lamp, and proceed to put on red and white bangles, a red *bindi* and *sindoor* (powdered mark in the hair), and to sprinkle holy water before chanting Sanskrit *slokas*. From the very outset, therefore, they are dressed not just as women, but as wives. While the performance appears to be beginning with a traditional invocation to the gods, this move is swiftly subverted; the women come to resemble devotees of Kali, the goddess of destruction. The colour scheme of the production is exclusively black, red and white, and the red accents in particular, associated with symbols of femininity and marriage, also simultaneously reference one of the most repeated words in *Macbeth*: blood.

While the production clearly flips the early modern performance condition of all-male casts, it moves one step further in its emphasis on the female perspective, making questions of gendered identity a central element of the performance. Though the performers do not cross-dress, their saris function as protean props and costumes and serve to mark charged moments that interrogate gendered identity. For instance, in the pivotal 1.5, as Lady Macbeth receives a missive from her husband, the performer undresses and the sari becomes the letter she reads as an 'unsexed' woman. However, she explicitly calls on *feminine* spirits in that famous speech, and the sari once again is draped on as she transforms into the hostess who 'look[s] like the innocent flower' (1.5.63). Throughout the production, therefore, the play troubles an easy separation between gendered identities, and, though it acknowledges the ambiguously coded 'man' (understood as both mortal and not-woman) in *Macbeth*, the adaptation works instead to suggest that the characteristics or qualities of femininity are themselves a disguise.

Vikram Iyengar's dance-drama, *Crossings* (2004–11), similarly appropriates and subverts idealized performance models of femininity in its adaptation of *Macbeth*.[7] Comprising four performers (three dancers and an actor), this all-female performance does not adapt the entire plot of *Macbeth*, but rather, through a fragmentary collage of text, music and dance, provides an exploration of the multifaceted character of Lady Macbeth, one that Iyengar views 'as the source of the ambition, which culminates in regicide and the moral horror that climaxes in the tragic ending' (Chakravarti and Ganguly 2010: 277). The title of the production, according to theatre reviewer Shanta Gokhale, indicates crossings that:

> happen between four performers who alternate as Lady Macbeth and, occasionally, Macbeth. They happen between three dance forms Kathak, Bharatanatyam and Manipuri; between dance

and drama, word and symbol, and most importantly between characters as they are and as they wish to be.

(Gokhale 2011: n.p.)

The title is also perhaps most importantly informed by the social expectations and constructions of gendered identities, as the play engages with the different facets and stereotypes of wifehood.

In their comparative analysis of two Indian Shakespeare dance performances – *Crossings* and *Wheel of Fire* – Paromita Chakravarti and Swati Ganguly argue that the productions 'deliberately deploy ugliness through the introduction of the parodic *shringara*, the subverted invocation and the hybrid grotesque figure of Narasingha' (2010: 284). *Crossings*, like *Macbeth Mirror*, grabs hold of the familiar and the sacred and inverts it; it upturns convention as the *shringara*, a performance tradition of adorning oneself for one's beloved, morphs into a preparation for regicide. Like *Macbeth Mirror*, this dance drama works to push back against expected conventions.

In the performance, for the informed and attentive audience, there are several evocations of elements and characters from Hindu mythology, from the liminal figure of Narasingha, the both/and and neither/nor who stands for Lady Macbeth's own ambiguously powerful and constrained position; to Draupadi, who bathes her hair in the blood of her enemy; to Putana, the *rakshasi* who attempted to poison Krishna. This mythological character, the 'child-killer' Putana who attempted to murder the infant Krishna by poisoning him through breastfeeding, provides an image of subverted motherhood, where breastmilk becomes its life-destroying antithesis that maps neatly onto Lady Macbeth's hypothetical imagery of infanticide: in both instances, the mother figures cruelly deny the infant nourishment in a grotesque reversal of maternal care.

I want to suggest, therefore, that the use of recognizable models and myths of femininity or the subversion of explicitly gendered roles in these productions allows us an alternative exploration of the gendered roles in *Macbeth*. If the Shakespeare play delineates socially constructed gendered roles, marking boundaries and punishing transgressions, these adaptations rest on a gynocentric approach to both the play and the nature of power itself, suggesting that Lady Macbeth's role is not simply one of the dominant critical interpretant of a masculine, desexualized woman but rather one that appropriates, twists and subverts expectations and conventions surrounding womanhood. In other words, if Shakespeare's *Macbeth* engages with the limits of what it means to be a man, these intertexts forward a reading of the play that implicitly and simultaneously engages with the question of what it means to be a woman.

Both *Crossings* and *Macbeth Mirror* are invested in exploring a refracted and fragmented femininity. Performers mirror each other, often reflecting a distorted version of what femininity is expected to be, crystallized in gestures, symbols of power. The performances thus force us to confront the fragility of idealized wifehood. Bharati Mukherjee's *Wife* is invested in similar questions. While the performances explicitly engage with the Shakespearean text in their exploration of these questions, the performances themselves are shot through with visual and sonic references to equivalent figures in the Indian mythic archive. Mukherjee's text, on the other hand, more implicitly engages with the Shakespearean text as one among several models that inform an analysis of the novel. These readings, in a field littered with other examples, serve to help trace a pattern of association between Shakespeare's heroines and Indian myth.

The intended audiences of all three adaptations comprise a group of people largely familiar with both archives: colonial and mythological. This group is also a visible and vocal, if not numerically strong, subsection of India's voting populace, and the exploration of gendered ideals in the cultural and literary context is not dissimilar to continuing political debates surrounding gender, citizenship and elected leadership. A distant reading of the 'proliferating network of relations that constitute "Shakespeare" at a given historical moment' (Lanier 2014: 26) can also therefore be extended to consider the ways in which this network is informed by, shaped by and influences its cultural context. While the field of Shakespearean performance has, over recent decades, been expanding in terms of the acceptance and acknowledgement of non-normative, intercultural, non-Anglophone and experimental productions, the opposite is true of plays, films and television based on Hindu mythology. The rise of Hindutva politics has resulted in a push to establish a form of canonical textual stability that is foreign to an archive founded on plurality, repetition and recycling. Goddesses dominate the Bengali Hindu pantheon; the religious calendar of a Hindu Bengali revolves around festivals dedicated to the goddesses of strength, destruction, wealth and learning (Durga, Kali, Lakshmy and Saraswati). Unlike in other regions of India, in Bengal the divine is explicitly feminized.[8] The current election campaign in the state of West Bengal sheds a light on precisely this aspect against the backdrop of a hotly contested battle between the BJP, the right-wing party in power at the centre, and the Trinamool Congress (TMC), the party currently in power at the state level. Drawing on an increasingly singular and masculine Hindutva ideology, the BJP's dominant slogan – *'Jai Shri Ram'* – praises the god Ram. Led by Mamata Banerjee, the only sitting female Chief Minister in India, the slogans deployed in response by the TMC remind their voters that Ram prayed to the goddess Durga and claim to revert to an earlier 'original' version of the greeting – *'Jai Siya Ram'* – that includes Sita too. Banerjee's strategy appears to rely largely on pushing back against a dominant discourse that, as in *Macbeth*, amplifies what it means to be a man, while displacing and silencing similar debate on what it means to be a woman. Yet this is a rhetoric that relies on a divine ideal, and there is an undeniable gap between the fictive, performative and mythological roles attributed to women and those they occupy in real life. As Dimple points out in the last lines of *Wife*: 'Women on television got away with murder' (Mukherjee 1987: 213). Lady Macbeth, Kaikeyi and Durga were all powerful and agential women, yet they represent the frequently vilified and venerated exception and not the rule.

Notes

1 See Richman 1991 for more details.
2 Kritibas Ojha's fifteenth-century *panchali* version remains one of the most popular Bengali versions of this narrative.
3 For a comparable discussion, see Mark Thornton Burnett and Jyotsna G. Singh's chapter in this volume.
4 This is not an uncommon trope and can be traced, in the Western canon, back to the biblical story of Adam and Eve.
5 Bharati Mukherjee received her PhD in Comparative Literature from the University of Iowa and taught literature and writing at university. In an interview, she talks of the influence of Shakespeare in her early

education: 'Of all English literature I was exposed to, Shakespeare's tragedies moved most. I could recite soliloquies by Macbeth, Hamlet, Portia, Shylock, King Lear, Cordelia with great feeling. I think it was the music of the lines, the sound of the words, that excited me. Elocution was my most favorite subject in school. I loved to read poetry out loud' (Mukherjee 2009: 83).

6 *Macbeth Mirror* (dir. Santanu Das, 2016) is available for viewing at: https://www.youtube.com/watch?v=1Pfvqqu8v4E (accessed 1 April 2021).

7 Images from *Crossings* and a production trailer can be seen at: https://vikramiyengar.in/portfolio/crossings (accessed 1 April 2021).

8 Durga Puja, the annual festival celebrating the goddess's defeat of Mahisasura, the 'buffalo demon', rests on the myth of Durga's origins. Created as an amalgam of all the most powerful gods as the ultimate force of good, Durga takes the form of a ten-handed woman to battle Mahisasura, who is protected by the boon that no male can defeat him. The annual festival is nonetheless figured as a ten-day visit to her natal home before returning to her marital abode, and she is worshipped in her role as mother, wife, daughter and daughter-in-law.

References

Chakravarti, P. and S. Ganguly (2010), 'Dancing to Shakespeare: Crossing Genre and Gender in the Tragedies', in P. Trivedi and M. Ryuta (eds), *Re-playing Shakespeare in Asia*, 271–90, New York and London: Routledge.

Desmet, C. and S. Iyengar (2015), 'Adaptation, Appropriation, or What You Will', *Shakespeare*, 11 (1): 1–10.

Gokhale, S. (2011), 'Understanding Lady Macbeth', *Mumbai Mirror*, 13 January. Available online: https://mumbaimirror.indiatimes.com/opinion/columnists/shanta-gokhale/understanding-lady-macbeth/articleshow/16092441.cms (accessed 1 April 2021).

Hansen, A. and K. J. Wetmore (2015), 'Introduction', in A. Hansen and K. J. Wetmore (eds), *Shakespearean Echoes*, 1–20, New York: Palgrave Macmillan.

Lanier, D. (2014), 'Shakespearean Rhizomatics: Adaptation, Ethics, Value', in A. Huang and E. Rivlin (eds), *Shakespeare and the Ethics of Appropriation*, 21–40, New York: Palgrave Macmillan.

Maqbool (2003), [Film] Dir. Vishal Bhardwaj, India: Kaleidoscope Entertainment.

Mukherjee, B. (1987), *Wife*, New York: Penguin.
Mukherjee, B. (2009), *Conversations with Bharati Mukherjee*, ed. B. C. Edwards, Jackson: University Press of Mississippi.
Richman, P., ed. (1991), *Many Ramayanas: The Diversity of a Narrative Tradition in South Asia*, Berkeley and Los Angeles: University of California Press.
Strange Illusion (1945), [Film] Dir. Edgar G. Ulmer, USA: PRC Pictures.
Valmiki (2018), *Ramayana: The Book of Wilderness*, trans. A. Sattar, Lanham: Rowman & Littlefield.
Venuti, L. (2007), 'Adaptation, Translation, Critique', *Journal of Visual Culture*, 6 (1): 25–43.

7

Romeo and Juliet meets rural India: *Sairat* and the representation of women

Nishi Pulugurtha

Indian cinemas, both regional and Bollywood, have seen many adaptations and appropriations of Shakespeare's *Romeo and Juliet*. Most adaptations have been great box office successes. The play *Romeo and Juliet* seems to be especially suited to Indian popular cinemas – families in conflict with one another, parents who create obstructions and restrictions, young lovers doomed to fail, quarrels, suicide and death. These are features that are an intrinsic part of the typical Indian film scenario.

The earliest Indian adaptation of *Romeo and Juliet* on film was *Ambikapathy*, a 1937 Tamil film directed by Ellis R. Dungan which was remade in 1957 by P. Neelakantan. Thea Buckley regards the 1937 film as 'a critical point in the evolution of regional Indian film and its inheritance of Shakespeare on screen' (2019: 200). The film, she notes, 'highlights relational dynamics between lovers who transgress socially sanctioned boundaries, setting up a conflict between individual and collective needs' (2019: 202). K. Balachander's Telugu film, *Maro Charithra* (1978), which was remade in Hindi as *Ek Duuje Ke Liye* (dir. K. Balachander,

1981), Mansoor Khan's *Qayamat Se Qayamat Tak* (1988), Manish Tiwari's *Issaq* (2013), Habib Faisal's *Ishaqzaade* (2012), Sanjay Leela Bhansali's *Goliyon ki Raas Leela: Ram-Leela* (2013), Aparna Sen's *Arshinagar* (2015) and Nagraj Manjule's *Sairat* (2016) are other films that use the Romeo and Juliet story.[1] The Marathi film *Priyatama* (dir. Satish Motling, 2014), the story of Parshya (Siddarth Jadhav) who belongs to the nomadic Potraj community and falls in love with the Patil (village leader's) daughter Gauri (Girja Joshi), locates the Romeo and Juliet story in Maharashtra in the 1950s. This film brings class and caste differences into its purview. However, while class differences are clearly referred to, the issue of caste is not.

This chapter examines the ways in which the woman protagonist has been represented in an Indian film adaptation of Shakespeare's *Romeo and Juliet*, *Sairat* (2016), a Marathi film directed by Nagraj Manjule. This love story of a lower-caste, poor fisherman's son and an upper-caste, Maratha, rich local politician's daughter became the highest grossing Marathi movie. Made on a shoestring budget of ₹4 crores (US$580,000), *Sairat* earned ₹82.95 crores (US$12 million) in Maharashtra. It earned a total of ₹110 crores (US$16 million) at the end of its theatrical run (Verma 2018: n.p.). Released in April 2016, *Sairat* is Manjule's second film and follows on from his *Fandry* (2013), which won the 61st National Film Award for Best Feature Film by a Director. In *Sairat*, Archana Patil/Archi (Rinku Rajguru), the heroine, is, in her agency, a character less often encountered in Indian cinemas. The first half of the film represents an independent young woman who defies conventions and stereotypes. Working to address questions of gender, the film, in a wonderfully nuanced way, also explores issues of caste and class conflict – Archana belongs to the Maratha caste while the hero, Prashant (Akash Thosar), is a Dalit. The film additionally brings into focus the horror of honour killings that have been seen in India in recent years.

Adapting Shakespeare

One of the reasons as to why Shakespeare's *Romeo and Juliet* has so often been adapted is, as Courtney Lehmann suggests, 'the profound sense of the tragic inevitability that fuels Shakespeare's play' (2010: 97). Aparna Sen, reflecting on why she chose the Romeo and Juliet story for her Bengali film, *Arshinagar* (2015), states that Shakespeare's play speaks of 'love in the midst of strife' and argues that only love can be an antidote to violence and intolerance (Parthasarathy 2016: 20). As Sisir Kumar Das notes of *Romeo and Juliet*:

> despite its tragic ending, [the play] provided a much closer approximation to the Indian experience of love and passion, social authority and individual frustration within the rigidities of caste and marriage rules. The twin lovers became a part of the Indian inventory of love legends that include Radha and Krishna, Laila and Majnu, Shirin and Farhad, Heer and Ranjha, Sohni and Mohiwal and Devdas and Parvati.
>
> (2005: 54)

Michael Pursell argues that 'Cinematic adaptation is necessarily a blend of the verbal and the visual, the ultimate aim being the integration of the visual realisation with the text so that each supports and enriches the other' (1980: 210). Film adaptations work on plays to create new texts and new ways of looking at and presenting Shakespeare. Extending the argument, Julie Sanders notes that adaptations work to make texts 'relevant' by 'proximation and updating' and a transposition that takes 'a text from one genre and deliver[s] it to new audiences ... in cultural, geographical and temporal terms' (2006: 19–20). For his part, Mark Thornton Burnett writes that:

> In the particular case of Shakespeare on film in his non-Anglophone manifestations, where there is no English lexicon to attend to, we are invited to be responsive to other verbal registers, to narrative strategies, and to emotional contours. These elements recall the plays, but not with any precise equivalence, meaning that we concentrate not so much on issues of nomenclature as questions about how categories of the Shakespearean are mobilized ... we also do well in adaptation studies to reflect on the extent to which Shakespeare variously explained and capaciously imagined functions in terms of cultural (and economic) capital.
>
> (2017: 1)

It is these various registers and strategies that form fascinating avenues to consider and explore when one examines texts that rework Shakespeare in different cultural and linguistic scenarios. I argue here that it is important to note the ways in which these registers and strategies function, in myriad forms, to reveal the re-configuration of Shakespeare in the Marathi film, *Sairat*. Shakespeare's plays themselves are reworking of stories and other narratives from different genres and are adapted, with alterations to the plot, in the representation of characters and in the alteration of history. As Douglas Lanier notes, Shakespeare's plays have a 'fundamentally adaptational nature' and can be seen as 'a version of prior narratives, as a script necessarily imbricated in performance processes, as a text ever in transit between manuscript, theatrical and print culture, as a work dependent upon its latter-day producers for its continued life' (2014: 29).

The reason as to why Shakespeare has been adapted in Marathi is the colonial presence and influence of Western education in India. Translations, adaptations, performances and recitations of Shakespeare were common in India since the mid-eighteenth century onwards.[2] Many of the translations changed names, locales and images, added elements of music, dance, new characters and story elements and did away with scenes thought not to appeal to Indian tastes. As in other parts of India, most Marathi plays initially were adaptations and translations from Sanskrit drama. However, there were plays translated from English, too, by Shakespeare in particular. Nanasaheb Peshwa translated *Hamlet* in 1857. After 1860, more plays by Shakespeare were translated into Marathi. The Marathi adaptation of Shakespeare is seen in the work of V. J. Kirtane. In addition, *Othello* was adapted in 1867 by the well-known dramatist, Mahadev Govindshastri Kohlatkar, while adaptations of *The Tempest* (1874), *King Lear* (1881), *A Midsummer Night's Dream* (1882) and *Romeo and Juliet* (1882) were very successful on the Marathi stage (Rajadhyaksha 1964: 83–94).

Sairat

Set in a village, Bitargaon, the film's title – *Sairat* – implies freedom and liberation and could also mean wild and reckless – all meanings are crucial to an understanding of the film and of Archi/Juliet's character. *Sairat* reinterprets Shakespeare's story of the 'star-crossed lovers' (Prologue, 6) and presents a 'hero' very different from that seen in other adaptations of the play in Indian cinemas. In an interview, Manjule states that *Sairat* is his reaction to Bollywood (Tilak 2016: n.p.). In a subtle way, Manjule challenges caste, class and gender stereotypes. He tries to present B. R. Ambedkar's idea of India to his audiences. Ambedkar's idea of India has been subject to discussion and debate by academics, activists and politicians. It envisions an idea of society free from divisions and bias based on caste, class and gender, a society in which every human being is able to exercise his/her basic human rights and privileges. Throughout *Sairat*, Manjule seems to be engaging with the idea of creating equal opportunities for all. As will be seen, this is why the first half of the film is set in the rural countryside where signs of prosperity are clearly visible.

Bitargaon is a village in the Solapur district of Maharashtra in Western India. (The film was, however, actually shot in Manjule's own village, Jeur, which is in the same district). Manjule himself figures as the cricket commentator in the opening scene. Bitargaon is like any other small village in this area: the economy is agrarian, and sugarcane is the chief cash crop. The first half of *Sairat* has many scenes shot in the sugarcane fields that provide a visually striking backdrop while clearly pointing to the importance of the powerful sugar lobby in the state. The heroine's father in the film is the village *patil* (chief) and belongs to the Maratha caste linked closely to the sugar lobby. We see him at work in the huge sugar market in the film as well. While caste hierarchies matter and are rigidly enforced, *Sairat* does reveal some interaction between different castes in the cricket matches and college classes – social interactions which are absolutely temporal.

A lower-caste young man, Prashant Kale (referred to by his friends as Parshya) falls in love with Archana Patil/Archi, a young woman from an upper-caste, upper class, rich family. Parshya is besotted by Archi in a way that recalls Romeo's lines from the play:

> Love is a smoke made with the fume of sighs;
> Being purged, a fire sparkling in lovers' eyes;
> Being vexed, a sea nourished with loving tears.
> What is it else? A madness most discreet ...
>
> (1.1.188–91)

Working in an equivalent capacity, the song, 'Yaad Lagla', beautifully captures the love-struck Parshya and the 'madness most discreet' evident in his actions. Newcomers Akash Thosar and Rinku Rajguru, the actor and actress, bring a raw energy to the characters. Archi is the spoilt daughter of the wealthy sugar baron and political kingpin in the village and moves around Bitargaon well aware of her status; Parshya, on the other hand, is a fisherman's son who belongs to the Pardhi caste (Olwe 2018: n.p.). He lives on the village outskirts in a dwelling that distinguishes the Dalit lived space from the upper-caste neighbourhood.

The lovers' story is framed within caste politics that threaten to wreck their love and lives. An awareness of this difference is constantly referred to by Parshya's friends, Salim Sheikh (Arbaz Shaikh) and Prashant Bhansode (Tanaji Galgunde), both of whom belong to marginalized communities (one is a Muslim and the other a Dalit). Salim and Prashant could be seen as versions of Benvolio and Mercutio. Prashant has a disability and hopes to fall in love, while the serious-minded Salim works in his father's garage. The two help Parshya and Archi and reach out to Parshya's family when things are going badly. What first draws Archi's attention to Parshya is the fact that he is a meritorious student in a co-educational college. Parshya writes poetry for the *College Wall Magazine*. Interestingly, the professor in the college teaches them the poetry of Marathi poet, Keshavsut (the pen name of Krishnaji Keshav Damle, 1886–1905), who introduced the sonnet into the Marathi language (Engblom 1988: 42–66). This and the fact that Parshya writes poetry suggest an association with *Romeo and Juliet* in which sonnets figure prominently. We might also recall here the melancholic lover, Romeo, and even Orlando carving his verses on trees. The blackboard, which can be seen just behind the professor as he recites lines from a Keshavsut poem that speaks of a new world order beyond class and caste borders, has written on it revealing statements and messages ('Social Inequality' and 'Black & White Together') as well as the title of a poem, 'I Have Seen Black Hands', by Richard Wright, the American Black author and activist. In this way, the film brings together visually and textually common themes running between discussions of race and caste. The professor also recites from the work of Namdeo Dhasal, a Marathi Dalit poet whose poetry reflects the realities of the lives of Dalits and speaks of the ways in which Dalits have been marginalized. In a world in which caste discrimination is soon to rear its ugly head, these are important registers. The professor, however, is soon at the receiving end of violence from Archi's brother, Prince (Suwaj Pawar), suggesting the latter's sense of privilege. When the affair becomes known, the professor advises Parshya to dump Archi, saying that this is exactly what the upper-castes would have done had the caste positions been reversed. In response, Parshya vehemently opposes the suggestion as he is in love. Prince stands in for Tybalt, using a sword to cut his birthday cake and expressing an aggressive hyper-masculinity. He is one of the male relatives who visits Archi at the end of the film and brutally decides her fate.

Caste questions

The term 'Dalit' brings into contention the idea of a 'politics of social reconstruction and change that draws on the teachings and philosophy of B. R. Ambedkar (1891–1956) and Jyotibha Phule (1827–1890)' (Bhatia 2010: 109). It carries with it an idea of people 'who have been broken, ground down by those above them in a deliberate and active way', with the term carrying a connotation of 'a denial of pollution, karma and justified caste hierarchy' (Jalote 2001: 33). Formally decided on at a conference in 1958, the term was judged an 'intentionally positive' one and chosen over others (such as 'untouchable') that had been in use before (Dharwadker 2005: 289). In spite of their differences, both Ambedkar and Gandhi spoke of and made the issue of the empowerment of Dalits an important part of the nationalist movement in India and 'ensured the constitutional abolition of untouchability in the written document [the Constitution of India] that was adopted in 1950' (Dharwadker 2005: 209). However, in spite of this, prejudice persists in the fabric of social life in India and writers have often used literature and performance as modes of speaking about caste and its implications. This has given rise in turn to Dalit literature that examines the lives of those who have been and still face prejudices on the basis of the caste into which they were born.

Indian cinemas, as a whole, have mostly elided caste as a theme. In post-independence Indian cinemas, films that address caste and caste oppression have been few. *Balayogini* (dir. K. Subramanyam,

1936), *Nandanar* (dir. Muruga Dossa, 1942), *Sujata* (dir. Bimal Roy, 1959), *Ankur* (dir. Shyam Benegal, 1974), *Rudraveena* (dir. K. Balachander, 1988), *Diksha* (dir. Arun Kaul, 1991), *Kotreshi Kanasu* (dir. Nagathihalli Chandrashekar, 1994), *Mukta* (dir. Jabbar Patel, 1994) and *Bandit Queen* (dir. Shekhar Kapur, 1996) are a few films that are centred around caste and caste oppression. Dalit cinema is a kind of cinema made by Dalit filmmakers who represent Dalit subjectivities and socio-cultural issues. Suraj Yengde notes that 'Dalit Cinema can be understood as a celluloid movement of visual creative art, made by Dalit film-makers, relating to Dalit subjectivities, inspiring socio-cultural criticism, and as a universal monument of time and space' (2018: 503). Nagraj Manjule's first feature film, *Fandry* (2013), and *Sairat* form part of this narrative. The hero of *Sairat*, Parshya, is a handsome young man who attends college and is a meritorious student. It is his securing high marks in examinations that first draws the heroine's attention to him. It is his role in the cricket match that wins the match for his team. By making the Dalit young man handsome, good looking and fair, the film challenges the conventional representation of beauty that is usually seen in the presentation of privileged and upper-class protagonists in Indian cinemas. Archi, the upper-caste young woman, is presented as dark-skinned. The film also questions the flamboyance of the masculine Indian film hero. Parshya, who looks so much like a 'hero', is beaten up by the men sent by Archi's father and is unable to retaliate or resist. Speaking of the issue of caste and caste oppression, the filmmaker has stated in interview: 'I realised that anger is not the answer to our struggles to confront caste, gender oppression and inequality … My endeavour in this film is to use a familiar template of love, caste and violence and make a plea for compassion and human kindness' (Tilak 2016: n.p.).

In the film, Parshya's parents are socially ostracized the moment the news of the affair becomes public. Later, they leave the village and move elsewhere where they have to face a *panchayat* (village council) too. There is distinct marginalization in their living conditions. For example, Parshya's family lives outside the village in a separately demarcated space; as S. R. Jalote states, 'In most Indian villages Untouchable living quarters, wells, and temples are still separate from those of the upper caste Hindus' (Jalote 2001: 38). When Archi arrives at their home in search of Parshya and asks Parshya's mother for a drink of water, it is important to note her friend's reactions: she does not approve of this Dalit family. In another scene in which Archi enters a temple and leaves her slippers outside, the camera pans in on flowers placed on the slippers. The scene speaks of the love between these two young people while also making an important statement about caste, as places of religious worship are often out of bounds for the lower castes.[3]

Forms and agencies

The representation of the hero and heroine in films in India clearly reveals inherent inequalities and stereotypes, with the hero imagined as being able to deal with everything that might come his way. As Jyotika Virdi notes, commenting on Indian cinemas, 'By decoding gender significance in the symbolic realm – in the imaginary – gender inequalities are exposed' (2003: 12). However, it is interesting to note that, in the second half of *Sairat* (when Parshya and Archi have run away to Hyderabad to escape the wrath of Archi's father and other upper-caste locals who are against their love affair, have set up home and are struggling to create a new life for themselves), Parshya resorts to domestic violence. Frustration in the way life shapes up disturbs the rosy imaginative life of love; Parshya doubts Archi and strikes her. He checks on her mobile phone, is angry that she frequently changes the password and asks for her password to verify callers.

Archi is fearless and mobile when we first see her – flamboyantly driving a tractor, taking her brother's motorcycle for a spin and challenging gender norms. She falls in love with Parshya and decides on their course of action when it becomes difficult for them to stay on in Bitargaon. It is she who first expresses her love for him and asks him for his mobile phone number. She drives a tractor to Parshya's home to make sure he knows where she will be so he can come and meet her. In addition, Parshya's sister expresses her surprise to her mother when Archi addresses her as aunt. It is Archi who decides on eloping – she takes jewellery from her home to help them financially. In an interview, Manjule states 'I am tired of a male order where women are props and wanted to give it a shake. The strong, independent women in the villages around me were inspirations for the female lead' (Tilak 2016: n.p.). On the other hand, Parshya is slow to realize Archi's intentions and read her actions and is shy in reacting to her. When the couple is caught and brought back, and Archi's father puts Parshya, his friends and family behind bars, Archi creates a furore in the police station and makes sure they are all released. She keeps saying that it was her plan to elope and hence she is to be arrested, if anyone is. When she sees Parshya, Salim and Prashant being beaten up, she jumps into the fray, snatches a revolver, and escapes with Parshya. However, it is to be seen that she challenges social norms mostly within the context of her own family and the space of the village. Later in the film, when they have moved to Hyderabad, she reverts to stereotypical gender norms as she gives in and forgives Parshya's abusive behaviour. While Parshya is unable to stand up to the upper-caste thugs who beat him up in Bitargaon, in Hyderabad, he abuses his girlfriend.

Lost in Hyderabad with no one to turn to, the young lovers find a kindly, older woman, Suman (Chhaya Kadam), who comes to their rescue and gives them shelter. This woman, a single mother whose husband deserted her, is the film's Nurse counterpart. Suman helps the lovers to find a place of their own and work. (A marriage takes place subsequently.) She is possibly the only other woman in the film with a degree of independence. Archi works her way up in the factory that she has joined, driving a scooter with her husband and child-pillion riding. The beautiful sugarcane fields, the river and the large swing that hangs from the tree give way to the slums of the big city in the second half of the film as the romance of the first half moves into the depiction of the realities of life in the second. Hyderabad could be seen as a version of the period of exile in *Romeo and Juliet* – a state of exile that soon becomes home.

In a scene in the first half, Archi, along with her friends, decides to go for a swim in a well and drives out the boys who are already swimming there. This 'well scene' reveals her authority and power, but it is important to note that her privilege also stems from the power her father wields in Bitargaon. When the lovers have a son, Archi names him Tatya, after her father. This could be seen as a reconciliatory gesture on her part; however, the caste reality of Parshya finds no equivalent expression. Archi's struggle is highlighted throughout. She complains about a stench in their room in Hyderabad but continues living there. When Parshya has to go to work, she asks him not to a couple of times. There is a sense of foreboding (it soon recedes as we see the two working their way up in the city) that recalls Juliet's lines:

> O God, I have an ill-divining soul!
> Methinks I see thee now, thou art so low,
> As one dead in the bottom of a tomb.
>
> (3.5.54–6)

Archi finds her circumstances difficult to adjust to and tells Parshya that she cannot live without him and misses her family and home too. Unlike Raj/Romeo (Aamir Khan) and Rashmi/Juliet (Juhi Chawla) in *Qayamat Se Qayamat Tak* (1988), who live in an abandoned temple after they have eloped together, Parshya and Archi are helped to adjust by Suman in Hyderabad. Archi learns Telugu, works, makes friends with factory colleagues and watches movies alone when Parshya is angry with her. There are times when she struggles between the decision to go back to her family and the desire to stay with Parshya.

From the start, it is Archi who takes the initiative. When she rides a tractor in Bitargaon, Parshya's mother's surprise is evident: Archi, she states, drives the tractor like a man. Archi gazes at Parshya in class, which makes him uncomfortable. The song in the background – 'Sairat Zaali ji' – is an expression of her desire and her love. Parshya does wait near her house to catch a glimpse of her early in the film, but he does it secretively. Later, Archi finds ways to meet Parshya and, when she catches him looking at her, makes it clear that she likes him too. When her cousin, Mangya (Dhananjay Nanavare), assaults Parshya, it is Archi who rebukes him and stops the assault. In an episode in which she refuses the letter delivered by a boy and sends it back to Parshya, it is clear that she is in charge. Her responses are such that Parshya is unable to comprehend them. Departing from Shakespeare's play in which Juliet sends her nurse as her messenger, in *Sairat* it is the boy who needs to be bribed by Parshya to act as his emissary. Like the Sapna/Juliet (Saritha and Rati Agnihotri) characters in *Maro Charitha* (1978) and *Ek Duuje Ke Liye* (1981) and Rashmi/Juliet (Juhi Chawla) in *Qayamat Se Qayamat Tak* (1988), Archi controls what she does until the affair becomes known.

Despite the fact that, in many interviews, Nagraj Manjule claimed that his film is woman-centric, it is to be noted that Dalit women are absent from it. Apart from a few scenes where they appear, these women barely speak and are generally present only when Archi is around. The female gaze in *Sairat*, a celebration of desire and of love, is Archi's alone. This is suggested in the last song in the film, 'Zingaat', a prelude to the ugly turn of events and a nod to the balcony scene in *Romeo and Juliet*: Archi dances in the balcony upstairs, and Parshya dances outside. The men dance outside, while the women dance within or on the balcony. This, like many other visuals in the film, suggests reinforcements of, and challenges to, gender hierarchies.

The end of the film is disturbing in a hauntingly nuanced way. The shot of the lovers' son, Tatya, walking away from the home leaving behind blood-stained steps takes us by surprise, a shocking reminder of patriarchal caste-based violence. Coming at a point when things seem happy and settled, the ending – in a familial setting – is a reminder of caste-based honour killings which, still reported, are a part of the reality of the Indian social fabric in rural as well as urban locations. Such killings, as Katerina Standish states, are 'often culturally sanctioned homicides or forced suicides that restore male family honour and result from culturally held beliefs that female members of society are the property of males' (2014: 113). Here, four male relatives, including Archi's brother, Prince, come to her home. The child is with a neighbour who has taken him to a nearby shop. The visitors come bearing gifts from Archi's mother. As she greets them, it is obvious she is delighted at what she believes is a gesture of reconciliation. The four men answer her questions but sit quietly as she makes tea. The camera pans the living space, revealing photographs of the happy family, of Parshya, Archi and their child. One visitor picks up an album and flips through the photographs, with no emotion. Parshya returns to see the men in his home; initially, he is taken aback but, when he speaks to Archi, she assures him that everything will be fine. The camera moves on to the neighbour walking back with the child: she greets another neighbour and drops the child in front of his home. As the child enters, the camera switches to the blood-splattered bodies of Archi and Parshya. The child cries and, not knowing what to do, walks out. The film is silent at this point, with no sound or music, not even the child's crying. As the child walks out of the house, the point of view shifts again to show his small bloody footprints. *Sairat* is unique in adaptations of *Romeo and Juliet* in featuring a child's perspective, and the innocent cries and bloodied footsteps serve to highlight the culture of hatred and violence. The new contexts of family comfort and warmth are replaced by a scene of destruction and death.

The role of Archi's family reveals the extent of patriarchal control over a woman's body, a control the family had been trying to exercise but could not because of Archi's resistance. Caste and family play important roles in marriages in India. A *pratilom* marriage (hypogamy) in which a woman marries a lower-caste man brings in the idea of pollution. Those who trespass societal norms of caste and class can be hunted down, beaten up or killed. In one scene in *Sairat*, as Archi and Parshya ride on a scooter, we see locals on the street beating up young men and women, a clear reference to the 'anti-Romeo' squads in India that, traditionally, have broken up Valentine's day celebrations (Harris 2018: 80–5). The episode reminds us of the presence of violence in the lives of Archi and Parshya – violence that rears its head at a time when least expected.

Caste, class and gender in *Sairat* are overlapping categories that result in discrimination. In addition, in an intersectional sense, complex prejudices are expressed via gender and caste ideologies that are an integral part of social practice. Although Archi belongs to an upper-caste family that has money and power, gender is the identifier that dictates how she is discriminated against. It is the men who decide how things are to be done, as is clearly seen in the scene in which Archi's father decides to remove all signs of her from the family's lives and smashes and destroys her photographs. Her mother is just an onlooker. The woman's body is seen as being owned by the patriarchal heads of the family who view it as a site of honour that is defiled by marriage to a man from a lower caste. This idea of the ownership of a woman's body clearly problematizes concepts of human rights, law and justice. Nevertheless, honour killings are perpetrated because they are judged legitimate punishments for the violation of caste rules. In *Sairat*, the relatives, including Archi's brother, come to her in her home with a specific agenda. The gifts are tokens only that mask their actual intentions. Archi and Parshya are killed in cold blood by family members indifferent to their happiness or their lives.

Conclusion

Sairat is mounted on a realistic scale with no lavish sets and costumes. On the contrary, the film depicts simple events and situations – a ladder being used to climb up the makeshift pavilion during a cricket match, the rich son cutting his birthday cake with a sword, a woman barging into the cricket match to drive her wayward son home, the courtship scenes unfolding against a backdrop of wells and sugarcane fields. *Sairat*'s box office success resulted in remakes of the film in other Indian languages as well, including the Bengali-language *Noor Jahaan* (dir. Abhimanyu Mukherjee, 2018), the Odia-language *Laila O Laila* (dir. Sushant Mani, 2017) and the Punjabi-language *Channa Mereya* (dir. Pankaj Batra, 2017). The Kannada remake, *Manasu Mallige* (dir. S. Narayan, 2017), had Rinku Rajguru reprising her *Sairat* role and did fairly well at the box office, while the Hindi remake, *Dhadak* (dir. Shashank Khaitan, 2018), failed. By making simply a Romeo and Juliet love story without any new elements, and by mounting it in a stereotypical Bollywood fashion, *Dhadak* did not appeal.

In *Shakespeare and the Problem of Adaptation*, Margaret Jane Kidnie describes adaptation as 'the addition of new material alongside substantial cutting and rearrangement' and transformation as 'the most extreme mode of innovation' where characters are made more simple and represented in relation to new sets of activities (2009: 3). *Sairat* functions in precisely these ways, also bringing important issues into visibility and offering commentary on contemporary Indian society. What Paromita Chakravarti notes with reference to recent Bengali adaptations of Shakespeare's plays is applicable to other Indian language adaptations that rework Shakespeare in multiple ways. Commenting on Bengali language adaptations, she notes, 'Shakespeare is not a signifier of a culture or identity but merely a resource to be used to narrate the story of millennial Kolkata and its denizens': Shakespeare, she argues 'provides a medium for articulating local identities and paradoxically, it is through these increasing forms of localisation that Shakespeare's universality survives' (2019: 177). *Sairat* brings the realities of honour feuds and killings, caste and caste oppression to the fore and challenges gender stereotypes. With its nuanced presentation and its wonderful music and score by Ajay-Atul, fresh actors who bring credibility to the story and its delivery, *Sairat* succeeded brilliantly with audiences in India (Pandhare 2016: n.p.). *Sairat* is Shakespearean in sweep, with its balconies, letters, characters hiding behind bushes and, most of all, the star-crossed lovers. As with other adaptations of Shakespeare, it reinvents an old story as a powerful and critical tale for our times.[4]

Notes

1 See 'Shakespeare Films in Indian Cinemas: An Annotated Filmography' 2019: 322–3.
2 For a comparable discussion, see Poonam Trivedi's chapter in this volume.
3 For a comparable discussion, see Thea Buckley's chapter in this volume.
4 I would like to thank *Talking Films Online*, a Facebook Group, for inviting me to moderate a discussion on the film on 19 December 2020 and to all members of the online audience for their wonderful comments and observations.

References

Ambikapathy (1937), [Film] Dir. Ellis R. Dungan, India: Salem Shankar Films.
Ambikapathy (1957), [Film] Dir. P. Neelakantan, India: ALS Productions.
Ankur (1974), [Film] Dir. Shyam Benegal, India: Blaze Film Productions.
Arshinagar (2015), [Film] Dir. Aparna Sen, India: SVF Entertainment/ Surinder Films.
Bandit Queen (1996), [Film] Dir. Shekhar Kapur, India: Kaleidoscope/ Channel 4.
Balayogini (1936), [Film] Dir. K. Subramanyam, India: Madras United Artists.
Bhatia, N. (2010), *Performing Women, Performing Womanhood: Theatre, Politics and Dissent in North India*, New Delhi: Oxford University Press.
Buckley, T. (2019), '"Singing is Such Sweet Sorrow": *Ambikapathy*, Hollywood Shakespeare and Tamil Cinema's Hybrid Heritage', in

P. Trivedi and P. Chakravarti (eds), *Shakespeare and Indian Cinemas: 'Local Habitations'*, 200–17, London and New York: Routledge.
Burnett, M. T. (2017), 'Adaptation, Shakespeare and World Cinema', *Literature / Film Quarterly*, 45 (2): 1–2. Available online: https://lfq.salisbury.edu/_issues/first/adaptation_shakespeare_and_world_cinema.html (accessed 15 March 2021).
Chakravarti, P. (2019), 'Cinematic Lear and Bengaliness', in P. Trivedi and P. Chakravarti (eds), *Shakespeare and Indian Cinemas: 'Local Habitations'*, 161–79, New York and London: Routledge.
Channa Mereya (2017), [Film] Dir. Pankaj Batra, India: White Hill Studios.
Das, S. K. (2005), 'Shakespeare in Indian Languages', in P. Trivedi and D. Bartholomeusz (eds), *India's Shakespeare: Translation, Interpretation and Performance*, 47–73, Newark: University of Delaware Press.
Dhadak (2018), [Film] Dir. Shashank Khaitan, India: Dharma Productions/Zee Studios.
Dharwadker, A. B. (2005), *Theatres of Independence: Drama, Theory, and Urban Performance in India since 1947*, Iowa City: University of Iowa Press.
Diksha (1991), [Film] Dir. Arun Kaul, India: NFDC Doordarshan.
Ek Duuje Ke Liye (1981), [Film] Dir. K. Balachander, India: Prasad Productions.
Engblom, P. C. (1988), 'Keshavsut and Early Modernist Strategies for Indigenizing the Sonnet in Marathi: A Western Form in Indian Garb', *Journal of South Asian Literature*, 23 (1): 42–66.
Fandry (2013), [Film] Dir. Nagraj Manjule, India: Navalakha Arts/Holy Basil Productions.
Goliyon ki Raas Leela: Ram-Leela (2013), [Film] Dir. Sanjay Leela Bhansali, India: Bhansali/Eros.
Harris, J. G. (2018), *Masala Shakespeare*, New Delhi: Aleph Books.
Ishaqzaade (2012), [Film] Dir. Habib Faisal, India: Yash Raj Films.
Issaq (2013), [Film] Dir. Manish Tiwari, India: Pen India Limited.
Jalote, S. R. (2001), *Contemporary African American Theatre and Dalit Theatre: A Comparative Study in Themes and Techniques*, Varanasi: Banaras Hindu University.
Kidnie, M. J. (2009), *Shakespeare and the Problem of Adaptation*, New York and London: Routledge.
Kotreshi Kanasu (1994), [Film] Dir. Nagathihalli Chandrashekar, India: G. Nanda Kumar.
Laila O Laila (2017), [Film] Dir. Sushant Mani, India: Finecut.
Lanier, D. (2014), 'Shakespearean Rhizomatics: Adaptation, Ethics, Value', in A. Huang and E. Rivlin (eds), *Shakespeare and the Ethics of Appropriation*, 21–40, New York: Palgrave Macmillan.

Lehmann, C. (2010), *Shakespeare's Romeo and Juliet: The Relationship Between Text and Film*, London: Bloomsbury.
Manasu Mallige (2017), [Film] Dir. S. Narayan, India: Rockline Productions/Zee Studios.
Maro Charithra (1978), [Film] Dir. K. Balachander, India: Andal Productions.
Mukta (1994), [Film] Dir. Jabbar Patel, India: Ashok Mhatre.
Nandanar (1942), [Film] Dir. Muruga Dossa, India: S. S. Vasan.
Noor Jahaan (2018), [Film] Dir. Abhimanyu Mukherjee, India: SVF Entertainment/Jazz Multimedia.
Olwe, S. (2018), 'Decades after Denotification, Pardhi Tribe Struggles to Shrug Off "Criminal" Tag', *The Wire*, 31 August. Available online: https://thewire.in/society/decades-after-denotification-pardhis-in-maharashtra-struggle-to-stave-off-criminal-tag (accessed 15 March 2021).
Pandhare, M. (2016), 'Youngsters to Protect Runaway Married Couples', *The Better India*, 4 June. Available online: https://www.thebetterindia.com/57175/sairat-inspires-group-protect-runaway-married-couples (accessed 15 March 2021).
Parthasarathy, S. (2016), 'The Bard Meets Bollywood', *Index on Censorship*, 45 (1): 18–21.
Priyatama (2014), [Film] Dir. Satish Motling, India: Modern Pictures.
Pursell, M. (1980), 'Zeffirelli's Shakespeare: The Visual Realization of Tone and Theme', *Literature / Film Quarterly*, 8 (4): 210–18.
Qayamat Se Qayamat Tak (1988), [Film] Dir. Mansoor Khan, India: Nasir Hussain Films.
Rajadhyaksha, M. V. (1964), 'Shakespeare in Marathi', *Indian Literature*, 7 (1): 83–94.
Rudraveena (1988), [Film] Dir. K. Balachander, India: Nagendra Babu.
Sairat (2016), [Film] Dir. Nagraj Manjule, India: Zee Studios.
Sanders, J. (2006), *Adaptation and Appropriation*, London and New York: Routledge.
'Shakespeare Films in Indian Cinemas: An Annotated Filmography' (2019), in P. Trivedi and P. Chakravarti (eds), *Shakespeare and Indian Cinemas: 'Local Habitations'*, 319–27, London and New York: Routledge.
Standish, K. (2014), 'Understanding Cultural Violence and Gender: Honour Killings; Dowry Murder; the *Zina* Ordinance and Blood-Feuds', *Journal of Gender Studies*, 23 (2): 111–24.
Sujata (1959), [Film] Dir. Bimal Roy, India: Bimal Roy Productions.
Tilak, S. G. (2016), '*Sairat*: Why a Doomed Love Story Has Become India's Sleeper Hit', *BBC News*, 7 June. Available online: https://www.bbc.com/news/world-asia-india-36457512 (accessed 15 March 2021).

Verma, S. (2018), 'Made in Marathi', *The Financial Express*, 22 April. Available online: https://www.financialexpress.com/entertainment/made-in-marathi/1141162 (accessed 15 March 2021).

Virdi, J. (2003), *The Cinematic Imagination: Indian Popular Films as Social History*, New Brunswick: Rutgers University Press.

Yengde, S. (2018), 'Dalit Cinema', *South Asia: Journal of South Asian Studies*, 41 (3): 503–18.

8

Dy(e)ing hands: The hennaed female agent in Vishal Bhardwaj's tragedies

Jennifer T. Birkett

Vishal Bhardwaj's *Haider* (2014) ends with a woman suicide bomber (Shakespeare's Gertrude) blowing herself up. Her hands are vibrantly dyed with henna, a remnant from her earlier wedding ceremony. Provocatively, all of Bhardwaj's tragic Shakespearean heroines kill, or are killed, with hennaed hands. While many scholars have looked at *Haider* (2014), *Omkara* (2006) and *Maqbool* (2003) as unique characterizations of female volition, and praised Bhardwaj's heroines' violent vivacity, none has speculated as to why these women are continuously caught red-handed. Given that Indian, as well as Shakespearean, performance history emphasizes hand gesture in association with agency, attending to these performative hands affords new interpretations regarding Bhardwaj's Bollywood take on Shakespeare's women. Specifically, I argue that Bhardwaj repeatedly reinvents the symbolic meaning of henna in these Shakespearean tragedies not only as a traditional wedding accessory but as a purposeful omen of violent vengeance for the tragic female agent.

By contextualizing these transcultural postcolonial films as both conventionally Shakespearean and traditionally Indian, Bhardwaj draws a connection between the female hand and intentionality. The performing hand evokes the longstanding Indian practice of *mudras*, a performative technique which treats the kinetic energy contained in hand gestures as a seal between the performer's mind, spirit and speech (Nair 1993: 34). Simultaneously, the hand also calls to mind the meaning of early modern English hand gestures, commonly understood to symbolize a person's intent and similarly utilized for dramatic performance (Rowe 1999; Refskou and Thomasen 2014; Karim-Cooper 2016). To borrow Jens Schröter's term, the performative hand in these films highlights the 'transformational intermediality' between Shakespeare's plays, Bhardwaj's films and their respective cultural histories, inviting an on-going dialogue between the texts and contexts (2012: 27). However, the emphasis on henna, as compared to hands only, further depicts these films as appropriations which translate a colonial source text for a postcolonial context, appealing to Indian audiences primarily. As Asam Sayed rightly points out, when adapting Western literary texts, Bollywood film directors often use 'culture-specific details' including context, mythology, music and dance to appeal to audiences (2019: 214). Utilizing culture-specific details, like henna, brings about the 'transculturation of indigenization', which Linda Hutcheon insists changes the meaning and overall impact of the source text drastically (2000: 142). In precisely this way, I argue that Bhardwaj's appropriation of henna in the context of his Shakespearean films not only changes the way we understand Indian cultural context, but also offers fresh readings of Shakespeare's *Hamlet*, *Othello* and *Macbeth*, specifically with regard to the female agent and her contribution to the play's climactic violence.

Bollywood, as a genre, frequently includes lavish wedding dance numbers, and thus – being a typical bridal custom – henna may seem a rather dull point of interest for these films. However, what should be a point of interest is that weddings occur in the films at all. While marriage acts as a source of conflict beginning both Shakespeare's *Othello* and *Hamlet*, neither *Hamlet*, nor *Othello*, nor *Macbeth* include wedding rituals during the timespan of the play. Bollywood cinema, on the other hand, is characterized by its on-screen wedding spectacle. Likely trying to fit the Bollywood genre, Bhardwaj notably tinkers with Shakespeare's timelines, setting weddings to precede the climactic events of Duncan's murder, Desdemona's strangling and Hamlet's revenge.

Given that Bhardwaj's films are considered among the first Bollywood-acknowledged adaptations of Shakespeare's texts, it is easy to label them as Bollywood films. Admittedly, I will refer to them as such throughout this chapter. However, Bhardwaj's take on Bollywood's conventional aesthetics is not entirely compliant with the genre's expectations. As scholars like Rosa García-Periago have noted, Bhardwaj critiques and advances typical Bollywood conventions in his Shakespeare-inspired Indian tragedies. One explicit way he achieves this is through the films' wedding ceremonies. Although both *Maqbool* and *Haider* include the typically vibrant song-and-dance numbers expected from a Bollywood wedding, Bhardwaj's marriage scenes swerve from the Bollywood mark. As García-Periago puts it, they '[do] not capture the Bollywood spirit' (2014: 70). This is partly because Bhardwaj chooses to appropriate Shakespearean tragedy, as compared to comedy. Overlapping the Bollywood trope of wedding spectacle with Shakespearean tragedy results in a challenging conflation between marital merriment and misfortune. At the centre of this conflation lies the wedding ritual of bridal henna. By blending the unexpected genre of Shakespearean tragedy and the typical Bollywood marriage spectacle, Bhardwaj imbues henna specifically, and the female hand more generally, with new symbolic meanings.

Customarily, the bride receives her henna (the *mehndi* stain) at the *mehndi* party, a pre-wedding celebration typically held the day before the marriage ceremony. The belief is that the stain cools the body down and invites joy, luck and blessing into the marriage. Common superstition also dictates that, the darker the henna, the better the husband. To ensure darker henna, and thus better husbands, brides undergo meticulous activities, including applying turmeric to lighten the skin, requesting their designs cover more surface area, pouring lemon juice over the stain and wrapping the body in cellophane for at least an hour. This is to say that, between having her body covered in turmeric, sitting still while someone paints her hands, feet, arms or legs, and then waiting for the lemon juice to seal the stain, the bride must sit idle for many hours.

Today, grooms may also opt to don henna and participate in inviting happiness into the marriage, but principally, the ritual is a rite of passage for the bride. Much like a bachelorette party, *mehndi* parties are female-dominated spaces. Brides looking to the Martha Stewart wedding blog, for instance, are told that the *mehndi* party is 'total girl power' (White 2017). But some scholars, like Rachel Sharaby, still see violent patriarchal structures dominating the ritual. As she suggests, the henna ritual 'expressed a rigid gender separation and a non-egalitarian system in which femininity was shackled in structural inferiority' (2006: 11). By acting as both physical and metaphorical inscriptions on the bride's body, these designs prescribe divinity, beauty and strength, but they also contribute to questions of ownership and identification. In order to revitalize the henna ritual as one which mobilizes women to act, then, Bhardwaj must appropriate henna as a traditional symbol of prescriptive prosperity and critique the ritual which requires female passivity and submission.

One way he accomplishes this is by harkening back to henna's mythical past. The origin of henna as a wedding tradition is difficult to trace. Rachel Sharaby notes that henna was present in Palestine during the biblical, Mishnaic and Talmudic periods, and that documentation shows Egyptians employed henna for embalming bodies and dyeing horsehair (2006: 14). The earliest written evidence depicting henna as a wedding custom, however, is from the Ugaritic Legend of Baal and Anath. Dating from the early Bronze age, this myth acts as an extensive metaphor depicting the agricultural cycles along the Mediterranean coast – where the henna plant grows natively. The connection between henna and marriage comes from the myth's depiction of springtime, where the women dye their hands before seeking husbands. However, the fertile springtime is not the only part henna plays in this agricultural myth. In the Fall, Anath, the myth's fertility goddess, adorns herself with henna prior to completing vengeance against Mot – the god of summer heat – who kills Anath's brother, Baal, the god of rain. The myth's depiction of Anath's revenge is visceral – describing her dismembering Mot, stashing the body parts in her clothing, and wading in his blood (Cassunto 1951). In the context of the myth, this butchery is interpreted to be a metaphor for the Fall harvest, where women de-head the grain and cut down the fields before the late rains come back (De Moor 1971). However, regarding Bhardwaj's films, this bloodshed provides a plausible model for reading henna as not merely a marital custom, but as a preparatory ritual for female proactivity and violence.

Scholars unanimously laud Bhardwaj for the unprecedented female intervention depicted in his climactic scenes.[1] Instead of distancing Lady Macbeth from bloodshed – killing no one, but herself – Bhardwaj puts Nimmi (Tabu), his Lady Macbeth, in the room, overseeing the murder of Abbaji (Pankaj Kapur) and shooting the guard point blank. In place of a Gertrude who drinks poison (knowingly or unknowingly), Ghazala (Tabu) steals the role of avenger from her son by detonating a suicide bomb. Instead of an Emilia who dies while Iago lives on, Bhardwaj surprises us with Indu (Konkona Sen Sharma) slashing Langda's (Saif Ali Khan) throat. Even Dolly (Kareena Kapoor), Bhardwaj's Desdemona, though still smothered by her husband, uses her last moments to draw blood from Omi's (Ajay Devgn) cheek. Each of these female avengers is prepared for their climactic violence with henna.[2] A seeming return to the Ugaritic depiction, this use of henna departs from providing good luck to the bride, and instead marks each female for terrible ends. When it comes to Bollywood Shakespeare, dyeing hands leads to death.

While the turbulent worlds of Mumbai's mafia ring in *Maqbool*, Uttar Pradesh's wild west in *Omkara*, and Kashmir's war-torn borders in *Haider* may force Bhardwaj's women to seek attention and redemption through violence, representing these women with hennaed hands is the director's choice. The following sections will consider the decisions Vishal Bhardwaj makes in *Maqbool*, *Omkara* and *Haider* to portray henna as an omen of violence and bad luck and to appoint the female avenger a seeker after agency denied by her patriarchal societies and even by Shakespeare, himself.

'Will these hands ne'er be clean?' – *Macbeth*

There is no wedding in *Macbeth*, no obvious reason for Bhardwaj to include henna in *Maqbool* (2003). And yet he does. Unexpectedly, the wedding featured in *Maqbool* is not the Macbeths'. In fact, Nimmi and Maqbool are not married at all. In what Mark Thornton Burnett rightly calls 'one of the film's most creative developments' and departures from Shakespeare's original text, Bhardwaj casts

Lady Macbeth in the role of Abbaji's mistress (2013: 58). What this affords is an additional layer of anxiety and motive to Abbaji's murder. Suddenly, the Macbeths are guilty not only of murder but also of a type of adultery. Both have a motive to kill, and both do so.

From the onset of the film, we are led to believe that Nimmi is sleeping with Abbaji to secure a role in his Bollywood films. Thus, when a younger, more attractive actress catches Abbaji's eye, Nimmi's job security is threatened, providing her with a motive beyond simply promoting Maqbool's position. This threat is visually apparent during the *mehndi* dance segment where Nimmi receives her henna. During this dance, the camera shifts between the outdoor female henna preparation – where Nimmi and Sameera (Masumeh Makhija), Abbaji's daughter, perform 'Jhin min jhini', a playful song about female flirtation – and the indoor male enjoyment of the new actress' dancing. This intercutting cinematography juxtaposes the female exterior space with the male interior gaze. Suddenly, the party no longer acts as a celebration of bride and groom, but as an amplification of the power struggle between Nimmi, Maqbool and Abbaji – a struggle which will lead to Abbaji's ultimate death.

Near the end of the song, the camera settles on Nimmi, lost in thought, staring intently at her hennaed palm. The camera invites the viewer to read the dye as a sign by providing an extreme close-up shot of Nimmi's fingers facing upward and tilted down towards the viewer, exposing her stained palm. Nimmi's mouth is visible, but her eyes are outside of the frame. The focal point is clearly her hand and the intricate henna detail. As Nimmi intently gazes upon her palm, the camera pans upwards revealing her eyes. She sings, 'His name, hidden in henna hues, burns my palm like a secret flame', while drawing her fingers in and turning her hands over to scan the knuckles and backs of the palms.[3]

At *mehndi* parties, henna artists often hide the letters of the groom's name in the bride's henna. The understanding is that the groom will search for the letters during the wedding night – providing a playful way of bringing him closer to the bride's skin. But Nimmi is not the bride, nor is Maqbool her groom. Thus, we can assume that either Nimmi requested the letters as a ploy or they have appeared without her knowing – an uncanny premonition of things to come. Whether planned or not, Nimmi takes advantage of the henna and her sexuality by immediately showing her palm to Maqbool and inviting him to find the letters of his name. This stokes his desire for her and the need to get rid of Abbaji. This moment also cues the audience to associate the hennaed hand with mischief and intrigue.

Rightly so, for it is Nimmi's hennaed hands which give the guard too much to drink, and it is with hennaed hands that she retires to Abbaji's bed. Although it is Maqbool who ultimately kills Abbaji, Bhardwaj's Lady Macbeth appears the more confident accomplice. While Maqbool closes his eyes to pull the trigger, Nimmi does not blink. That is, until blood splashes across her face. In this moment the camera closes in on Nimmi drawing her palm to her cheek, returning the attention to her hand. Its ruddy colour, the way the henna design drips down her fingers, all invite the viewer to read the henna as an extension of blood. When Maqbool flees, Nimmi finishes the job. While Shakespeare also tasks Lady Macbeth with finishing Macbeth's dirty work by placing the daggers on the guard, Bhardwaj's Nimmi goes one step further. Her red hands grab the gun stored underneath Abbaji's pillow, as she, not Maqbool, kills the guard.

Because of Lady Macbeth's iconic association with red hands, one might expect Bhardwaj to depict Nimmi delivering the line – 'Out, damned spot' (5.1.35) – with hands actually stained red. And yet, he does not go for low-hanging fruit. While Nimmi's hands are hennaed during the bloody act of Abbaji's murder, they are not hennaed at her death. This decision to draw attention to Nimmi's red hands at Abbaji's death and away from them during her madness signals a shift between Abbaji's death and her own. That difference is Nimmi's agency and proactivity. While she kills the guard and aids in killing Abbaji, she does not kill herself. Unlike Shakespeare's Lady Macbeth, Nimmi's death does not come by way of her own hands. Her death is caused by Maqbool's removing her from medical care too soon following childbirth. In this moment, she is not the actor, but the acted upon. While Nimmi does not die with ruddy fingertips, the symbolic nature of henna as a token of violent volition remains intact. The lack of henna at her death, but especially the striking attention to henna leading up to Abbaji's murder, attests to its connection with Nimmi's increased proactivity and violent fervour.

'Our new heraldry is hands, not hearts' – *Othello*

Throughout *Omkara* (2006), Dolly/Desdemona's henna gives off an aura of mystery and warning – subtly appearing and disappearing in various scenes. Its most explicit entrance occurs when she draws her hands to her face, horrified by the dead snake dropped into her pot of turmeric – an omen of bad luck. Following this moment, we consistently see hennaed hands during Dolly's wedding ceremony and ultimate smothering. While Othello and Desdemona are married for the majority of Shakespeare's play, Bhardwaj's Omi (Othello) and Dolly (Desdemona) do not marry until the very end of the film. Setting the wedding ritual, once again, right before the most climactic scene, Bhardwaj preps his Desdemona (Dolly) and Emilia (Indu) with henna for their violent endings, and subsequently deconstructs the typical Bollywood convention of marriage spectacle.

Dolly's henna is first spotted during the opening montage depicting Dolly and Omi falling in love. In the shot, Dolly stands in front of a mirror with hennaed hands, stroking the bloodstain on her shoulder left by a wounded Omi. Notably, the henna was not on her hands when Omi left the bloodstain on the nightdress, nor is it seen in the segments following this moment in front of the mirror. This suggests some time lapse between the night Omi collapses on Dolly's shoulder, and this night she stands in front of the mirror (this night, given the fact that she is hennaed, is likely the night before her intended wedding to Rajan [Deepak Dobriyal], Bhardwaj's counterpart to Shakespeare's Roderigo). The presence of henna conveys that the evening before she is supposed to marry Rajan, Dolly has still not washed Omi's blood from her dress. Instead, she rubs the stain with pleasure. In other words, this appearance of henna affords a connection between Dolly's marriage (symbolized by her henna) and death / sexual desire (symbolized by the blood stain), appropriately ominous for a character who will die because her husband believes she is sexually deviant.

Dolly's henna reappears again briefly during the conventional Bollywood love song, composed and sung by Bhardwaj, but the appearance is fleeting. The song 'O Saathi Re' draws a dangerous line between passion and violence, emphasized by Dolly and Omi's accompanying violent foreplay. As Bhardwaj's voice paints the sensual image of a lover scolding his beloved until she is scared and crying 'sweet tears', we see Dolly throwing furniture at Omi and chasing him with a shotgun. The song's lyrics continue to imagine the lover stitched into his beloved's body, so that when she twists, he is bruised, 'torn to shreds', but she, still attached, must go with him wherever he goes. For a film which ends with Omi smothering Dolly on their marital bed, the conflation of passion and violence in this scene is thematically provocative, but so too is Dolly's assertiveness in participating in that violence. By portraying Dolly's playful retaliation, Bhardwaj hints that Dolly might not be merely 'a bruised dove, ben[t] meekly to the implacable jealousy of the s***t Othello, and receiv[ing] her death, while kissing the hand which gives it', as the actress, Charlotte Vandenhoff, performed the role in 1851 (R. 1851: 168).

Visually, even if only briefly, Bhardwaj also hints that henna plays a role in Dolly's capacity for retaliation. In one shot during the musical montage, Dolly and Omi are lying together in the straw with perfectly clean hands, and in the next, Dolly's hands are seen hennaed, gripping the arms of a press while Omi grips her. Dolly uses her hands to push Omi off, freeing her body from his and returning to her task. When the camera cuts to the two caressing inside the house, the henna has disappeared completely. This appearing and disappearing of Dolly's henna does not lead us to any chronological cohesion like the opening sequence affords, but its supernatural quality, especially in the midst of a love song fraught with violent affection, further associates henna with female fortitude and associates Omi and Dolly's wedding with bad luck – much like the priest's inability to find an auspicious wedding date, and the dead snake which falls into the turmeric pot. Whether the henna in both of these early scenes is intentional or simply a continuity error does not negate the powerful visual association between henna, bad luck and violence which culminates in Dolly's smothering and Indu's revenge, where henna is more prominently displayed.

In one specific shot following Dolly and Omi's wedding nuptials, the camera provides a close-up of Dolly's hands next to a small candle. Her palms press up against a green wall, leaving behind two red handprints as the image fades to black. Like henna, this wedding custom is meant to bring joy as the bride enters her new home. The bright red colour, either from vermilion or *alta*, intentionally resembles blood – purportedly connecting the new wife with symbols of fertility (blood being present during birth). However, it is sometimes claimed that this custom, like henna, holds superstition. Supposedly, the angle of the impressions, specifically whether the prints tilt or not, prophesies whether the bride will be a 'good' wife. Considering Dolly's hands as an omen for her tragic end, Bhardwaj uses this shot to highlight the ambiguous anxiety which plagues the play. Receiving a mere glimpse of these prints before fading to black leaves the viewer questioning, like Omi, whether Dolly is virtuous or not. While the blood red impressions may not cleanly evidence Dolly's loyalty, they do emblematically depict what is about to befall her. Like the candle, Dolly's light is about to go out, leaving only a bloody handprint behind.

Contrasting Bhardwaj's smothering scene with his source text reveals a complex portrayal of Desdemona's agency in her final moments. While Shakespeare presents Desdemona verbally pleading for her life, adamantly assuring that 'I never did / Offend you in my life, never loved Cassio ... never gave him token' (5.2.58–9, 61), Bhardwaj's Dolly is markedly silent, neither confessing nor denying Omi's accusations. Omi further removes Dolly's ability to defend her honour by presenting her with a false dilemma. A distant echo of Othello's decisive command to 'confess thee freely of thy sin', even when confession 'Cannot remove nor choke the strong conception / That I do groan withal', Omi says he will only spare Dolly's life if she pleads guilty (5.2.53, 55–6). Even if this false dilemma logically evidences acquiescence as a pronouncement of innocence, Dolly's response of 'with pleasure, you are free to take my life' perpetuates the image of a Desdemona who submits to her husband's will, even in death. In this manner, Bhardwaj's script surprisingly appears to strip Shakespeare's Desdemona of her voice, her dissent and her agency, instead of bolster it.

However, while Bhardwaj may limit Dolly's speech, he grants her hands greater consideration. When Omi covers Dolly's mouth with a pillow, her hennaed hand, covered in glistening bangles, reaches up to his face and digs into his skin. The camera emphasizes the importance of this gesture by placing Dolly completely out of the frame except for her hand. In this manner, her hand acts as a synecdoche. Incapable of utterance, her hennaed fingers gesture her final plea. She draws three streaks of blood – a handprint of her three fingers – before her hand drops limply off the bed. This bloody handprint left by a ruddy hand highlights an increased proactivity for this typically submissive Shakespearean heroine. While Dolly's violence does not kill Omi, her intention to cause pain by scratching his face – either in attack or self-defence – moves us away from a Desdemona who exonerates her husband by claiming 'Nobody. I myself ... hath done / This' (5.2.121–2) to one who intends to fight back.

Of course, Bhardwaj's Dolly is not the first to envisage a Desdemona resorting to physical violence. Nineteenth-century European actresses, like Fanny Kemble and Ellen Terry, also sought to portray Desdemona as 'strong, not weak', by fighting off their Othello counterparts, and subsequently fighting against eighteenth-century stipulations that Desdemona ought to be meek and submissive (Terry 1969: 129). But Bhardwaj's Dolly responds not only to European performance history, but also to traditional Indian portrayals of Desdemona as the husband-worshipping wife. Through accentuating Dolly's capability to retaliate with her hands, even while still submitting modestly with her voice, Bhardwaj speaks back to these traditions, both complying with and critiquing the expectations for this Shakespearean heroine.

Dolly's death, of course, is no surprise. The bad omens (henna included), plus the very fact this film claims to be a retelling of *Othello*, all forewarn that she will die. However, what is unexpected is the Emilia character's turning into an armed assailant and enacting vengeance for Dolly and Omi's deaths. As in *Maqbool*, Bhardwaj fudges character relationships in order to shift allegiances. Indu, here, is not Dolly's maid, but Omi's sister. This informs a familial duty to avenge Omi and Dolly's deaths and complete violent action towards Langda (Iago). Bhardwaj's Omi does not deliver justice as Shakespeare's Othello might in wounding Iago. While Indu slaps Langda twice, Omi merely tells him that 'Death will only help free your soul' and allows him to leave. The male protagonist cannot, or will not, be an avenger for justice here – but the female Indu will. She has, as Mike Heidenberg insightfully suggests, an 'empowered activeness that rivals anything her husband or brother display' (2014: 99). Because of this, she assumes the prominent role that Emilia lacks in *Othello*. Although active in voicing opinion and restoring truth, Shakespeare's Emilia ultimately dies by her husband's sword. Iago lives on after the curtain falls. Bhardwaj's Indu, on the other hand, slashes Langda's throat, significantly altering the source text. While Heidenberg wants to see Indu as the vengeful goddess Durga, and Asma Sayed visualizes the goddess Kali, I read her much like Anath, a hennaed female turned fiery slayer (2019: 220). With sickle raised over her head, she becomes, as Poonam Trivedi rightly suggests, 'the instrument of justice and moral retribution, something which has been found lacking in Shakespeare's ending' (2019: 33).

With Dolly's henna acting as an omen of tragic ends, we assume that Indu's henna marks her for death also. And yet Bhardwaj leaves Indu's ending open for interpretation. She is last seen wailing and looking down a well – the camera looking up at her. Mark Thornton Burnett suggests that Indu throws Langda's body down that well (2013: 81), and Mike Heidenberg sees her as merely venting grief (2014: 98–101), but Lalita Pandit Hogan (2010: 58) and Poonam Trivedi contend that Indu will throw herself into the well, 'righting the wrongs ... by taking her own life' (2019: 35). During a Q&A session, Bhardwaj revealed that he intended a final shot with the sound and image of something falling into the water. However, the team chose to cut this ending out, leaving the audience to imagine Indu's fate for themselves.[4] Still, whether Indu pushes Langda's body, or throws her own, down the well, her ending is undeniably violent and intentional. Adorned with henna, Indu delivers justice by avenging her sister-in-law's death, and plausibly sacrifices her own life as a redemptive measure. By endowing both Dolly and Indu with violent determination and hennaed hands, Bhardwaj delivers a new way of considering *Othello*'s female victims and their tragic ends, a way in which female agency is crucial to restoring justice and resolving domestic tragedy.

'The treacherous instrument is in thy hand' – *Hamlet*

In the 5 October 2014 issue of *Indian Express*, Bhardwaj relates that '*Haider* is an extension of what [he] attempted in *Maqbool* and *Omkara*' (Singh 2014). Certainly, *Haider* (2014) is an extension of his granting Shakespeare's females a more active role in the tragedy. In what Abhishek Sarkar calls 'a remarkable departure from Shakespeare', Bhardwaj has Ghazala (Gertrude) hijack Haider's

(Hamlet) mission by detonating a suicide bomb, killing herself, blasting off the Claudius figure's legs and providing an ending far 'more drenched in blood than is possible on stage' (2017: 39). Unsurprisingly, she detonates the bomb with red hands.

Throughout the film, Bhardwaj incorporates red accents as an intentional aesthetic choice, most often associating the colour with violence. The viewer is first cued to the association during the Jhelum river song, which informs the viewer that 'Red, your colour, is red', and 'Blood, blood, blood, blood has become the colour of the time'. Red accents appear explicitly in costume design – especially for the women. The most blatant example is Arshia/Ophelia's (Shraddha Kapoor) red scarf, which leaves bodies wherever it goes.[5] Repeatedly connecting the colour red with blood and death, Bhardwaj conditions the viewer to do the same with Ghazala's red henna by the end of the film.

Red stands out in the final scene as blood splatters across snowy terrain. Ghazala's henna, her scarf and the blood all stand in heightened contrast to the film's predominantly black-and-white colour scheme. Noticeably, Ghazala's henna – as compared to Dolly's or Nimmi's – is blatantly more red than orange or brown. This saturation is especially surprising given the time that passes between Ghazala's wedding and this final scene. Just as in *Omkara*, Bhardwaj moves the wedding from the beginning of Shakespeare's play to much later in this film. However, given the time lapse between Ghazala's wedding and the suicide mission, it seems implausible that her henna could still be so potently red in the graveyard – even if she used lemon juice and cellophane. This contradiction is evident at Parvez/Polonius' (Lali Parimoo) burial, where Arshia's henna from the same wedding has faded significantly, but Ghazala still has seemingly blood-washed fingertips. I suggest Bhardwaj gives special care to ensure Ghazala's henna resembles blood in that final scene when she becomes the avenger, making her henna a proleptic symbol, like the other red accents, foreshadowing her part in the bloody graveyard scene.

Her active role in the final scene is further foreshadowed by her part in the ghost's final visit. In a similar way to Shakespeare, Bhardwaj allows ambiguity to permeate the final ghost encounter. But where Shakespeare presents a Hamlet claiming to see the ghost with a Gertrude who claims to see 'Nothing at all' (Q2, 3.4.129), Bhardwaj more explicitly teases the audience with the real possibility that Ghazala sees her late husband's spectre while Haider is unconscious. Unsurprisingly, Ghazala's hennaed hand is visibly present in the midst of this scene. When Haider's father enters the bedroom, he removes Ghazala's hand from his son's sleeping body. Talking to an unconscious Haider, the ghost tells him to 'aim your bullets at those cunning, deceiving eyes that entrapped your mother'. Although Haider is the intended recipient of this message, the camera focuses on the wide-awake Ghazala, whose eyes stare intently at the ghost. Immediately, the shot shifts to morning, where Haider wakes up, presumably wondering if the ghost's visit was all a dream. Ghazala remains asleep beside the bed, her hennaed hand resting, once again, over his, inviting uncertainty as to what occurred.

Presenting the final ghost's visit as a possible dream both provocatively retains and removes Shakespeare's ambiguity regarding whether Gertrude ever sees the ghost. It omits the debriefing conversation between Gertrude and Hamlet, and subsequently sets aside Gertrude's admission that she saw and heard 'nothing but ourselves' (Q2, 3.4.131). In doing so, Bhardwaj leaves us questioning whether the visit was merely Haider's drowsy illusion, or if Ghazala wakes up to the reality of her son's situation – the reality that her current husband murdered her previous one. This stresses a 'writing back' against Shakespeare's original work. It suggests, as Margaret Jane Kidnie advocates, that Shakespeare's 'works are entangled in the present ... potentially *always* written again through production' (2009: 102). Consequentially, this also allows for possible premeditation to Ghazala's violent act in the final scene, expanding her role in suggesting she might know, or suspect, more than we believe.

The fact that Ghazala comes into the graveyard with so many red markers, including her henna, should cue the audience to expect her death, but perhaps not the surprisingly proactive manner in which she dies. Shakespeare's Gertrude may or may not intentionally drink poison to save Hamlet; Gertrude's insistence that 'I will [drink from the cup], my lord. I pray you pardon me' (Q2, 5.2.275) leaves us with ambiguity, but Bhardwaj's film does not. With her hennaed hand in the foreground, Ghazala tells Haider that 'Revenge does not set us free', and that 'Freedom lies beyond revenge', before walking out of Haider's holdout towards Khurram/Claudius (Kay Kay Menon) and his men. With that same ruddy hand, she removes her black cloak to reveal a suicide vest with eight metal grenades. Ghazala becomes the final solution to bring about justice, but also to save her son. Acting in this way, she emerges, as Paromita Chakravarti suggests, a heroine of 'premeditated agency' who enacts vengeance 'on her own terms' (2016: 131). Ghazala, the hennaed avenger, finishes the job that Haider will not.

Conclusion

Unlike Dolly and Nimmi's henna, which intricately spreads all across their hands, Ghazala's henna is far simpler, largely consisting of two solar circles on the backs of her palms. While today's brides generally cover hands, arms and feet, ancient Vedic custom prescribes that henna was originally applied solely to the palms, symbolizing the inner and outer sun – an awakening of one's inner light. As Farah Karim-Cooper unpacks in her engaging book regarding the hand in Shakespearean performance, early modern hand gestures also indicated a person's inner will (2016). Being the preeminent bodily metaphor for human action, hands were believed to prove someone's guilt (as seen in Lady Macbeth's bloody hands), seal a deal with a handshake, bind a matrimonial promise and witness devotion to God through religious ritual. Giving one's hand was giving one's consent and commitment. This is perhaps best evidenced in John Bulwer's *Chirologia,* where the physician insists, 'What we put our hand unto we are infallibly understood to *will* and *intend*' (1644: 54). As Indian and Shakespearean amalgamations, Bhardwaj's females clearly intend their violent acts. But Nimmi, Dolly and Ghazala's red hands reveal more than guilt: they reveal their newly determined will.

Poonam Trivedi notes that twenty-first-century Indian Shakespeare films repeatedly return to this theme of female avengers (2019: 23–44). What cinema scholars like Carol Clover and Göksel Basak suggest is that, when 'victim-heroines' (to modify Clover's coinage) claim revenge to right wrongs, they represent progress in male-dominant, patriarchal cinema conventions (Clover 1993: 4).[6] Bhardwaj's cinematic use of non-Western contexts, as well as concepts, provides progressive, interpretative possibilities for considering Shakespeare's heroines and their agency as well as for considering typical Bollywood conventions. He invites a re-reading of Shakespeare that enhances Lady Macbeth's part in

Duncan's murder, provides Desdemona and Emilia the right to retaliate against domestic abuse, and allows Gertrude the chance to right wrongs. In *Maqbool, Omkara* and *Haider*, Bhardwaj changes timelines, shifts relationships, and stages choreography, cinematography and cosmetics to ensure his heroines are caught red-handed in pro-activity. In doing so, Bhardwaj's tragedies invite his viewers to not only reconsider Shakespeare's female characters, but to reconsider henna as not merely a custom that requires the idleness of brides, patiently hoping for good husbands, but as a custom that once empowered a goddess to tear her enemy limb from limb in the restoration of justice.

Notes

1 See Hogan 2010; Burnett 2013: 55–86; Heidenberg 2014; Chakravarti 2016; Trivedi 2019.
2 Poonam Trivedi coins this term in relation to Bhardwaj's heroines (2019: 23–44).
3 I quote from DVD English subtitles.
4 Poonam Trivedi recalls that Bhardwaj responded to this question during a Q&A session via Skype at the 'Bard in Bombay: Shakespeare in Indian Cinema' conference hosted by Simon Fraser University, Vancouver, November 2015, and also in person at a similar session at the 'Indian Shakespeares on Screen' conference, London, April 2016 (2019: 35).
5 The scarf is visibly present when the Salman brothers (Rosencrantz and Guildenstern) die, when Parvez (Polonius) is shot, and when Arshia (Ophelia) commits suicide.
6 This progress, Carol Clover claims, stems directly from the women's liberation movement; 'feminism that is, has given a language to [the female's] victimization and a new force to the anger that subsidizes her own act of horrific revenge' (1993: 4).

References

Bulwer, J. (1644), *Chirologia, or, The Naturall Language of the Hand Composed of the Speaking Motions, and Discoursing Gestures Thereof*, London: Thomas Harper.

Burnett, M. T. (2013), *Shakespeare and World Cinema*, Cambridge: Cambridge University Press.
Cassunto, U. (1951), *The Goddess Anath*, trans. I. Abrams, Jerusalem: Magnes Press.
Chakravarti, P. (2016), 'Theatre Reviews: *Haider*', *Shakespeare Bulletin*, 34 (1): 129–32.
Clover, C. J. (1993), *Men, Women and Chain Saws: Gender in the Modern Horror Film*, New Jersey: Princeton University Press.
De Moor, J. (1971), *The Seasonal Pattern in the Ugaritic Myth of Ba'lu*, Kevelaer: Butzon and Bercker.
García-Periago, R. (2014), 'The Ambiguities of Bollywood Conventions and the Reading of Transnationalism in Vishal Bhardwaj's *Maqbool*', in C. Dionne and P. Kapadia (eds), *Bollywood Shakespeares*, 63–86, New York: Palgrave Macmillan.
Göksel Demiray. B. (2012), 'The Avenging Females: A Comparative Analysis of *Kill Bill Vol.1–2, Death Proof* and *Sympathy for Lady Vengeance*', *CINEJ Cinema Journal*, 1 (2): 29–35.
Haider (2014), [Film] Dir. Vishal Bhardwaj, India: UTV Motion Pictures.
Heidenberg, M. (2014), 'No Country for Young Women: Empowering Emilia in Vishal Bhardwaj's *Omkara*', in C. Dionne and P. Kapadia (eds), *Bollywood Shakespeares*, 87–101, New York: Palgrave Macmillan.
Hogan, L. P. (2010), 'The Sacred and Profane in *Omkara*', *Image and Narrative*, 11 (2): 49–62.
Hutcheon, L. and S. O'Flynn (2000), *A Theory of Adaptation*, London and New York: Routledge.
Karim-Cooper, F. (2016), *The Hand on the Shakespearean Stage: Gesture, Touch and the Spectacle of Dismemberment*, London: Bloomsbury.
Kidnie, M. J. (2009), *Shakespeare and the Problem of Adaptation*, London and New York: Routledge.
Maqbool (2003), [Film] Dir. Vishal Bhardwaj, India: Kaleidoscope Entertainment.
Nair, S. (1993), 'Hands that Speak Volumes', *UNESCO Courier*, September: 34–7.
Omkara (2006), [Film] Dir. Vishal Bhardwaj, India: Shemaroo Video, Big Screen Entertainment, Panorama Studios.
R., E. F. (1851), 'Portrait Gallery (No. VIII): Mr. and Miss Vandenhoff', *Tallis's Dramatic Magazine*, April: 165–9.
Refskou, A. S. and L. Thomasen (2014), 'Handling the Theme of Hands in Early Modern Cross-Over Contexts', *Early Modern Culture Online*, 5: 31–51. Available online: https://doi.org/10.15845/emco.v5i0.1291 (accessed 16 February 2021).
Rowe, K. (1999), *Dead Hands: Fictions of Agency, Renaissance to Modern*, Stanford: Stanford University Press.

Sarkar, A. (2017), 'Haider and the Nation-State: Shakespeare, Bollywood, and Kashmir', *South Asian Review*, 37 (2): 29–46.

Sayed, A. (2019), 'Adaptation as Translation: The Bard in Bombay', in J. Locke Hart (ed.), *Shakespeare and Asia*, 213–28, London and New York: Routledge.

Schröter, J. (2012), 'Four Models of Intermediality', in B. Herzogenrath (ed.), *Travels in Intermedia[lity]: ReBlurring the Boundaries*, 15–36, Hanover: Dartmouth College Press.

Sharaby, R. (2006), 'The Bride's Henna Ritual: Symbols, Meanings, and Changes', *A Journal of Jewish Women's Studies & Gender Issues*, 11: 11–42.

Sherman, C. R., B. Copenhaver and P. Lukehart (2000), *Writing on Hands: Memory and Knowledge in Early Modern Europe*, Seattle: University of Washington Press.

Singh, H. (2014), 'Kashmir is the Hamlet of my film', *Indian Express*, 5 October. Available online: https://indianexpress.com/article/entertainment/bollywood/kashmir-is-the-hamlet-of-my-film (accessed 1 June 2021).

Terry, E. (1969), *Four Lectures on Shakespeare*, ed. C. St. John, New York: B. Blom.

Trivedi, P. (2007), 'Filmi Shakespeare', *Literature / Film Quarterly*, 35 (2): 148–58.

Trivedi, P. (2019), 'Woman as Avenger: "Indianising" the Shakespearean Tragic in the Films of Vishal Bhardwaj', in P. Trivedi and P. Chakravarti (eds), *Shakespeare and Indian Cinemas: 'Local Habitations'*, 23–44, New York: Routledge.

White, C. (2017), 'Attending a Mehndi Party? Here's Everything You Need to Know', *Martha Stewart Weddings*, 15 May. Available online: https://www.marthastewart.com/7892206/traditional-mehndi-party (accessed 16 February 2021).

PART FOUR

Critics and creatives

9

Embattled bodies: Women, land and contemporary politics in *Arshinagar*, a film adaptation of *Romeo and Juliet*

Rosa García-Periago

Arshinagar ('*Town of Mirrors*'), Aparna Sen's 2015 film adaptation of *Romeo and Juliet,* represents the director's second cinematic encounter with Shakespeare after her successful *opera prima*, *36 Chowringhee Lane* (1981), which revolves around an Anglo-Indian elderly teacher, a kind of female Lear, whose life is characterized by despair and loneliness. Aparna Sen's cinema draws on many different traditions. Bengali writers such as Bankim Chandra Chatterjee and Ishwar Chandra Vidyasagar, who wrote on women in earlier periods, influenced her cinema. Sen's cinema has also been read in relation to parallel cinema. And it bears the traces of her contact with the Bengali intelligentsia. Her father, Chidananda Dasgupta, was one of the founders of the Calcutta Film Society in 1947, and Aparna Sen subsequently carried 'forward a high cultural legacy of Bengali art' (Bakshi and

Dasgupta 2017: 191) into her cinematic work. If the 1950s saw the emergence of Indian parallel cinema with Bengali auteurs such as Satyajit Ray, Mrinal Sen and Ritwik Ghatak, the late 1970s and 1980s were distinguished by the revival of a new wave of Indian parallel cinema productions (labelled commercially designed arthouse movies) with filmmakers such as Shyam Benegal, Gautam Ghose and, of course, Aparna Sen. Aparna Sen's cinema seems to promote a distinctive kind of cinematic vision in which women play a crucial role, their parts are expanded and they are granted a transformative agency.

A particular feature of *Arshinagar* is a female-centred perspective. Sen's films embrace a wide range of women's identities and backgrounds, whether these reveal themselves in religion, ethnicity, education or caste/class. The director's resilient female characters are discovered as rebelling against patriarchy and their own constrained social and cultural circumstances. In addition, emerging from the director's commitments is an espousal of social causes and a will to entertain the possibility that differences between Hindu and Muslim communities can be overcome. The articulation of aesthetics and gender in Sen's films shares features with cinematic works by other women filmmakers, such as the Indian diasporic Deepa Mehta or Shamim Ara, from the (Pakistan) Lahore film industry. In this way, a film such as *Arshinagar* makes visible aspects of 'women's solidarity' (White 2015: 23), including assertive heroines who defy customs and the established order; political ideas; sexual desire and particular locations, such as the room on the roof or the terrace in Bengali households, thereby recalling a cosmopolitan women's film culture. Dealing with a contemporary crisis (tensions between Hindu and Muslim communities) through a love story, *Arshinagar* explores the relationship between female bodies and national ideologies, female bodies being stamped in the film as contested spaces. At the same time, *Arshinagar* reflects on female bodies as ciphers of the regional or 'Bengaliness'.[1] Bengaliness might be understood as a '*construct* of the supposedly consolidated entities of Bengali-speaking peoples' (Chakraborty 2014: 4), and, in *Arshinagar*, Bengali women function as political expressions of the nation and the region at one and the same time.

Arshinagar favours a discourse of female bodies and the nation that breaks with traditional imaginings of women as one-dimensional national symbols. Inside the discourses of 'Bollywood' cinema, women's bodies tend to be idealized as vehicles for notions of national purity and dignity. Chastity becomes a crucial trait, symbolizing 'national honour' and providing 'the moral code for the lives of women in the nation' (Banerjee 2017: 10). Female agency is generally curtailed, the focus instead being on women as reproducers of dominant ideologies. Such forms of representation bring to mind, too, nationalist movements in which women can reproduce 'the boundaries of national groups and acculturate their children to function within them' (Ranchod-Nilsson and Tétreault 2002: 6). By contrast, although *Arshinagar* explores national preoccupations, it does so with no equivalent idealization of the nation or women's bodies. Women in the film exercise agency, with their bodies functioning as sites of conflict and contestation. Women characters in *Arshinagar* analogize a riven nation rather than a unified territory. In addition, they represent a wide range of positions: higher status – Dadijaan (Waheeda Rehman) – and lower status – Fatema (Swagata Mukherjee) – and Hindu – Ronojoy/Romeo's mother Madhu (Jaya Seal) – and Muslim religions – Julekha/Juliet (Rittika Sen) and her grandmother, Dadijaan (Waheeda Rehman) – highlighting the complexities of national affiliation and the impossibility of any attempt at homogenizing via women's identities. *Arshinagar*, then, looks to embodiment as an indicator of national crisis and contemporary politics.

The political landscape of *Arshinagar* is implicitly gendered in a way that marks out the film as a Shakespearean adaptation. In fact, following Robert Stam's argument, *Arshinagar* represents a transformation of the source text, for texts 'generate other texts in an endless process of recycling, transformation, and transmutation, with no clear point of origin' (Stam 2000: 66). Given that the play is not an object, but a 'dynamic process that evolves over time in response to the needs and sensibilities of its users' (Kidnie 2009: 2), *Arshinagar*'s engagement with the source text results in the generation of a new text created from a productive interplay. *Arshinagar* modifies the 'original', adds, but also cuts; it alters and rewrites the text at length. So, *Arshinagar* imagines the Capulets as the Muslim Khans and the Montagues as the Hindu Mitters, the ancient grudge being recast to prioritize religion as a defining component. The grudge is perpetuated by the violent, ruthless and stubby-haired Tayyab Khan/Tybalt (Jisshu Sengupta). *Arshinagar* imagines Romeo as Ronojoy Mitter (Dev), a long-haired rock singer and reluctant fighter, Mercutio as the aggressive and cocky Monty (Anirban Bhattacharya), and Friar Lawrence as a schoolteacher. When Ronojoy meets the angelic Julekha Khan/Juliet at an *Eid* banquet, they fall in love and turn into the fabled star-crossed lovers, only to worsen longstanding familial disagreements based on religion and business rivalry. The film consistently expands the narrative, as when it explores another pair of lovers in the past – Ronojoy's mother, Madhu Mitter, and Julekha's father, Sabir Khan (Koushik Sen). Sen transposes Verona to a mirror for Kolkata ('Mirrorville'), but, rather than imagining it 'through the romantic aura of bourgeois nostalgia', envisions the location 'as a site of bitter class and communal struggle' (Chakravarti 2021: 109), and such an interpretation is emphasized in an ending that favours high-angle shots of the brutal killing of the protagonists. But the narrative expands again via the addition of female characters, such as Dadijaan, the stylish Muslim grandmother, and the puppeteer; played by the same character who plays Fatema/the Nurse (Swagata Mukherjee), she, like Dadijaan, is a grandmother. Even the Juliet and Lady Capulet counterparts are given new and different nuances and places, with Julekha/Juliet seeking out forms of independence and belonging from the start. In this sense, fresh perspectives are provided and additional alleyways and possibilities for the text opened and explored. The film inevitably makes us think anew about Shakespeare.

More generally, *Arshinagar* can be examined against a backdrop characterized by ongoing instabilities exacerbated by 'the growing might of a right-wing central government since 2014 and its stated goal to build a Hindu nation' (Chakravarti 2021: 110). Transposing the ancient grudge between Capulets and Montagues to the longstanding Hindu-Muslim divide, the film makes for a particularly intense and timely relocation of a conflict in which women's roles carry significant ideological freight. Accordingly, this chapter looks at the gendering of *Arshinagar*'s political landscape. Whether it be the Muslim Juliet in the present or Romeo's Hindu mother in the past, women are subjected to expressions of antipathy towards what is perceived to be the 'other', thereby making visible the tragic consequences of aspiring to agency (as the first section discusses). At the same time, as the second section explores, *Arshinagar* goes beyond the Hindu-Muslim divide to contemplate related political controversies such as the local government's land acquisition policy, which is played out on the body of Fatema/the Nurse. Clearly, *Arshinagar* points to inequalities among different classes and the difficulties of cohabitation in contemporary India. Bodies definitely matter in the presentation of a national crisis and global and local politics. The actions women's bodies perform as ciphers of politics in *Arshinagar*, and the ways in which bodies enact the political world, are the subjects of this chapter.

Women's bodies and community politics

The prologue to *Romeo and Juliet* describes how 'Two households, both alike in dignity ... From ancient grudge break to new mutiny' (Prologue, 1, 3), and from a backdrop of conflict the action of *Arshinagar* springs. The two rival gangs are the Mitters and the Khans, glaring red and black colours marking separate domains, even the different households. The Mitters are identified by bright red, whereas the Khans are marked by black, perhaps because this colour can be associated with Muslim communities. In addition, Hindu and Muslim religious differences inevitably inflect the dialogue. The gangs make their money from drug smuggling and shady businesses. Overseeing the operations of both gangs (and bringing different slum and market settings together) is the figure of the puppeteer (unnamed and dressed in bright colourful clothes), who also plays Fatema/the Nurse: her doubled role has a merging function. Through the puppeteer, *Arshinagar* foregrounds a female voice and female representational authority. The puppeteer, or narrator, serves to describe and represent a world of horror, upset and prejudice. Distinctively, the film includes as part of the score the song, 'Bari'r Kacche Arshi Nagar' ('The Town of Mirrors Near My Home'), which was composed by Lalon Fakir, a nineteenth-century Bengali philosopher, author and saint known, as Taarini Mookherjee notes, 'for his religious tolerance and pluralism' (2019: 1). In this way, *Arshinagar* repurposes a nineteenth-century song in a contemporary plea for interculturalism. The song's lyrics describe a neighbour who is present, but cannot be seen, and the phenomenon of having another self within your own. Such mirroring ideas are made manifest in the doubling of the actress playing the Nurse and puppeteer roles. And, at other level, the notion of repetition draws attention to the repetitive nature of Hindu-Muslim conflicts that are at the film's heart.

Following in the footsteps of films such as *Qayamat Se Qayamat Tak* (dir. Mansoor Khan, 1988), a Bollywood adaptation of *Romeo and Juliet*, Sen's *Arshinagar* intersects two generations of pairs of lovers, stressing continuing expressions of intolerance. When the narrative combines the present and the past, the different sets of lovers are distinguished by their different clothing, characteristic of their religion. Ronojoy's mother, Madhu Mitter, wears a yellowish *salwar kameez* and a shawl, while Julekha's father, Sabir Khan, wears a typical Muslim outfit (a *serwal*, white cotton pants and a *thobe*, a white gown). When we move into the present, Julekha appears wearing a veil covering her hair (connoting Islam), whereas Ronojoy wears more contemporary clothes. The film also localizes and 'Banglaises' *Qayamat Se Qayamat Tak*, which itself is an adaptation of an earlier South Indian film. The two Juliets in the film (Julekha Khan, the Muslim and younger Juliet, and Ronojoy's mother, the Hindu and older Juliet) are victims of a Hindu-Muslim impasse. Filling in for what Shakespeare's play does not tell us (the origins of the grudge), the film in the opening shot shows a close-up of Madhu Mitter's face when looking at a note that reads 'Marry me' and which she keeps in a safe. Via flashback, the narrative recalls her past in which she enjoyed a romance with Sabir Khan/Capulet. Despite the earlier efforts of Khan and Ronojoy's mother to tie the knot, this cross-boundary relationship, the film makes clear, is forbidden by their respective families. That this romance lies outside 'the realm of possibility' can be seen in the way 'that it appears within a tale that is itself self-consciously presented as fictional' (Harris 2018: 84). The implication is that a relationship between a Muslim Romeo and a Hindu Juliet is out of the question and can remain in the realm of illusion only. In keeping with the suggestion, the *mise-en-scène* introduces notes of Brechtian alienation which are underscored in the film's mixing and matching of realism and artifice. Actual rooftop scenes that were filmed in Lucknow are shot against obviously artificial backdrops of towers and spires, exemplifying this paradoxical combination perfectly. Moreover, the fictional tale is returned to in the ways in which the film reveals the consequences of the characters' actions. While Sabir Khan turns into an exaggerated patriarch, even stricter than his parents in forbidding his daughter's romance with Ronojoy,

Ronojoy's mother sinks into despair. The impossibility of their union affects her psychologically to the extent that she fosters the idea of Ronojoy's emancipation and elopement with Julekha to avoid further woe.

'Gender relations are implicated in the contexts of politics', states Tamar Mayer (2004: 157), a formulation that seems particularly relevant to the representation of Julekha Khan. Through Julekha, *Arshinagar* suggests that the complicating factor in the central romance remains religion. In a discussion of the director, Kaustav Bakshi and Rohit K. Dasgupta write that Sen's female characters move away from 'submissive, law-abiding, conformist characters'; they are heroines that transgress 'moral codes' (2017: 199). In line with Juliet, Julekha is precisely such a figure. When she is introduced in *Romeo and Juliet,* Juliet presents the analogy of her love as a bird, claiming that she will not look deeply into Paris' heart to find love 'to make it fly' (1.3.100). A bird is free to choose where to fly, and Juliet, it is implied, lacks freedom to allow her heart to fly where it desires in pursuit of love. Interestingly, *Arshinagar* introduces its heroine through an emblematic scene in which Julekha has a tattoo of bird wings etched on her back (only Fatema accompanies her, and clearly there is no parental approval). The tattoo is revealing: it seems to empower her to achieve liberation, and the wings suggest a will to soar, to escape, to secure a different kind of mobility. Such qualities are seen in Julekha's resistance to the arranged marriage with Parvez/Paris (Shataf Figar), her disobeying her father's orders, and cross-dressing scenes, suggestive of an alternative history to that experienced by Ronojoy's mother. In addition, when informed of the romance between her father and Ronojoy's mother, she approves the prospect of inter-community liaisons: 'why can't Hindus and Muslims marry if Christians and Hindus do marry?' she asks. If Christians and Hindus marry, other cross-community romances should be allowed, her argument goes. However, Julekha ends up as another innocent victim (the pink hues of her outfits are here perhaps indicative) of the Hindu-Muslim divide, an unavoidable death amidst disruption. Women are long-time sufferers, and nothing, it seems, has changed in the thirty-year difference between the two generations of lovers; Partition precipitated a breakdown in relations between the two communities, and the wound has not yet healed.

Jonathan Gil Harris notes that 'Indian adaptations of *Romeo and Juliet* sometimes hint at a historical trauma that they do not address explicitly: Partition and its aftermath' (2018: 83). *Arshinagar* is a case in point, as it is set in contemporary India but looks back to the historic Partition between India and Pakistan via the character of the stylish grandmother. As a *khandaani* Muslim woman (a higher status within the Islamic community), she wears 'black and grey shararas paired with lace and chiffon dupattas' (Sen 2017: n.p.). A *dupatta* is a shawl-like scarf or veil singling out elegance; its fabric may vary in accordance with one's class and one's budget. The grandmother's pain radiates outwards and she functions as a powerful image of how trauma is felt for generations to come. The inclusion of the grandmother in the narrative (she is lacking in Shakespeare's *Romeo and Juliet*) allows for a journey that takes the film backwards and forwards, since, given her age, she was clearly born before Partition. She represents, in fact, a kind of 'old Muslim household', and not least because she speaks 'Urdu and Hindustani' (Chakravarti 2019: 312) simultaneously. In addition, her son is the permanent reminder of conflict – his romance was doomed to failure. Via flashbacks, the film reveals the main opponent to that relationship was none other than Dadijaan, and, in a meeting with her husband and son, she blames Ronojoy's mother for intending to forswear her religious vows. In her words, 'a woman who forswears her religious vows cannot be true to her husband and spouse'. Inevitably, the grandmother conceives of women in ideological terms, reading into the woman's body national and religious boundaries. Yet, at the same time, *Arshinagar* constructs the grandmother as an instrument of transformation and change. What brings this change of heart about is a resentful comment from her son to Julekha bewailing the impossibility of a Hindu and Muslim union. The camera zooms in on her face, showing bewilderment, and, against the weight of pessimism, Dadijaan's evolution is a breath of fresh air. In the midst of acrimony, Dadijaan's support of her granddaughter's romance exorcises her guilty past and puts affirmation in the place of adversity. The emblematic scene of grandmother and granddaughter embracing each other wearing white represents a moment at which female spaces and alliances raise prospects of a more hopeful future. Crucially, the meeting of grandmother and granddaughter enables Julekha to move forward and attempt a new life with Ronojoy. Solidarity, however, does not end here, for Fatema equally proffers assistance, two women coming together to enable Julekha in a doubled structure. Such

FIGURE 9.1 *The tragic* dénouement *of* Arshinagar *(dir. Aparna Sen, 2015). Courtesy of Aparna Sen and Shree Venkatesh Films*

an arrangement is consistently repeated in the film, either through parallelism (like Dadijaan, Fatema also has a granddaughter) or through scenes of cross-dressing. Julekha's empowerment fosters sorority, and, in conflicted terrain, female spaces, networks and support are the antidote to turmoil.

Despite the greater role of female intervention, and moves to facilitate the relationship between Ronojoy and Julekha, their romance collapses under the weight of a greater force, contemporary society and its internal contradictions. *Arshinagar* rewrites the ending of Shakespeare's *Romeo and Juliet*, but it rejects any ameliorative alternative; if anything, tragic complexions are amplified. While, in *Romeo and Juliet,* the last time the protagonists see each other alive is in 3.5, Ronojoy and Julekha, at the close of the film, briefly see each other standing at each side of a level crossing and wait to reunite. Their happiness, however, is momentary only; agency quickly evaporates, and the lovers are killed by passing rioters. In an ironic finale, marked by constant shot-reverse-shots, the Muslim Juliet, dressed as a Hindu man with a turban and a moustache, is killed by Muslim rioters, and the Hindu Romeo, dressed as a Muslim woman in a black *burqa*, is shot by Hindu rioters while looking at his beloved's corpse in a powerful close-up. Instead of killing themselves in a final act of self-determination, the lovers are constructed as subjected to the whims and projections of society, the realms of romance and political disorder bleeding into each other in a spectacle of communal disharmony. The riots are encouraged by the land-grabbers, or capitalist entrepreneurs, so that the real villains of the film are not so much specific Hindu/Muslim agitators as the global/capitalist figures who push them into violence. The film's condemnation of the expression of differences is self-evident here, especially since the two communities are mirror images of each other and can easily be swapped, as the ending demonstrates. While Shakespeare's *Romeo and Juliet* closes with Escalus' observation that the 'story' (5.3.309) of *Romeo and Juliet* is the tragedy *par excellence*, *Arshinagar* suggests that its tragedy is condemned to be repeated. It has already been repeated generation after generation, in fact, as in the love story between Ronojoy's mother and Julekha's father. After the funeral procession in which black and white tones predominate in high-angle shots, the ending takes on a further suggestiveness in intermingling the realms of reality and illusion. When Ronojoy is shot, the note with the lovers' plans for their joint living space floats away on the breeze until it is collected by Fatema, here in her interchangeable role of puppeteer. The film's two dimensions are finally juxtaposed. Hence, the doubling casting device is made explicit in such a way that the ambivalences of cross-dressing earlier are emphasized. *Arshinagar* highlights, at the close, the paradoxes that categorising produces at the same time as it hints at the contemporary complexions of identity. In so doing, the film alerts us to the reflections, distortions and repetitions that characterize India's ongoing political narratives.

Women's bodies, urban crises and Bengaliness

Emerging from the previous discussion, this section argues that *Arshinagar* discharges national *and* regional preoccupations. It suggests that urban crises are played out on women's bodies and that, in the process, notions of Bengaliness are negotiated. In this connection, the film presents itself as a salient instance of Mark Thornton Burnett's thesis that, in world cinema, 'Localization takes on a gendered complexity' (Burnett 2013: 128). Female bodies as signifiers of the regional are given particular emphasis in the slum sequences. The camera tracks the figure of the Nurse so as to tell a different story to the main plot and to highlight how a state policy of land acquisition is mired in social conflict and class rivalry. The song, 'Kala Paisa Wala' ('Black Money People') has the virtue of communicating in a succinctly economic way the dynamics of the situation. Filth, malfunctioning drains and run-down houses fill the slum, and yet this is the only place most of the 'Mirrorville' city-dwellers can call home. 'Kala Paisa Wala' is an operatic song that denounces the government's malfeasance and its subscription to profit; in Taarini Mookherjee's words, it 'critiques the upper classes' corruption and their exploitation of the lower classes' (2019: 7). In fact, the government in *Arshinagar* – aided and abetted by the Mitters and the Khans – is planning to demolish the slum and build a mall. What seemed a fantasy world, impossible to associate with any actual location, serves, in fact, to frame the film within Bengal, representations of rapacious acts of land acquisition inevitably bringing to mind 'real' cases within the Indian state. Singur and Nandigram are well-known West Bengal locations for anti-land acquisition struggles. Violence and major rebellions took place in these areas in 2007 in response to government plans 'to set up a chemical hub by acquiring something like 14,000 acres of fertile agricultural land' (Nigam 2011: 39). Despite state pressure, a considerable number of farmers and sharecroppers in the area refused to acquiesce and precipitated agitation in order to retain their properties. Arrestingly, women played a significant role in the disturbances.

Here, the song, 'Kala Paisa Wala', with its line of men and women and Fatema at the centre, works to bring these larger West Bengal incidents into the filmic frame. If the Singur and Nandigram movements were characterized by the participation of subaltern groups in terms of class, caste and gender, *Arshinagar* takes energy from these and related expressions of discontent. Like their real-life counterparts, the men and women of the slums of *Arshinagar* raise their voices and attempt to block the bulldozing of a school. As the violence intensifies, and slum-dwellers fall to the ground, the camera zooms in on Fatema again, and the narrative delves into her story. Hers is a set of experiences that is shaped not only, as Helma Lutz, Maria Terrera Herrera Vivar and Linda Supik state, 'by gender but also by other social categories' (2011: 8); hence, Fatema's exclusion needs to be contextualized inside a nexus of relations of rule and systems of discrimination. In keeping with this focus, the film discovers Fatema in terms of images of marginalization (dirty streets) and situates her predicament according to a logics of class difference. It is Fatema's condition as a slum-dweller in a violent environment that prompts her to escape with her granddaughter and ask for Dadijaan's help (a woman who is herself bound in by patriarchal dictates yet can still benefit from an upper-class lifestyle). In an emblematic scene with Fatema and her granddaughter and Dadijaan and Julekha (to which viewers have access through a veil), Fatema asks for assistance and is allowed to stay in the house while the disturbances escalate outside. Camerawork parallels two grandmothers (Dadijaan and Fatema) with their respective granddaughters (Julekha and Fatema's granddaughter) in a singular and expressive scene. The episode marks a celebration of a union of women belonging to different classes, representatives of the margins being elided with figures of privilege in a unique shot which gestures to gendered support networks. Via cross-class alliances, *Arshinagar* again aspires to an alternative dispensation.

Matching its foregrounding of women's bodies and local politics is the film's representation of the Baul singer (Parvathy Baul) at two key mirroring moments (these bracket Ronojoy and Julekha's love story). Baul is an oral musical tradition from the Bengal region and emphasizes the spirituality of the body rather than that of the mind. According to Bhashkar Bhattacharya, the central concept of Baul philosophy is 'Truth within the body', a microcosm of the universe in which all the 'elements of existence reside' (1993: 148). The first of these moments features the Baul singer against the backdrop of the funfair, the lovers having just met during a Khan party in a cross-dressing encounter (Julekha dressed as a Hindu young man and Ronojoy dressed as a Muslim young woman). Crucially, because the Baul singer sings the previously mentioned song, 'Bari'r Kacche Arshi Nagar' ('The Town of Mirrors Near My Home'), its motifs of strangeness and familiarity reverberate outwards, reflecting on the lovers and raising the possibility of relations based on mutual acceptance. Given the cultures of fear and intimidation that have arisen in India, mainly since the destruction of the Babri Masjid in 1992 (this sixteenth-century mosque in Ayodhya, Uttar Pradesh, was demolished by Hindu nationalists) and the 2002 Gujarat riots (a three-day period characterized by inter-communal violence triggered by the burning of a train), a discourse of this kind, and a subscription to the idea of the neighbour, remains pertinent and timely. The second mirroring moment occurs at the close, just prior to the *dénouement*, when the cross-dressing scene is repeated. In the midst of internecine violence, the second song the Baul singer sings, 'Aami Aami Kore Barai' ('I Roam around Talking only of Myself'), centres on mirroring and hence the potential for harmony/ reciprocity. It is performed at the point where the Hindu temple at the centre of the slum is purposely burned down so that the mall can be built. In both cases, the singer occupies filmic space via bodily emphases – an *ektara*, ankle bells, the drum around her waist, her bare feet and, especially, her flying, dreadlocked hair – and vocal power.[2] Baul music preaches 'tolerance and oneness' (Nettl and Rommen 2016: 118), and this is precisely the message of the songs the Baul singer performs, which function as a kind of prologue/epilogue. Irrespective of the complications of religion and gender, loving relations and pacific possibilities are entertained in the second song, the surrounding strife serving only to highlight its themes. In an otherwise depressive milieu, a distinctively female voice is prioritized, and it is one that is animated by its location in praxes of place, politics and Bengaliness.

The film also depicts – and takes to task – the ways in which, inside the operations of local politics, women are identified as targets of attack. Although political corruption is a symptom of ill-governance throughout India, the state of West Bengal was especially affected in 2016 when members of the Trinamool Congress (TMC) were recorded accepting bribes in exchange for extending favours to a fictitious company.[3] In view of the film's representation of the involvement of the Mitter and the Khan families in bribery, an allusion to a fraught political context can be intuited. The middle-aged and Escalus-like politician (Paran Bandopadhyay) who appears in *Arshinagar* endlessly negotiates with the Mitters and the Khans, shedding light on the importance of money over ethics and the fact that the world is up for sale (as the song 'Kala Paisa Wala' suggests). Even if the action discovers scenes in which compensation is (seemingly) negotiated for the slum-dwellers, it simultaneously makes clear that women are seen as objects to be abused and saleable items. A distinctive moment is when Tayyab/Tybalt ambushes a couple with their daughter, pressures them to sell their property and threateningly cuts the mother's hair. A further instance of the equation between women and transaction centres on Julekha Khan, for her father aims at an arranged marriage for the sake of his business. Referencing Shakespeare's play, Paris is remodelled as Parvez, Julekha's suitor, and any relationship between them is imagined in purely economic fashion. If the initial conversation between Capulet and Paris in *Romeo and Juliet* gestures to Juliet's wishes ('My will to her consent is but a part' [1.2.16]), *Arshinagar* strips out Julekha's participation from her father's discourse, placing emphasis instead on the exercise of rule as an exclusively male preserve. Parvez/Paris lives in Dubai – the cradle of 'real-life' crime bosses, such as Chhota Shakeel or Dawood Ibrahim, and the preferred port of call for some Indian companies and many Indian labourers looking for work – and he is clearly involved in suspect dealings (as indicated in his conversations with Sabir Khan, Julekha being part of the deal).

Despite the fact that women are envisaged as transactionable – and public – commodities, *Arshinagar* throughout, but particularly so in its latter stages, elaborates an alternative scenario that points up Julekha's agency. Through her, the film declares the importance of a personal sphere and an individual agenda and accentuates the ways in which she goes against male-imposed norms. In the two relevant sequences, the attention to cross-dressing is revealing as we see foregrounded notions of fluidity and transference; identity markers of religion and gender appear as flexible and negotiable, even as processes of performativity. *Arshinagar*, in fact, destabilizes the distinctions between Hindu/Muslim, man/woman, natural/artificial and depth/surface; as Taarini Mookherjee writes, 'markers are easily shifted and exchanged ... [the lovers] each bear the markers not just of the other's gender, but also the other's faith – a sort of doubled cross-dressing' (2019: 5–6). *Arshinagar*, in short, raises pertinent questions about gender and religion and, through the act of rewriting Shakespeare, contemplates the possibility of gendered and religious signifiers being dissolved. If subjects function as mirror images which reflect inner selves, it is suggested, then a fairer, more equitable world can be anticipated. This is a world that subscribes not to a one-dimensional concept of the nation but, instead, to free-standing, performative scenarios. Crucially, the idea that markers of identity are flexible is crystallized in the film's investment in Bengali culture and images. According to Shormishtha Panja, *Arshinagar* 'deploys regional rather than pan-Indian traditions in music and dialogue, traditions that would require annotation not just for a non-Indian viewer but even for an Indian viewer from outside Bengal' (575). A unique brand of Bengaliness, which shows itself in *Arshinagar* in interrelated regional references, is promoted via filming locations. Some of these are emancipating and suggestive of plural identities, as in those episodes set in 'the *chhader-ghar* (room on the roof) or the terrace', which, 'in joint Bengali households', functions as 'a place of word-making for Bengali women' (Bakshi and Dasgupta 2017: 194). The relationship between Julekha's father and Ronojoy's mother is filmed almost entirely in a recreated terrace in one of these households. In addition, Julekha and Tayyab/ Tybalt's mother (Roopa Ganguli) also forge a strong bond when they are represented as moving to the terrace to talk about the past. In this way, *Arshinagar* both cultivates the regional and embraces negotiable categories of identity in its elaboration of women's bodies, agencies and material experience.

Conclusion

Arshinagar looks to question the contemporary Indian moment through the lens of Shakespeare's *Romeo and Juliet,* 'a play that depicts love in the midst of strife' (Parthasarathy 2016: 20). Although the plotting of a Romeo and Juliet love story along the Hindu/ Muslim divide is not novel (several adaptations, such as *Bombay* [dir. Mani Ratnam, 1995], have used the play to flag precisely this theme), it is Sen's exploration of the conjunction between women's bodies and political instability that makes her film distinctive.[4] Her adaptation departs from conventional representations of women – which see in them symbols of the nation's dignity and purity – and gestures, instead, in Srimati Mukherjee's words, to more liberating 'processes of meaningful exchange' (2016: 133). Moreover, in the 'how' of its workings out, *Arshinagar* takes up dissident positions. It urges us to think again about its Shakespearean source and to reflect on the ways in which women characters might be marshalled, extended and invented. As such, the film demonstrates how, as Mark

Thornton Burnett states, 'location is invariably indissoluble from questions about women's status and agency' (2017: 206), even as it also deploys tropes of embodiment to interrogate India's political landscape.

Because it is tuned to explore national and regional crises, Shakespeare's *Romeo and Juliet*, in *Arshinagar*, takes on fresh dimensions. The play is revitalized in the adaptation's examination of systems of local power politics that themselves are shaped by nationalist ideologies. Nor are the concepts of region and nation that the film engages with necessarily homogeneous or idealized. For example, the older metaphor of woman as nation is taken apart in an ending that emphasizes only difference and ambivalence. Via Julekha, *Arshinagar* disavows the notion of women as cultural reproducers, for her escape from 'Mirrorville' is a key component of the action and is imitated, in turn, by other women from her family. Elsewhere in the film, the to-and-fro between different women's voices and classes illuminates complexities of identification and the intransigence of social and political conflict. This is most obviously signposted when Ronojoy (in the disguise of a *burqa*-clad woman), crying over Julekha's body (in the disguise of a Hindu man with a turban), is murdered by those of his own faith, this climactic moment bringing to a head the film's anatomization of a riven world. Tamar Mayer argues that 'the nation cannot be discussed in gender-neutral terms' (2004: 153) since it has an 'intimate relationship to gender' (2004: 156), and, in the gendered interplay of the film's ending, a powerful impression of nation divided, and a community antagonized, is afforded.

Arshinagar gives the 'story' (5.3.309) of *Romeo and Juliet* a local habitation and a name. 'Mirrorville' is, in many ways, a microcosm of India itself, and the fictional Bengali city's enmities and troubles indicate larger crises: the Mitters and the Khans are reflective and symptomatic. As has been suggested earlier, the effect, even if there are interludes of affirmation and solidarity, and despite summoning of other scenarios, is to underscore the sense of a dystopian universe. For all her agency, for instance, Julekha is still mindlessly slaughtered (the suicide narrative, as in Shakespeare's play, is excised). More broadly, in its status as a woman-helmed adaptation, *Arshinagar* marks a departure in the representation of women on Indian screens. The film asks us to think through Shakespeare's figurations of women in the light of its representation of a city/region/nation in crisis and in relation to an adaptation in which 'addition, expansion, accretion, and interpolation' (Sanders 2016: 18) are made manifest. At the centre of that crisis are female bodies, but without the attendant reification and consumerism that characterizes some expressions of 'Bollywood' cinema. Functioning in these ways, *Arshinagar* places on display a rewriting of Shakespeare that resonates with the contemporary at the same time as it prompts a reappraisal of the practices of cinematic authorship.

Notes

1. For a comparable discussion, see Taarini Mookherjee's chapter in this volume.
2. An *ektara* is a one-stringed musical instrument to which a drum is attached.
3. The controversy erupted in March 2016 when a portal uploaded videos of TMC politicians accepting bribes. TMC is an Indian political party, mainly based in West Bengal.
4. For a comparable discussion, see Jennifer T. Birkett's chapter in this volume.

References

Arshinagar (2015), [Film] Dir. Aparna Sen, India: SVF Entertainment/ Surinder Films.

Bakshi, K. and R. K. Dasgupta (2017), 'From *Teen Kanya* to *Arshinagar*: Feminist Politics, Bengali High Culture and the Stardom of Aparna Sen', *South Asian History and Culture*, 8 (2): 186–204.

Banerjee, S. (2017), *Gender, Nation and Popular Film in India: Globalizing Muscular Nationalism*, London and New York: Routledge.

Bhattacharya, B. (1993), *The Path of the Mystic Lover: Baul Songs of Passion and Ecstasy*, Rochester: Destiny Books.

Bombay (1995), [Film] Dir. Mani Ratnam, India: Amitabh Bachchan Corporation Limited/Madras Talkies.

Burnett, M. T. (2013), *Shakespeare and World Cinema*, Cambridge: Cambridge University Press.

Burnett, M. T. (2017), '"Shining the Light on Women": Recreating the Comedies in Matías Piñeiro's Film Adaptations of Shakespeare', *Adaptation*, 10 (2): 192–209.

Chakravarti, P. (2019), 'Interview with Aparna Sen', in P. Trivedi and P. Chakravarti (eds), *Shakespeare and Indian Cinemas: 'Local Habitations'*, 304–16, London and New York: Routledge.

Chakravarti, P. (2021), 'Globalising the City: Kolkata Films and the Millennial Bard', in P. Trivedi, P. Chakravarti and T. Motohashi (eds), *Asian Interventions in Global Shakespeare: 'All the World's His Stage'*, 104–23, London and New York: Routledge.

Chakraborty, M. N. (2014), *Being Bengali: At Home and in the World*, London and New York: Routledge.

Harris, J. G. (2018), *Masala Shakespeare: How a Firangi Writer Became Indian*, New Delhi: Aleph Books.

Kidnie, M. J. (2009), *Shakespeare and the Problem of Adaptation*, London and New York: Routledge.

Lutz, H., M. T. Herrera Vivar and L. Supik (2011), 'Framing Intersectionality: An Introduction', in H. Lutz, M. T. Herrera Vivar and L. Supik (eds), *Framing Intersectionality: Debates on a Multi-Faceted Concept in Gender Studies*, 1–23, London and New York: Routledge.

Mayer, T. (2004), 'Embodied Nationalisms', in L. A. Staeheli, E. Kofman and L. J. Peake (eds), *Mapping Women, Mapping Politics: Feminist Perspectives on Political Geography*, 153–69, London and New York: Routledge.

Mookherjee, T. (2019), 'Theorizing the Neighbor: *Arshinagar* and *Romeo and Juliet*', *Borrowers and Lenders*, 12 (2): 1–21. Available online: https://openjournals.libs.uga.edu/borrowers/article/view/2374 (accessed 15 March 2021).

Mukherjee, S. (2016), *Women and Resistance in Contemporary Bengali Cinema*, London and New York: Routledge.

Nettl, B. and T. Rommen (2016), *Excursions in World Music*, 7th edn, London and New York: Routledge.

Nigam, A. (2011), *Desire Named Development*, New Delhi and New York: Penguin Books.

Panja, S. (2020), 'Critiquing Globalization: Transnational Technologies in *Arshinagar*, Aparna Sen's Bengali Adaptation of *Romeo and Juliet*', *Shakespeare Bulletin*, 38 (4): 573–92.

Parthasarathy, S. (2016), 'The Bard meets Bollywood: How India's films use Shakespeare to tackle controversy', *Index on Censorship*, 45 (1): 18–21.

Qayamat Se Qayamat Tak (1988), [Film] Dir. Mansoor Khan, India: Nasir Hussain Films.

Ranchod-Nilsson, S. and M. A. Tétreault, eds (2002), *Women, States, and Nationalism: At Home in the Nation?*, London and New York: Routledge.

Sanders, J. (2016), *Adaptation and Appropriation*, 2nd edn, London and New York: Routledge.

Sen, Z. (2017), 'Waheeda Rahman to share screen with Dev in *Arshinagar*', *Times of India*, 12 January. Available online: https://timesofindia.indiatimes.com/entertainment/bengali/movies/news/waheeda-rahman-to-share-screen-with-dev-in-arshinagar/articleshow/46296830.cms (accessed 2 January 2021).

Stam, R. (2000), 'Beyond Fidelity: The Dialogics of Adaptation', in J. Naremore (ed.), *Film Adaptation*, 54–76, London: Athlone.

36 Chowringhee Lane (1981), [Film] Dir. Aparna Sen, India: Film-Valas.

White, P. (2015), *Women's Cinema, World Cinema: Projecting Contemporary Feminisms*, Durham and London: Duke University Press.

10

Where the wild things are: Shifting identities in *Noblemen*, a film adaptation of *The Merchant of Venice*

Mark Thornton Burnett

The Indian film *Noblemen* (dir. Vandana Kataria, 2018) is framed by water. We begin in a school swimming pool or, rather, we begin underwater as the camera focuses on a group of furiously thrashing male bodies. Three teenage boys, it seems, are attempting to drown another teenage boy, and a sense of panic is encapsulated in a soundscape of muffled noise and bursting bubbles and a montage of choked leaves and desperate movement. Water connotes distress in a dark and shocking appropriation of the 'sadness' (1.1.5) of Antonio in *The Merchant of Venice*: 'Your mind is tossing on the ocean' (1.1.7), Salarino opines. The bright blues and dark greens of the swimming pool are picked up in the film's overall colour scheme. For example, in a later scene in a dormitory, the blue and green hues of the walls and bedspreads have watery associations. Just as suggestive is a sequence on a terrace in which our attention is directed to bright blue and green flowerpots decorating a pathway. Even in the classrooms, the greenish tinge of the blackboard hints at water-infused environs. As a water-surrounded city, Venice is also refracted in the film's interiors – in transformative moments in bathrooms and shower cubicles and in the drama studio in which a model of a Renaissance galleon is proudly displayed ('argosies with portly sail ... woven wings' [1.1.8, 13]). These colours, locations and properties keep the swimming pool opening at the forefront of an audience's mind at the same time as they conjure the idea of maritime Venice.

Such inventive utility is testimony to the playfully allusive ways in which this woman-helmed film engages Shakespeare.[1] Director Vandana Kataria co-wrote *Noblemen* with Sunil Drego and Sonia Bahl and in this, her first directing venture, drew on her background as a designer, novelist and second-unit director to craft a unique adaptation of *The Merchant of Venice*. *Noblemen*'s dialogue comprises two languages – English and Hindi – and dips in and out of the Shakespearean text (which is always in English) with varying degrees of application and intensity. The film foregrounds three 'set-piece' speeches ('Hath not a Jew eyes?' [3.1.53], 'The quality of mercy' [4.1.179] and 'So may the outward shows' [3.2.73]) at pivotal moments alongside a background of quotation from the Bassanio role. The latter is made credible because Shay (Ali Haji), the boy we encounter in the swimming pool, is rehearsing the part of the Venetian lord/adventurer for the school play. Distinctively, then, *Noblemen* rewrites *The Merchant of Venice* by putting Bassanio at its heart and making this character a newly important resource. In a manner reminiscent of *Dil Chahta Hai* (dir. Farhan Akhtar, 2001), and through a series of character parallels, plot twists and scenic recreations, *Noblemen* and *The Merchant of Venice* join company in a mutual exploration of male friendship, homoeroticism, competitions between men and revenge, to the extent that the energies and ambitions of the text are radically repurposed.[2] A series of spiralling events centred around the effects of bullying – and recalling in some ways the actions of William Golding's novel, *Lord of the Flies* (1954) – eventually works to demonstrate that toxic masculinity is not born but made. As the film's opening on-screen proverbial expression has it, 'A monster, when left unchecked, creates an even bigger monster'. The quotation is not credited, but it carries nevertheless the weight of a moral pronouncement and a narrative prediction. The fact that *Noblemen* has been made available via Netflix may not be unrelated. As Ramon Lobato and

Amanda D. Lotz write, the platform makes possible connections between 'traditional screen studies knowledge' and 'wider debates ... that play out in distinct ways across national and disciplinary boundaries' (2020: 133).[3] This chapter argues that *Noblemen* borrows from the Shakespeare-in-high-school film genre in order to find local and national meaning in what has, up to now, been almost entirely a US phenomenon. In so doing, the film places the Indian teenager at centre stage.

I

Noblemen is set in the fictional Noble Valley High, an elite Indian private boarding school in Mussoorie, Uttarakhand, in the foothills of the Himalayas, and the connection with *The Merchant of Venice* is sustained in the lensing of the architecture. The concentration on Gothic-inspired features such as arches, colonnades, dark recesses, courtyards, squares with trees and stone staircases keeps alive the concept of Venice, while an aerial shooting style that showcases panoramas of sepia-coloured rooftops equally affirms the school as a kind of cityscape in miniature. Propelling the storyline is the promised 'Founders' Day' production of *The Merchant of Venice*, the occasion an eloquent reminder of ideological currents running between Shakespeare, colonial and postcolonial praxes, and memorialization. The production of the play, it is suggested, is an instrument through which the school's subscription to history, and to a hide-bound *raison d'être*, is celebrated.[4] In keeping with location and plot, then, *Noblemen* discovers a world of intense hierarchy and traditionalism, as intimated in shots of notices on the walls extolling hard work, a headmaster cast in a militaristic vein ('Carry on', he instructs, like an archetypal sergeant major) and places that express the residues of empire (the swimming pool is adorned with the school motto, 'Truth Courage Strength'). Injunctions and mottos alike are realized in English, the *lingua franca* of private education in India and a route, as Barbara D. Metcalf and Thomas R. Metcalf write, to 'professional elites ... politics [and] ... government employment' (2006: 119, 135).

In its subscription to setting and elevation of the performance motif, *Noblemen* mimics the Shakespeare-in-high-school genre, as witnessed in films such as *Ten Things I Hate About You* (dir. Gil Junger, 1999), *'O'* (dir. Tim Blake Nelson, 2001) and *She's the Man* (dir. Andy Fickman, 2006), adaptations of *The Taming of the Shrew*, *Othello* and *Twelfth Night*, respectively. But it combines these influences with borrowings from a sub-genre – the film in which a high school drama society stages a Shakespeare play with resounding success. Examples here include *Dead Poets Society* (dir. Peter Weir, 1989) and *Get Over It* (dir. Tommy O'Haver, 2001) in which a psychically regenerative production of *A Midsummer Night's Dream* is the climactic endpoint.[5] Commenting on Shakespeare plays in films, Sarah Hatchuel notes that 'a scene or scenes from a Shakespeare play may be inserted to echo the film story as a whole ... as mere outlets for emotion ... [or] to sponsor anti-intellectualism' (2016: II, 1946). Combining both genres outlined above, *Noblemen* flits in and out of correspondences with *The Merchant of Venice*, invites and sometimes frustrates parallels with the key players and suggests, ultimately, a landscape of shifting identities. Furthermore, the film, bucking the trend of some of its generic counterparts, flips a comedic orientation, no doubt in part because the generic affiliation of *The Merchant of Venice* is itself so unstable. Crucially, and simultaneously, *Nobleman* looks to 'real-life' events of intimidation, bullying and violence in Indian private schools as part of a critical rationale. In 2014, for example, Scindia School in Gwalior, Madhya Pradesh, was 'caught up in [a] ... crisis after one of its students allegedly attempted suicide ... owing to bullying by his seniors ... [the school] expelled three senior students ... and ... debarred two of its employees' (Dutta 2014: n.p.). Echoing and responsive, *Noblemen* finds in its engagement with Shakespeare an opportunity to analogise interconnections between colonial legacies, sexuality and contemporary political conservatism.

At an immediate level, *The Merchant of Venice* figures in a range of character identifications that are reflected in names. Even if cast as Bassanio in the school play, Shay, the unruly-haired, wide-eyed and shy tenth-grader, bears a resemblance to Shylock, and, as the film develops, it foregrounds his underlying qualities of sensitivity, vulnerability and same-sex attraction for Murali (Kunal Kapoor), the drama teacher. Meanwhile, Antonio and Bassanio are shadowed in Arjun (Mohammed Ali Mir) and Baaadal (Shaan Groverr), high-achieving seniors who excel at sport and are envisioned as school heroes.[6] Implicated in *The Merchant of Venice* via their names' alliterative similarity, they are at the top of the schoolboy hierarchy (Arjun is captain of the football team and head of the army cadet corps) even as they are also represented as dysfunctional in their bullying behaviours. What *Noblemen* charts is the effect of bullying on Shay, as he moves from an appreciative and generous young man to an embittered and murderous force. Early on, when asked in a drama studio discussion to debate what *The Merchant of Venice* is 'about', he states that he does not favour 'revenge' as a strategy for dealing with conflict: there is 'no need', he reflects. Instead, he prefers empathy and compassion, qualities that are indicated, most obviously, in his adoption of the finch as a pet, emblazoned with the school's colours. And, in keeping with his pacific outlook, Shay is a member of 'Gandhi House'. But, as *Noblemen* makes clear, Shay turns to violence when identified via the school's inimical structures of discrimination as victim/target.

The equation between Shay and Shylock is developed over several scenes, including the opening which, in retrospect, suggests how easily assault masquerades as play. A barely sublimated aggression here accords with the never seen, but emotively reported, vilification accorded Shylock in the play; as he states, 'oft / In the Rialto you have rated me ... You call me misbeliever, cut-throat dog, / And spit upon my Jewish gaberdine' (1.3.104–5, 109–10). Consonant with the construction of Shay as abused, *Noblemen* discovers him in an ever-worsening series of injurious situations. He is exploited as a 'wimp', forced to collect drugs for Arjun and to engage in parodic recitations of the school motto. Such situations serve to ratify schoolboy 'values' of loyalty and the importance of keeping confidences. As Shylock insists that his 'bond' is respected, so does Shay dutifully observe the ties that bind him to his seniors. Hence, setting out on his drugs assignment, he counsels himself with Bassanio's words, saying: 'Yes, here I tender it for him in the court, / Yea, twice the sum. If that will not suffice, / I will be bound to pay it ten times o'er, / On forfeit of my hands, my head, my heart' (4.1.204–7). In this appropriation of the passage, Shay is constructed as giving voice to the kinds of devotion that ensure and perpetuate abusive relations. And, as in the play, bonds between men are premised on modes of economics and exchange, schoolboys rather than merchants functioning as financial representatives and proxies. The status of Shay as victim/target extends outwards to encompass his friends and allies. Paralleling the play, *Noblemen* introduces Ganesh (Hardik Thakkar), Shay's closest companion, as a type of Gratiano: his overweight body functions as the ideological counterpoint to the seniors' trim, athletic forms. At once, Ganesh is a familiar high-school type akin, for instance, to Rowley Jefferson in the cartoon fiction series, *Diary of a Wimpy Kid* (2007–20). At another level, his presence in the film localizes and legitimates acts of regional and caste marginalization. Subjected to repeated acts of brutalization, as when he is hit in the groin, poked and mockingly offered bananas, Ganesh is designated the 'fat dark boy'. In a film in which language works to signify status, Ganesh's preference for Hindi, as opposed to English, marks him out as 'other' and, like Shay, as the object of violent attention.

All the film's interactions are of a piece with the bullying culture that *Noblemen* examines and interrogates. At the start, the camera pans over the murals surrounding the swimming pool: they show images of the fanged, beaked and clawed monsters from Maurice Sendak's famous children's picture book, *Where the Wild Things Are* (1963). The suggestion, at the same time as chaos and mayhem are anticipated, is that these 'wild things' are always already in the school milieu, as instanced in acts of aggression that have become entirely routinized. If these are evident in the culture, they are also apprehended dialogically in threats of humiliation and punitive accusations of difference. Typical is the scene in which Arjun (his name also suggests the erstwhile hero-warrior of the *Mahabharata*), announcing his selection for the state's youth football team, parades down the table on a red tablecloth and exclaims: 'get ready to get your arses whipped in the final!'. The language here conjures a spectacle of humiliation while simultaneously endorsing a culture of conformity verbalized in hyper-masculinist terms. At the same time, the camera's pan over the cups and trophies in the background of the dining hall makes clear that victory and reward are indivisible from praxes of persecution. Bullying, in being ignored by the teachers, is implicitly accepted as an unalterable fact of school life.

The action of *Noblemen* accelerates when Shay secures the part of Bassanio, to the chagrin of Baaadal, who also covets the role. Ably aided by Arjun, Baaadal attempts to force Shay to abandon the part and the production. 'The play belongs to Baaadal', Arjun insists, his statement of Shakespearean ownership crystallizing a personal history of privilege. Entitlement, indeed, is everywhere apparent. At the end of the film, for example, at his public arrest, Baaadal protests, reasoning that 'the Commissioner of Mumbai Police is my Papa's best friend'; earlier, in a similar attempt to inveigle authority and promote himself, he assures the drama teacher, 'my Dad can help ... being a movie star ... whatever you want'. In such exclamations, the film takes to task the idealised Shakespearean notion of a 'nobleman', revealing instead an outlying context of corruption and malfeasance. (And it is one of the film's symptomatic ironies that, eventually, Baaadal succeeds in securing publicity, although not on stage.) But Shay will not relinquish the role: persuasion does not work, with the tenth-grader clinging to his Shakespearean identity with a Shylock-like intransigence. As a result, brutality amplifies: Shay has a fork pushed down his throat, he is casually kicked and stamped on, he is made to march without a break, carrying a heavy rucksack. This latter scene, glossed as 'training ... to be a man', makes manifest the interlocking codes of militarism and masculinity on which the institutional ethos depends. Equally powerfully, it stands as the most obvious instance of the invisibility of abuse.

At first, as Bassanio, Shay finds sensitivities within his part. The lines, often in voiceover, are consistently reimagined. When burying the finch that the seniors have killed, for example, Shay asks himself, 'Do all men kill the things they do not love?' (4.1.65), his question indicating an appalled recognition of the callousness in his midst. By the same token, in the dormitory, he anticipates the return to school of his friend, Ganesh, who has left following a suicide attempt: 'I am married to a wife / Which is as dear to me as life itself' (4.1.277–8), he reflects. In the play, of course, these lines indicate a tug of conflicted allegiances; in *Noblemen*, by contrast, Bassanio's words are reapplied to indicate Shay's unshakeable commitment to his treasured friend. However, as the film progresses, Shay takes on greater affinities with Shylock, not least when he is locked out of the dormitories. Names suggest themselves here in punning capacities (Shay-lock/Shy-lock), as Shay is obliged to seek refuge at the drama teacher's lodgings and to accept his offer of a rug (a type of gabardine) to protect him from the cold. The identification is further reinforced in a shot of a splendid Victorian edition of *The Merchant of Venice* open at an illustration of Shylock leaving the courthouse. Not only does the scene operate to fetishize the status of the Shakespearean book; it simultaneously affirms, as Shay's dawning awareness indicates, that the connection with Shylock centres on narratives of exclusion. The moment of recognition also serves to clarify the ways in which Bassanio's words come to provide Shay with less and less solace, and as much is established in the scene in which he is raped by Arjun with a prosthesis. Flashing fluorescent lights, and glimpses of pornography on the walls of the senior study, make for a horrifying episode, with the gagged Shay being held down on a table by Arjun's cronies as he screams in pain. There can be no coming back from the experience, no further recuperative use of Shakespeare, and Shay now relinquishes the production: 'I don't think I should be doing it', he discloses in an admission of performative defeat.

II

For *Noblemen*, *The Merchant of Venice* proves a resonant text with regard to statements of longing ('My purse, my person ... Lie all unlocked to your occasions' [1.1.138–9]) and constructions of compromised masculinity ('I am a tainted wether of the flock' [4.1.113]). Even as it romanticises bounty-hunter Bassanio and his heterosexual project to win Portia, the play remains a narrative in which the action is enabled by the dynamics of same-sex desire. Writing of Antonio and Bassanio, Alan Sinfield highlights notes of 'intimacy ... intensity ... excess [and] ... amatory sacrifice' (2006: 54, 55), and a similar conjunction of characteristics can be seen in *Noblemen* in the scene in which Arjun and Baaadal lie closely together on a bed to smoke a joint and discuss 'girls'. Their exchange reverberates with the charged language of 1.1 and, given that *Noblemen* is an adaptation, also recalls other adaptations of *The Merchant of Venice*, including Michael Radford's 2004 film version in which Bassanio (Joseph Fiennes) and Antonio (Jeremy Irons) retire to a bedroom to conduct their Portia-driven dialogue.

Homoerotic attraction is at its most pronounced in Shay's feelings for Murali, the drama teacher. At the second rehearsal with the cast, Murali steps up on stage to deliver the Prince of Morocco's opening speech, taking off his shirt to illustrate his argument about a general social levelling: 'Mislike me not for my complexion, / The shadowed livery of the burnished sun, / To whom I am a neighbour and near bred' (2.1.1–3). Critical tradition focuses on the racial politics of this self-identification, but, in a further radical application of the play, *Noblemen* seizes on the speech to represent a sexual awakening. Kunal Kapoor, who plays Murali, is an established 'Bollywood' star, and the film exploits his intertextual glamour in an episode in which the lighting privileges his smiling expression and the camera angle (from below) accentuates his imposing presence. With arms outstretched, and jumping up and down on stage, the bearded and wavy-haired Murali is shot in such a way as to make him physically alluring. It is at this moment that Shay is overtaken by desire, having to leave the studio when he finds himself aroused. At the same time, however, the coming-into-awareness is hedged about with complication, with Shay's retreat into a dark corridor suggesting the irreconcilability of homoerotic projection and school morality.

Any suggestions of sexual acknowledgement are additionally complicated by contexts of homophobia, expressions of antipathy that find legitimation in the charges of effeminacy which fill schoolboy discourse. Hence, Shay is branded a 'mummy's boy'; he is a 'fucking faggot' and 'cock-sucking rat'. Cocaine-snorting is all too often the prompt for expressions of toxic masculinity and male rage. But, just as explosively, it is an encounter with Shakespeare in the drama studio that occasions the furious release of pent-up emotions. As his friends are increasingly mistreated, Shay's resentments gather, to the extent that, in a therapeutic exercise to get into character, he is encouraged to growl and roar at his classmates: 'That's it ... feel the anger ... come out of it', Murali instructs. The focus on mirrors in this episode, as well as red-filtered lighting, emphasize that, for Shay, this is a pivotal development. Not so much the withdrawn tenth-grader here as an infuriated beast, Shay is taken out of his former self, and confronted with an alter ego, changed by a process that forces him to look within.

III

While charting a trajectory to atrocity, *Noblemen* insists on making other – positive – paradigms available. Most importantly, Shay is joined in the cast by Pia (Muskkaan Jaferi), the daughter of a junior schoolteacher, who takes on the Portia role. For Pia, the play has a dreadful relevance. Showing Shay the scars of abuse she suffered at her father's hands, she reveals that 'My father, he was much worse to my mother', conjuring a history, as in *The Merchant of Venice*, of a young woman labouring under the dictates of a persecutory patriarchy. Crucially, Pia offers Shay friendship and alternative notions of selfhood. Painted in warm browns, the house she lives in with her mother is set high above the hills and surrounded by greenery. In an archetypal construction of *The Merchant of Venice*, the home evokes Belmont and, in Jyotsna G. Singh's words, 'mythic associations ... a pastoral retreat [and] a green world' (2000: 148). More specifically, Pia makes available to Shay a discourse around the concept of mercy. When, for example, the tenth-grader briefly earns the respect of his classmates in the wake of Arjun's public apology (a specious gesture, or Shakespearean trick, as it turns out), he is greeted by Pia, who, in the early morning light between the trees, quotes Portia's lines almost in full: 'The quality of mercy is not strained: / It droppeth as the gentle rain from heaven / Upon the place beneath ... It is enthroned in the hearts of kings, / It is an attribute to God himself' (4.1.179–81, 189–90). Clarifying the local relevance of the well-known speech, she adds, 'I'm talking about the Arjun apology'. If only momentarily, a merciful dispensation is countenanced in an otherwise hostile environment, Pia's appropriation of Portia's words suggesting the restitution of naturalized relations, shared ideals and healing effects. Previously an onlooker only, Pia comes into her own at this point, announcing, like her Shakespearean counterpart, her redefinition, to cite Carol Leventen's discussion of the play, as 'something rich and powerful' (1991: 71). In his response, Shay captures the jubilant mood, declaring in public in a procession to school Bassanio's lines: 'I ... Have ... been this day acquitted / Of grievous penalties ... We freely cope your courteous pains withal' (4.1.403–5, 407). Happy in the (as it turns out false) knowledge that the tyrannies of Arjun and Baaadal have ended, and anticipating the cessation of abuse and accusation, Shay alights on Bassanio's equivalent sense of release. In this affirmation of mercy, and in the approbation Shay's delivery of Bassanio's lines receives, an alternative mode of being in the world presents itself.

As well as Pia, another alternative is embodied in the drama teacher. With his casual polo neck and knitted jacket, and in his predilection for dispensing with 'inhibitions', Murali is also envisaged as at odds with the system. His drama studio is adorned with a carnival mask (instancing Shakespeare's Venice-set play), superhero toys (suggesting immersion in popular culture), flying Hindu deities and a globe (signifying Shakespeare's theatre).[7] These function as talismanic objects, ciphers for Murali's dedication to Shakespeare but also for his alterity and internationalism. In conduct, Murali is set apart, practising *tai chi* as an index of his absorption in other cultural registers; not for him the school's institutionalized militarism. Not surprisingly, then, Murali's dramaturgy is of a radical kind. To cite Richard Burt on the high school film genre in which a drama society stages a Shakespeare play, Shakespeare is a 'metaphor for rebellious, passionate, non-conformity ... supported by teachers ... opposed to ... corruption [and] ... discipline' (1997: 250). Matching filmic antecedents, Murali is represented as aspiring to a performative dimension in which his students are 'in the moment' and in which there is 'no caste, no sex, no religion'. The principles underlying his vision are spelled out in his excited rendition, in a further drama studio rehearsal scene, of Shylock's 'Hath not a Jew eyes?' address. The delivery of the speech hints at a biographical trajectory (as a postcard on display in his lodgings suggests, Murali is a Sri Lankan Tamil, part of a community that, historically, has conflicted with the Sinhalese majority, leading to mass migration). Certainly, in the film, Murali is viewed critically: 'I've never trusted that smooth-talking Tamilian. No background in education, no recommendations ... always suspicious', the deputy headmaster (Ivan Rodrigues) states. A north-south dialectic inserts itself here as does the spectre of caste discrimination. At another level, Murali as Shylock symbolizes resistance; several scenes earlier, Ganesh is taken to hospital after his suicide attempt, suggesting that the Shakespearean word operates retrospectively as a mode of protest. Finally, Murali's charismatic performance impresses itself on a rapt Shay, as his reaction shots indicate. Recognizing the speech's import, Shay internalizes the applicability of its sentiments, the idea being that, in his awakening sexuality, he responds powerfully to the rejection of ostracization and a plea for egalitarianism. Whichever way Murali/Shylock is read, a speaking out against injustice is abundantly apparent.

Yet, as the action of *Noblemen* reveals, the paradigms enshrined in Pia and Murali fail. Their alternative perspectives are singularly unsuccessful. For Pia, she is unable to make a meaningful connection with Shay, with whom she has fallen in love. His rejecting her in the hospital – 'You're not one of us ... You're not a boy and you will never understand' – catapults Pia into a transformation in which, sobbing and distraught, she cuts her hair in the mirror. The sequence suggests both a traumatized effort to become a boy and an attempt to be one with an all-male establishment. In *The Merchant of Venice*, of course, the cross-dressed Portia/Balthazar is an empowered figure who turns the tables on the Venetian legal establishment; in contradistinction, in *Noblemen*, Pia's impersonation of a boy marks her nadir. Her descent into isolation and disempowerment is signalled in her art. As she shears her locks, for example, the camera pans over her felt-tip, and starkly red and black, cartoons scattered on the floor showing images of Shay, 'Home' and bullying seniors. These outlets for expression – cries in a crisis – are returned to as illustrative backdrops over the final credits. Here, additional cartoons appear with injunctions and quotations from the play, such as 'Open Your Eyes', 'Say Something' and 'One half of me is yours, the other half yours' (3.2.16). Yet these post-narrative materializations of Pia – her efforts at communication – announce no substantive change. Rather, they ratify the patterns of closing-down we have seen already, as attested to in the lyrics of the accompanying song ('What's the point in it all? ... We're tearing each other apart') and in the ways in which red and black stains spread outwards to swamp the screen.[8]

After his highpoint (the performance of 'Hath not a Jew eyes?'), Murali, similarly, is cast out: the out-of-the-blue climax to the film demonstrates how he is killed at Shay's hands. Having confessed to Murali that he has been raped, Shay runs after the drama teacher, who has left his lodgings to confront Arjun, the rapist. But, in a turnaround that demythologises any notion of his unassailability, Murali himself is beaten up and thrown into the swimming pool near-unconscious. In a series of rapid crosscuts, interspersed with red visuals and shaky photography suggestive of psychic shock, the closing sequence mixes and matches an extended history – Shay's drowning, rather than rescue, of his teacher, his framing of the seniors (he impersonates an accusatory Murali in a phone call to the headmaster), and the subsequent arrest of Arjun and Baaadal for murder. The escalation of the action into an unexpected outcome is jarring and disorienting even if it is still underpinned by Shakespearean imperatives. For, even if Shay is revenged on the seniors, this is at the cost of the teacher who has attempted his enablement. More forcefully than any bond with a teacher, the ending discovers the catastrophic working out of Shay's need for self-preservation, his desire to belong as a 'nobleman'. As he exclaims, bowing to institutionalism, 'I have no choice, there's nothing I can do'. In this sense, Shay is represented as an even more heinous 'monster' (the term is picked up from the opening quotation in Pia's reflection, 'These monsters need to be arrested') than his persecutors. And, as we are pushed via the *mise-en-scène* into an uncomfortable confrontation with the face of Shay in the water, we are taken back to the underwater scene of the start. The choking greens and blues of the opening recur, but perspectives are now flipped (it is Shay rather than Murali who looks down into the swimming pool's murky depths). The question of who the wild things are is opened up anew. Once again in his maritime medium, Shay now looks to camera not with terror but with an even more terrifying blankness and inscrutability.

Conclusion

If, in the drama studio, Shakespeare is the prompt for utopian imaginings and alternative futures, underlying attitudes make clear the remoteness of this possibility. Shakespeare, as *Noblemen* constructs him, cannot and does not bring about a better world. Writing on the representation of Shakespeare productions on film, Russell Jackson notes that individual performances occasion 'personal transformation' and enable 'cathartic and therapeutic' experiences (2013: 3, 127). This is vehemently not the script of Kataria's adaptation in which Murali's schema of a hierarchy-free society, a place rising above difference, can only ever be a fantasy. Any redemptive aspirations notwithstanding, the structures of Noble Valley High remain remarkably resistant to reformation. Rather, institutional power re-establishes itself in a manifestation of elitism more repressive than before. In the film's closing minutes, the new headmaster, the promoted deputy, addresses the school in the quadrangle, announcing: 'things need to be broken and tamed ... boys need to be disciplined to become men ... the Founders' Day celebrations are cancelled'. The conjunction of need and authority expressed here reinstates the worse praxes of masculinity and punishment with the effect that Shakespeare is pushed out. Running against the grain of the genres it references, *Noblemen* concludes with a Shakespeare production not so much deferred as abandoned.

In part, the system can renew itself because of the cycles of abuse which the film dramatizes (and to which the plot stands as testimony). Although the ending is jumbled up, it is clear that one act of intimidation precipitates another and that violent histories are part of a continuum. Pursuing the opening fictive quotation about the creation of the monster, *Noblemen* discovers how bullies originate in being bullied themselves. For example, Arjun, too, when his grades slip, must deal with an incandescent father and is threatened with losing his school place. (He learns at the patriarch's hands.) Similarly, the deputy headmaster, looking out at the scene of Shay's being forced to march, reflects: 'This will make a fine man of him ... We've all been through it ... Look what it did for me'. Such disciplines of 'making men' also, of course, make the victims and scapegoats necessary for the system to continue – in this sense, the Shylock story is everyone's story.

The idea is played out in a series of metatheatrical inserts (a kind of epilogue) that are spliced into the closing moments: these show an imagined production in which Shay performs Bassanio's speech about the deceptiveness of appearances. Initially shot partially clothed and from the back, an angle that recalls the film's absorption in homoeroticism, Shay prepares for his individual part, the mirrors that surround him bringing to a head the question of shifting identities. Distinctively, as Shay dresses and then ascends the stage, he takes on a stereotypically queer persona, with a white face, extravagant ruff, red lips, dark stockings, and capacious cloak: the tenth-grader comes into his sexuality but only in solitary mode. In its filmic context, the speech makes sense as an articulation if not rationalization of a need to conceal the queer subject, stressing, as it does, 'outward shows', a 'world' that is 'deceived with ornament', a legal system that 'Obscures ... evil', religious institutions that hide 'grossness', 'cowards' that assume 'valour's excrement' and 'beauty' that can be 'purchased' (3.2.73, 74, 77, 80, 83, 87, 88, 89). Despite recent examples to the contrary, many Indian cinemas, as Thomas Waugh writes, have demonstrated 'an avoidance pattern with regard to explicit same-sex discourses and identities', camouflaging 'homoeroticism in particular' (2002: 193). And this in a political context in which consensual homosexuality in India was only decriminalized in 2018, the year in which *Noblemen* was released (Safi 2018: 27). In this connection (and reflecting the ways in which the film expresses the isolated Shay/Bassanio), the representation of Antonio towards the end of Michael Radford's 2004 film adaptation of *The Merchant of Venice* suggests itself: the merchant walks listlessly through the Belmont palazzo alone with no part in the connubial celebrations. At the same time, *Noblemen* is distinctive in that, in contrast to Radford's envisioning of same-sex desire, it installs Bassanio as queer and, as the film concludes, at centre-stage. As Bassanio, Shay takes over from Murali, and Pia, having rejected all other models; indeed, his being privileged works to displace 'Hath not a Jew eyes?' as the emotional core of *The Merchant of Venice*, substituting for it instead and as climax the casket scene. Operating thus, *Noblemen* incorporates Bassanio not as a character of sensitivity but a subject of duplicity: to cite Pia's reflections at the start of the film when she hears the news that Shay has been cast, 'he doubly sees himself' (5.1.244). In the discussion of what *The Merchant of Venice* is 'about', Shay gets to the heart of the play, but the message he takes away with him concerns itself with the concealments, compromises and atrocities required of him to secure his status as a 'nobleman'. Kataria, in this radical and internationally pitched adaptation, reflects on the postcolonial Shakespeare in India by rewriting genres, gesturing to the here-and-now and intervening in ideologies that are themselves in dispute. In so doing, her film canvasses and critiques the ways in which individuals and communities come together and divide, leaving us with the wild things not on their fantastic island but integrated into the fabric and cultures of the contemporary Indian world.

Notes

1 Other inventive uses are found in visual detail: the finch Shay adopts suggests Jessica, also likened to a 'bird' (3.1.26), while the ring Shay's mother (Soni Razdan) displays to him during a video-call references Shylock's 'turquoise' (3.1.111).
2 Noting the film's coded references to *Much Ado About Nothing* and *Troilus and Cressida*, Madhavi Menon argues for its 'preoccupation with ... deviant desire ... that cannot be named' (Menon 2008: 80, 83, 85).

3   It is important to note, as Ramon Lobato notes, that 'Netflix is unaffordable for all but the most affluent Indians ... a price Netflix is willing to pay to remain a premium product' (2019: 126).
4   In the educational calendar in India, 'Founders' Day' is the occasion on which the founders of a school or college are remembered.
5   There is no equivalent tradition of such films in Indian cinemas, although *Ratha Thilagam* (dir. Dada Mirasi, 1963), *Sorgam* (dir. T. R. Ramanna, 1970) and *Isi Life Mein* (dir. Vidhi Kasliwal, 2010) include insets of college, rather than school, productions of, in order, *Othello*, *Julius Caesar* and *The Taming of the Shrew*. For a scintillating discussion of the last film, see García-Periago 2016: 109–27.
6   Baaadal owes the extra 'a' in his name to his father's wish to honour an astrologer's prediction.
7   The flying/superhero theme is reinforced in Shay's likening of himself and Ganesh to Batman and Robin and in the backstory of Shay's disabled mother, formerly a Wing Commander in the Indian Air Force.
8   The song is a rearranged version, with new lyrics, of 'Yeh Duniya Agar Mil Bhi Jaye' from the film, *Pyaasa* (dir. Guru Dutt, 1957).

References

Burt, R. (1997), 'The Love That Dare Not Speak Shakespeare's Name: New Shakesqueer Cinema', in R. Burt and L. E. Boose (eds), *Shakespeare the Movie: Popularizing the Plays on Film, TV, and Video*, 240–68, London and New York: Routledge.

Dead Poets Society (1989), [Film] Dir. Peter Weir, USA: Touchstone/Silver Screen.

Dil Chahta Hai (2001), [Film] Dir. Farhan Akhtar, India: Excel Entertainment.

Duttta, A. (2014), 'Within the Walls: How the Practice of Ragging Throws Light on the Covert Ways of Boarding Schools', *MailOnlineIndia*, 30 August. Available online: https://www.dailymail.co.uk/indiahome/indianews/article-2738684/Within-walls-How-disturbing-practice-ragging-throws-light-covert-ways-boarding-schools.html (accessed 1 April 2021).

García-Periago, R. (2016), 'More Than an Indian Teen Shrew: Postcolonialism and Feminism in *Isi Life Mein*', *SEDERI*, 26: 109–27.

Get Over It (2001), [Film] Dir. Tommy O'Haver, USA: Ignite/Morpheus.

Hatchuel, S. (2016), 'Plays-within-the-film', in B. R. Smith (ed.), *The Cambridge Guide to the Worlds of Shakespeare*, II, 1946–53, 2 vols, Cambridge: Cambridge University Press.

Isi Life Mein (2010), [Film] Dir. Vidhi Kasliwal, India: Rajshri Productions.
Jackson, R. (2013), *Theatres on Film: How the Cinema Imagines the Stage*, Manchester and New York: Manchester University Press.
Leventen, C. (1991), 'Patrimony and Patriarchy in *The Merchant of Venice*', in V. Wayne (ed.), *The Matter of Difference: Materialist Feminist Criticism of Shakespeare*, 59–79, Ithaca, New York: Cornell University Press.
Lobato, R. (2019), *Netflix: The Geography of Digital Distribution*, New York: New York University Press.
Lobato, R. and A. D. Lotz (2020), 'Imagining Global Video: The Challenge of Netflix', *Journal of Cinema and Media Studies*, 59 (3): 132–6.
Menon, M. (2008), *Unhistorical Shakespeare: Queer Theory in Shakespearean Literature and Film*, New York: Palgrave Macmillan.
Metcalf, B. D. and T. R. Metcalf (2006), *A Concise History of Modern India*, 2nd edn, Cambridge: Cambridge University Press.
Noblemen (2018), [Film] Dir. Vandana Kataria, India: Yoodle/Saregama.
'O' (2001), [Film] Dir. Tim Blake Nelson, USA: Daniel Fried, Chickie the Cop and Dimension Films.
Pyaasa (1957), [Film] Dir. Guru Dutt, India: Guru Dutt Films.
Ratha Thilagam (1963), [Film] Dir. Dada Mirasi, India: National Movies.
Safi, M. (2018), '"A Great First Step": Elation in India after Gay Sex is Legalised', *The Guardian*, 7 September: 27.
She's the Man (2006), [Film] Dir. Andy Fickman, USA: DreamWorks/Lakeshore.
Sinfield, A. (2006), *Shakespeare, Authority, Sexuality: Unfinished Business in Cultural Materialism*, London and New York: Routledge.
Singh, J. G. (2000), 'Gendered "Gifts" in Shakespeare's Belmont: The Economies of Exchange in Early Modern England', in D. Callaghan (ed.), *A Feminist Companion to Shakespeare*, 144–59, Oxford and Malden: Blackwell.
Sorgam (1970), [Film] Dir. T. R. Ramanna, India: Sri Vinayaga Pictures.
Ten Things I Hate About You (1999), [Film] Dir. Gil Junger, USA: Touchstone/Mad Chance.
Waugh, T. (2002), '"I Sleep Behind You": Male Homosexuality and Homoeroticism in Indian Parallel Cinema', in R. Vanita (ed.), *Queering India: Same-Sex Love and Eroticism in Indian Culture and Society*, 193–206, London and New York: Routledge.
William Shakespeare's 'The Merchant of Venice' (2004), [Film] Dir. Michael Radford, UK: UK Film Council/Arclight Films.

11

Women punctuating Shakespeare: Campus theatrical experiment, the Shakespeare Society and the insider/outsider dialectic

N. P. Ashley

The role of imperial theatre and education in introducing Shakespeare to India is well-established: much has been written about Shakespeare plays in the Raj playhouses of Calcutta in 1775 and the incorporation of Shakespeare into the curriculum of Hindu College, Calcutta, starting in 1822 (Bosman 2010: 285–301; Harris 2018: 14).[1] But the entity that brings theatre and education together, campus theatre, has received insufficient critical attention. Examining campus theatre illuminates both the ways in which Shakespeare has been adapted in India and the place of Shakespeare in performance in Indian educational programmes.[2]

A quick look at any survey of Shakespeare in India brings up student performances of Shakespeare's plays. Typical is the account in an article on Shakespeare and Bengali theatre:

> In 1837 Bengali students staged the Court Scene from *The Merchant of Venice* in the Governor's House, in 1852 and 1853

the students of the Metropolitan Academy and David Hare Academy staged Shakespeare's plays, while the ... students of the Oriental Academy staged in the Oriental Theatre Shakespeare's *Othello* in 1853, *The Merchant of Venice* in 1854 and *Henry IV* in 1855.

(Bhattacharya 1964: 29)

Providing another example, Rosa García-Periago, discussing the 'rebirth' of Shakespeare in India around 1964, traces the journey of the noted playwright, Utpal Dutt, through campus theatre:

Utpal Dutt began his theatrical career with amateur productions of Shakespeare's plays at St Xavier's College, such as *Hamlet* (1943). Drama at St Xavier's College in Calcutta was extremely influential, and contributed significantly to the performance of Shakespeare in India.

(2012: 60)

Bringing things up to date, Jonathan Gil Harris, in his 2018 study, *Masala Shakespeare*, writes about student productions in Ashoka University, where he teaches, and the productions by Delhi Zakir Husain College staged as part of the Shakespeare Society of India competition (253–4). These stray examples demonstrate the entrenched place of campus theatre across the historical spectrum in India, from some of the earliest expressions to the latest manifestations.

The subject of this chapter, the Shakespeare Society (or English dramatic society) of St Stephen's College, Delhi, has also been mentioned in the critical record. For example, in an online broadcast organized by the Folger Shakespeare Library, Modhumita Roy ties campus Shakespeare to traditions of Anglophilia, reflecting: 'So this very prestigious college, St Stephen's College in Delhi, started a Shakespeare Society in 1924 and there, the idea is that you ... "faithfully" produce Shakespeare on stage' (Singh and Roy 2016: n.p.). Her remarks serve to remind us of the College's origins. St Stephen's College was established in 1881 by the imperial British government, with the objective of producing colonial administrators. For its part, the stated mission of the Shakespeare Society was to instil in students an interest in Shakespeare in such a way that performance could function as a key element of the College's mission – and a means of cultivating English – in India.

Campus theatre, like campus youth, is a phase: formative energies dissolve into the artistic/political entities the students go on to become. Campus theatre, then, is largely seen as a visiting place, a training-ground or stepping-stone and no more. But Andrew James Hartley, in the introduction to his *Shakespeare on the University Stage* (2015), makes a more subtle distinction between campus theatre and professional/amateur models of theatre:

> College/University productions of Shakespeare (by which I mean those staged at institutions of higher learning attended voluntarily after any compulsory education) emerge out of quite different materials and cultural conditions elsewhere, being more directly tied to the vagaries of academic life in intellectual, aesthetic and fiscal terms. Most importantly, their identities hinge on the unique properties of the college or university which constructs their audience.
>
> (2015: 1)

These so-called 'unique properties' will probably remain unique until such a time when we have a more theorized grasp of the theatrical work of colleges and universities. Without paradigms, any understanding of campus theatre will remain sketchy, if not inadequate. In a country like India, where theatre traditions can tend to be insular, the site of campus theatre, with guaranteed rehearsal room and a ready-made audience, offers all kinds of rewarding opportunities. Yet, because largely run by a floating population of students, this type of theatre does not always receive adequate critical investment.[3] As Peter Holland argues, 'Lack of archival research' (2015: 10) also makes concepts and histories fragmented, leaving campus theatre simply a place in which learning is experienced and about which memories gather.

This mirage-ish zone might well have been avoided had I not myself been exploring intersections between campus theatre and Shakespeare for almost a decade now. As a member of the English faculty at St Stephen's College, and as the Staff Advisor to the Shakespeare Society (a role I have occupied for some years), I have had to find ways of historicizing and theorizing my experience, both as insider and outsider in relation to student-led, extra curricular projects. This becomes particularly challenging because my attempt, as a man, in this chapter is to explore questions of women's presence and to reflect on what my role has meant and what it entails. And this is at an institution in which traditions have been remarkably male. The College only became co-educational in 1975, with some women students pejoratively recounting early experiences (Dewan 2012: n.p.). Given this background, as I argue in this chapter, to promote a kind of experimental Shakespeare, and even a college theatrical Shakespeare, necessitates a number of negotiations. The chapter first explores how the Shakespeare Society has played a crucial role in terms of the presence of women in the College over time. It then discusses three of the Society's recent Shakespeare adaptations – 'The Blue Pencil' (an ensemble piece, 2011), the full-length adaptation, *The Tempest* (2013), and 'The Speeches of *The Tempest*' (a short play, 2015) – to ascertain how these specific productions assist in developing an understanding of campus theatricals, the spaces women occupy in college and the contributions they make to Indian sites of Shakespeare.

Indian Shakespeares as they play themselves out in campus theatre are not curious accidents but exigencies. If classrooms were spaces of memorization and magisterial professorial performances which could impress an unfamiliar world on students, campus theatre societies, by contrast, ushered in lighter moments of conversation and debate. Relevant here is a document (27 May 1899) in the St Stephen's College archives about the formation of a society entitled, 'The Falstaff', a name suggestive of the Shakespearean character that faculty members wanted to have foregrounded for the Society and its activities. It reads:

'THE FALSTAFF'
1. That this Society be called 'The Falstaff'.
2. That it will consist of any professors who may wish to join and twelve student members to be duly elected by vote, preference in such election being given to senior students.
3. That a Secretary be elected annually whose business it shall be to keep a record of plays read, parts assigned, absentees and to collect subscriptions.
4. That any member absenting himself three times in succession without sufficient reason will cease to belong to the Society.

5. That there be an entrance fee of eight annas, and a quarterly subscription of six annas, which shall be expended after any necessary expenses have been met, upon a copy of Shakespeare to be presented annually to that student who in the opinion of the professors is the best reader, not having already received such a copy.

27 May 1899.[4]

This document mentions only play reading, not theatrical performances, with the Society run according to monies contributed by faculty and students alike, placing it outside college funding mechanisms (and this continued for decades). Interestingly, although the St Stephen's College magazine has a section titled 'College Chronicle' in the 1920s, which documents college activities, none of these magazines mentions the activities of 'The Falstaff'. This could mean that, despite the serious-sounding by-law, the Society was seen as informal and self-sufficient.

A rather different set of associations is suggested in an article in the December 1922 issue of the college magazine. Kali Charan Mathur's 'The Stage in India: Some Suggestions' makes some extraordinary claims about women actresses:

> It would be in the best interest of the stage and the people to give the part of women to youths 'with unbroken voices' for a long time to come, and to dispense off with the actresses altogether. Their presence is unbearable even in ordinary plays but it becomes utterly intolerable when religious plays are being staged. How improper, ridiculous and insulting it is for these actresses to play the parts of pure and pious women like Sita, Diropadi, Mira Bai and others! ... It is high time to get rid of the whores of society and to purge the stage of them altogether.
>
> (1922: 13)

The 'youths', according to Mathur, will be able to bring out 'the sheer poetic value of the author's conception' (1922: 13), a dimension which, in his view, is weakened by the realism and robust emotion of the 'actresses'. Mathur goes on, however, to instruct readers that 'the boy-actors would need to be highly trained ... especially when they would be required to represent a girl who has assumed the disguise of male attire' (1922: 13). Indian theatres have always featured actresses and female dancers on stage, and this kind of making invisible of female bodies looks as if it is borrowed from the conventions of the Elizabethan playhouse, though the author is not specific about his debt. Such positions could be seen as Victorian morality imbibed from colonial education, a hangover from an earlier period. However, any argument about the cross-dressing of Shakespearean characters misses the point that the actors of the sixteenth and seventeenth centuries invariably *had* to cross-dress!

In 1924, the Rev. H. Wilson Padley, formerly of St John's College, Cambridge, joined St Stephen's as a faculty member, and he was to have a considerable impact. That same year he organized and had staged 'The Trial Scene' from *The Merchant of Venice* in response to a call by the then Acting Principal to deliver an entertainment comprising a scene from Shakespeare and an Urdu play (performed by the 'Dramatic Society'). Intriguingly, the subsequent 1925 report, written by Padley, and reflecting on the foundation of the Shakespeare Society, mentions that Nerissa was played by Sham Narain, a young male student, as 'coy and roguish' (1925: 27). The following year, according to the chronicle section of the college magazine, Padley celebrated the newly inaugurated Shakespeare dinner:

> The first annual Shakespeare Dinner was held at the College Hall on February 13th, at 7.30 PM. Almost all our members were present ... We were privileged to entertain some of the workers for *The Winter's Tale* – our musicians, scene-shifters, stewards and makers up. After dinner, two scenes were performed. The Lady Macbeth sleep-walking scene by Radhika Narain, S. C. Sircar and Uma Shankar and the Wooing of Katherine from *Henry V*, by Mr and Mrs C. B. Young who were 'tyrannically clapped for't' so that they had to repeat the last part.
>
> (Padley 1926: 34–5)

A faculty member's wife, Mrs Young did act in a staged scene. In an all-male environment, and via a scene from a Shakespeare play performed for dinner guests, this marks for the first time the cultural and acting presence of a woman in the College. We might also bear in mind here the helpers and assistants at the dinner. Most of these individuals would not have known English, nor would they have been Anglophiles, suggesting both variations in, and the complexions of, the audience but also a shared space in which faculty, students and non-teaching staff came together. In addition, as performance is not about textual meaning but energies and impulses, the faculty member and his wife had to repeat the performance.

In these early performances, the female characters were played by men. A 1932 review, signed by M., and referencing by name male students in crossed-dressed parts, confirms the practice:

> The playing of the women's parts is a more difficult business – and what women! Amar K. Sen made the old Duchess of York almost seem likeable, and Kapadia looked well as the Lady Anne, but he clearly found her an unconvincing person.
> (1932: 46)

The review makes sense in context and inside a system in which women were unavailable for performance. But this was to change for a period in the 1940s. In 1928, since there were no Anglican colleges where women could study, St Stephen's became co-educational for post-graduate students and, between 1943 and 1949, admitted female undergraduate students. During this six-year period, the Shakespeare Society recruited its first female secretary, Joy Michael (*née* Christian). She puts her name to a report in the 1946 volume of the college magazine, the year in which *As You Like It* was staged, and it is clear that a number of women, who could have been from the College, participated:

> Our special thanks to Mrs Krishnaswamy who has very kindly helped us not only in playing the part of a charming Celia, but for her invaluable aid in many other spheres. We also thank Miss Sheila Rollston and Miss Shantala Bahadur for consenting to take the parts of Phoebe and Audrey.
> (Christian 1946: 56)

Joy Christian also acknowledges in the report the women who helped with the costumes, an element otherwise missing in accounts of the Society during these years. Christian ends her report with an Eliot-like call to future generations. Treating the society like an institution, she takes on the mantle of Henry V in an exhortation addressed to the players to come, including, we might assume, women:

> Though we come and go, the Shakespeare Society, like Tennyson's brook flows on eternally. Therefore beware, ye later generations, that the banner be not defiled. Add to it further glories and a greater and nobler tradition.
> (Christian 1946: 57)[5]

One might further speculate that the presence of women in the College resulted in changes to the layout of buildings and accommodation. A recent history of the College refers to 'E-13, Allnutt North' as 'the Shakespeare Society room (the only room in Residence open to women' (Vepa and Vishvanathan 2011: n.p.). All of the Allnutt residence blocks in the College have historically been out-of-bounds for female students, but, as a designated Shakespeare room, 'E-13' gave women exclusive access via their Shakespearean involvement. This in turn suggests that, from an early date, the Society entered into gendered negotiations about the nature of college spaces.

That co-educational moment was a brief one. By 1949, the College had ceased to be co-educational. The Shakespeare Society, however, did not wish to return to the convention of men cross-dressing, and found a way out through establishing an alliance with a local (women's) college. To cite a discussion by Ashish Roy:

> Thankfully, Miranda House, founded in 1948, a year prior to [St] Stephen's reversion to all-male status, proved the locus of a broader University-wide change and, indeed, a 'magical' Shakespearean bond. 50s onward, MH provided the female leads for virtually every Shak Soc production, with brave 'interlopers' from Lady Shri Ram College helping the course.
> (2011: 153)

The Miranda House connection is affirmed in a later account of preparations for a production of *Henry V*. The Secretary, R. Chetsingh, writes in the 1952 volume of the college magazine (now christened *The Stephanian*) that 'the ladies from Miranda House, who were very kindly allowed to act for us, began to learn French' (1952: 27). In this regard, a report from the 1970s by the Principal of the College is striking for what it does *not* tell us:

> We are grateful to the Principal of Miranda House for continuing to kindly allow her pupils to act on stage. Once, nearly two decades ago, the Principal withdrew the permission for her ladies to act in one Shakespeare play. That year (1955), we were compelled to do *The Taming of the Shrew*.
> ('Annual Report' 1974–5: 55)

This suggests that, with the exception of one year, there was a system in place by which the women students of another college became the leading ladies of Shakespeare Society productions. As far as the participation of Miranda House was concerned, students taking parts were confined to female lead roles. And the reviews printed in *The Stephanian* give a flavour of how male reviewers viewed these actresses. For example, Peter Preston writes in a 1962 review:

> The ladies, as always, brought grace, beauty and clear speaking to their parts. None could blame Reagan and Goneril for looking rather young for the daughters of an octogenarian – each in their own way conveyed something of their sensual and cruel ... temperaments.
> (1962: 50)

If Preston concentrates on matters of age and appearance, Benjamin Gilani singles out issues of plausibility and authenticity. His review of a 1972–3 *Hamlet* runs:

> Liletta Keswani as Gertrude came across very strongly when she opened her mouth for the first time but very soon forgot she was supposed to be a queen and walked through the rest of the play as if she were a model.
> (1972–3: 77)

By contrast, in a later – anonymous – review of *The Comedy of Errors*, it is precisely an absorption in the part that is identified.

The now celebrated film director, Mira Nair, is mentioned for her student performance:

> Mirabai Nair, as Adriana, lived up to her fast-growing reputation ... she played the virago to the hilt, her outraged femininity coming across with all its bathos ... how about *The Taming of the Shrew* next year, Shakespeare Society?
> ('Shakespeare Society's *Comedy of Errors*' 1975–6: 22)[6]

Interestingly in these reviews, *The Taming of the Shrew* is mentioned twice, first as something of a duty and then as a provocation. In addition, and perhaps echoing the play's misogyny, the reviews underline stereotypical constructions of women who are seen either as pretty stage presences or as cantankerous entities. Regardless of the experience of the actresses, or the nature of the performance space, the male eye/reader sought through Shakespeare a familiar critical idiom that is ultimately antithetically angled.

It was in 1975 that the paradigm shift occurred. In 'Stephanian Diary', Mukul Manglik writes:

> The decision awaited within and without Stephania with mixed feelings of dread and enthusiasm was finally implemented in July 1975 – St Stephen's turned co-ed ... Within college and apart from a handful of favourable opinions, reactions against students were singular – disappointment and disgust.
> (1975–6: 5)

The comments suggest that there were two combating traditions within the Shakespeare Society: one fluid, unofficial performance tradition with its capacity to infiltrate through into spaces of gender stratification, the other fixed, mainstream textual tradition that framed women in limiting ways.

It was against this background that I arrived at St Stephen's College, although I was unaware of the Society and its place in the institution's curricular life. For myself, a late learner of English from a rural part of India at what was traditionally known as an elite, Anglophilic and urban college, I initially felt something of an outsider. When I was appointed as the first ever Staff Advisor to the Shakespeare Society, joining the then Society President, Ashish Roy, I was told by the then Principal, Rev. Valson Thampu, that 'We used to take pride in the fact that the Shakespeare Society was the only Shakespeare Society this side of the Suez Canal'. There was a challenge before me, therefore; at the same time, I was essentially clueless since, despite a decade-long participation in school/campus theatre, I had neither acted nor directed Shakespeare. The popular impression of the Society as a club of individuals from the city elites of South Delhi did not help either: 'The only qualification required to be in Shakespeare Society is a South Delhi address', a running joke went. The Society was at a difficult point, and the annual Shakespeare production had not taken place in the last two previous years.

My first task was to make sure that the annual Shakespeare production was reinstated. *Othello*, the 2011 production, was set in the time and place of the original play and, as concept, imagined Iago as the body through which the Venetian aristocracy's racism and fears of miscegenation were expressed. To externalize the idea, a sextet – a grouping of six characters – featured as a spectral presence, Mikhail Sen playing the lead role. Some way into the production process, I sensed an allegorical connection. Just as characters in the play are shaped by cultural undercurrents, so was I in some ways being shaped by the spectral presences of a production that, along with the student directors, Tanima Sharma and Rajiv Naresh, I had helped devise. An outsider, I was also an insider. Shakespeare, St Stephen's College and campus theatre were all spaces I was now occupying while, at the same time, being experientially and structurally outside them.

At this point in time, the College had greater numbers of female students than male students, and, as reading practices in the humanities had altered, it seemed important to bring in a different kind of development and for the Society to be recalibrated. It was the moment for students to own the Shakespeare they had been exposed to in the classroom, not the Shakespeare who was known for his grand soliloquies but the Shakespeare who could be understood through post-colonial, deconstructive and, in particular, feminist readings. I wanted to make a bridge between textual readings and performance and, to achieve this, suggested an ensemble piece featuring selections from Shakespeare and directed by women students. My feeling was that, in the context of male traditions, and from a cursory look at the history of the Society, creating a space for women directors could mark a departure. The stipulation that only women could direct did result in a few dissenting murmurs (presumably because of a perception that faculty members were interfering with student activities), but I only became aware of these at a later stage, and everything else went smoothly. Directors were given free rein to work with Shakespeare as they wished, with all of the selections/scenes being rolled into one ensemble piece under the aegis of the Shakespeare Society. Six selections/scenes by nine directors/co-directors were approved, and eight of the nine were from the English department. Once the scripts came in, I asked my women colleagues, Giti Chandra, Deepti Bhardwaj, Manpreet Kaur, Maitrayee Roychaudhary, Priyasha Mukhopadhyay and Vebhuti Duggal, to mentor the directors; since the Shakespeare Society never had a female Faculty Advisor/President in its history till then, this was also a first.

When the scripts were submitted, it struck me that the applicants/participants were trying to edit and punctuate Shakespeare, so I suggested the title, 'The Blue Pencil', referring to the proverbial blue pencil of the editor. The programme for the ensemble piece featured two images on the cover. To the left was the lower part of a male body dressed in Venetian breeches and shoes and revealing the handle of a sword; to the right was an equivalently dressed woman wearing a petticoat and bodice, the difference being that hands were crossed and headphones displayed. Although the woman's body lacked a face, the confidence of the posture, and the gesture of 'checking out', were unmistakable. Also characterizing the ensemble piece was the way in which we added a prelude: this showed the writing Shakespeare, played by a male student, being interrupted, and encircled, by the women directors. They put an end to his actions with a collective shout, thereby becoming players themselves in the selections/scenes that ensue.

All six selections/scenes, knitted together into one ensemble piece, were adaptations. Two of them worked by jumbling up Shakespearean lines to comic effect. For example, Naintara Rana and Arushi Gupta directed *Romeo and Juliet* and used lines from *Romeo and Juliet*, *As You Like It*, *The Merchant of Venice*, *Henry V*, *Macbeth*, *Antony and Cleopatra*, *Othello* and *Hamlet* both to parody romantic love and to point up the Shakespearean quotations that circulate in an Anglophilic Indian academy. The selection/scene showed Juliet (Vishaka George) sitting in a chair on the famous balcony and Romeo (Reuben George) standing next to her: assorted interlocutors are nearby and interject with comments.

The second *Romeo and Juliet* selection/scene, directed by Pooja Anna Pant and also selectively deploying lines from the play, was imagined as a play rehearsal: the story goes off-track because the players fail to understand the script. A book of Shakespeare is an important prop, with lines that illuminate the lovers' complaints and taunts being taken too literally, resulting in Romeo and Juliet unwittingly killing each other (they have no knowledge of how the 'real' play ends). In this connection, Margaret Jane Kidnie's comments on the 'scholarly impulse toward fixity' are illuminating: 'performance', she notes, 'constitutes a very different type of "text" from dramatic literature' and can be seen as a 'never contained ... liberating space of infinite creative potential' (2000: 458). Applying these suggestions, the students in the ensemble piece acted out the conceptual interplay engendered by Shakespeare's literary iconicity at the same time as they registered the archetypal presence of Romeo and Juliet in their lives. Or, to adapt Italo Calvino's remark in *If on a Winter's Night a Traveller* (1981), Romeo and Juliet have become a kind of book 'that Everybody's Read So It's as if You Had Read Them, Too' (1981: 5), meaning that students are able to draw on knowledge of, and take advantage of, various Shakespearean constructions. The students edited to perform and performed their edits. The disconnected canonical Bard associated with school, the deconstructionist tendencies of College lessons and floating notions in contemporary culture – all formed part of the parodic mix. A bridging of classes, sensibilities and identities was, I felt from my position in the wings, unapologetically celebrated.

Other entries in the ensemble of selections/scenes explored questions about the possibilities (or impossibilities) associated with gendered identities. Here, I have in mind the adaptations of *A Midsummer Night's Dream*, directed by Sohini Basak, Sukhalakshmi Gooptu and Urvashi Bahuguna, and *The Merchant of Venice,* directed by Urna Mukherjee, which located their interpretations in the America of the 1920s and the England of the 1950s, respectively. For the directors, these periods were particularly suggestive. Both selections/scenes centred on choices. For example, Puck, the bartender in the adaptation of *A Midsummer Night's Dream*, served in a semi-directorial capacity in a pub of the roaring 1920s ('The bar becomes a space to play out these multifarious gender relations', ran the programme note) and welcomed women who came in pursuit of love. Similarly, the adaptation of *The*

Merchant of Venice made clear how Portia was only able to choose among incompetent and unworthy suitors in the post-war England she inhabited: this, according to the director's programme note, was 'a bleak time for feminism'. Finally, a selection/scene directed by Tanya Sharma telescoped the murder/death scenes of *Othello* and *Romeo and Juliet* in the form of a letter written by Death to a personification of Love (*eros* and *thanatos* are intimately intertwined). With this adaptation, as in the others, working with if not against Shakespeare provided access to new spaces and generated fresh impressions.

Throughout the process of adaptation, self-consciousness was self-evident. This was most obvious in the *Macbeth* selection/scene which, directed by Rebecca Sarah John, scripted by Jaideep Pandey and mentored by Maitrayee Roychaudhary, took the form of a making-of-*Macbeth*-the-movie narrative. Taking place somewhere in India, the selection/scene figured the Macbeth counterpart as the director and the Lady Macbeth counterpart as his wife. The director (Chhayankdhar Rathore) is unhappy with the soft and unthreatening way in which the actress (Ahona Palchaudhari) delivers Lady Macbeth's lines: he requires her to be unspeakably villainous. For her part, the actress is of the opinion that Lady Macbeth does everything for Macbeth, just as she does for her husband, including compromising her own integrity to secure his career advancement. By the end of the selection/scene, the actress realizes that, since the director cannot understand or value Lady Macbeth's sacrifices, he is incapable of appreciating hers. Nora-like, she walks out of the theatre, intoning to herself Lady Macbeth's lines as though they were a powerful freedom chant, 'To cry, "Hold, hold"' (1.5.52). Her declaration, and abandonment of a feeble but still protesting husband, made for an exciting conclusion to this selection/scene, the last of the ensemble: a woman leaves the stage, a stage associated through College history with many grand Shakespeare productions, delivering familiar lines but with a new political content and energy. In a discussion of 'woman-crafted Shakespeares', defined as 'the power to shape Shakespeare and to reshape the institutional hierarchies and barriers or "mechanisms of exclusion" that surround (women)', Sujata Iyengar considers the ethical and political issues thrown up by adaptation as follows:

> Does 'Shakespeare' offer an invaluable convenient cultural shorthand for dominant or elite cultures and an imitable

polysemic richness that makes it useful to analyze present-day problems ... or by turning to Shakespeare, do we merely replicate the established terms of the discussion and reinforce hide-bound canonical, Eurocentric, and male privilege when we could more productively move away from Shakespeare to other writers, historical eras, and geographical periods?

(2016: 507)

These are still questions before the Shakespeare Society, and one performance of one production, however conceived, does not change the character of a collective, invert an impression or remake a legacy. Yet, at the same time, the *Macbeth* adaptation, and the ensemble piece as a whole, triggered thought and helped pave the way for future directions.

One of the selection/scene directors, Pooja Anna Pant, went on to direct the 2013 annual production, *The Tempest*. In this production, the student team's focus was on developing two Miranda characters – one was the subdued favourite, the other was the assertive and defiant daughter. This doubling lent the production a woman-centric dimension, an element that, in the Shakespeare Society, was becoming more significant. As Staff Advisor, I made suggestions, and offered direction, with the students taking prompts on board and changing them in such a way that the past of the Society was rewritten. The younger Miranda in this production – the favourite – made me think about the friendship that must have existed between her and Caliban during their childhood and before their estrangement. The coming together of the indigenous inhabitant of the island and the white female colonialist was a threat to Prospero, the enlightenment hero. This was the period in which campaigning against interfaith marriages was taking place; under the conspiratorial pretext of 'Love Jihad', it was argued that Muslim men were part of a crusade to woo and convert Hindu women for the purposes of Holy War. Clearly, in fact, the real imperative was to repress romantic love and interfere in the lives of youth. A campaign started in Kerala, South India, in 2009, reached the villages of Uttar Pradesh, North India, and was a factor in the process that led to murders and demographic displacement in Muzaffarnagar in 2013. Within such contexts, a politicized kind of feminism was becoming a useful tool against hyper-masculine rhetoric and majoritarian ideologies in India, and the shift in orientation and performance content of the Shakespeare

Society allowed for particularly creative and interventionist acts of adaptation.

This full-length production of *The Tempest* was the precondition for a shorter, slimmed down version of the play staged two years later. In 2015, the Society came up with the idea that the whole play might be synopsized in fifteen to twenty minutes: accordingly, the action, directed by a woman student, Radhika Goswami, was telescoped down to Miranda (Srishti Gawtham), wearing a white gown, and Caliban (Edwin Joseph), wearing only a towel, staring at the audience and delivering their lines without ever looking at each other. To fill in for the backstory, a chorus-cum-Ariel entity made up of four women students was introduced. Although all the dialogue was taken from the 'original' play, some of the lines given to Caliban and Miranda belonged to Prospero and other characters. Crucially, this synopsized *Tempest* explored the transformation of a young, happy-go-lucky woman whose emotional centre shifts to her lover/husband and away from her father even as Caliban suffers confusions and collapse. After the story of the 'original' unravels through them, Caliban and Miranda sing the epilogue as one: they turn towards each other, suggesting the reclamation of a lost bond ruined by social and cultural pressures: 'As you from crimes would pardoned be, / Let your indulgence set me free' (Epilogue, 19–20). As I watched both player-singers and thrilled to the marvellous highs and lows of the music (flowing, as it were, with their voices), I felt the space and life of campus theatre experiment had taken me beyond the insider-outsider dialectic and into a sphere of mutuality. Now, I could think of myself as a link in a recovered and developed tradition, a witness to exciting student negotiations between text and performance, and a contributor to a chapter about women and Indian Shakespeares.

Notes

1. For a comparable discussion, see Poonam Trivedi's chapter in this volume.
2. As a starting point, see Kumar and Kour 2019: 44–51.
3. On the one hand in India, there is a fully fledged and state-funded experimental theatre; on the other hand, there are sporadic and private-sponsored productions.

4   This original but uncatalogued document was accessed in the St Stephen's College Archives Shakespeare Society folder.
5   Joy Michael returned to college to work with students of the Shakespeare Society and pursue alumni projects. See Sen 1973–4: 6–10.
6   Other luminaries of the Shakespeare Society include historian and former Pakistan Minister for Education, I. H. Qureshi, former Indian minister and diplomat, Shashi Tharoor, former Indian cabinet minister, Salman Khurshid, actors Roshan Seth, Benjamin Gilani and Konkona Sen Sharma, quiz show host Siddhartha Basu, historian Mukul Kesavan and documentary-maker Sanjay Kak.

References

'Annual Report' (1974–5), *The Stephanian*, Annual, 85: 55–9.
Bhattacharya, S. K. (1964), 'Shakespeare and Bengali Theatre', *Indian Literature*, 7 (1): 27–40.
Bosman, A. (2010), 'Shakespeare and Globalization', in M. de Grazia and S. Wells (eds), *The New Cambridge Companion to Shakespeare*, 2nd edn, 285–301, Cambridge: Cambridge University Press.
Calvino, I. (1981), *If on a Winter's Night a Traveller*, New York: Harcourt.
Chetsingh, R. (1952), 'Shakespeare Society', *The Stephanian*, 61 (3): 27–50.
Christian, J. (1946), 'Shakespeare Society', *The Stephanian*, 38 (1–3): 56–7.
Dewan, S. (2012), 'Of Chick Charts, Hen Charts and Other Such Women's Stories', *Kafila*, 8 May. Available online: https://kafila.online/2012/05/08/st-stephens-college-the-class-of-85-saba-dewan (accessed 15 March 2021).
García-Periago, R. (2012), 'The Re-Birth of Shakespeare in India: Celebrating and Indianizing the Bard in 1964', *SEDERI*, 22: 51–68.
Gilani, B. (1972–3), '*Hamlet*', *The Stephanian*, 82: 76–9.
Harris, J. G. (2018), *Masala Shakespeare: How a Firangi Writer Became Indian*, New Delhi: Aleph Books.
Hartley, A. J. (2015), 'Introduction: Tragedians of the City, Little Eyases or Rude Mechanicals?', in A. J. Hartley (ed.), *Shakespeare on the University Stage*, 1–10, Cambridge: Cambridge University Press.
Holland, P. (2015), 'Campus Shakespeare: Fragments of History, Fragments of a Concept', in A. J. Hartley (ed.), *Shakespeare on the University Stage*, 10–27, Cambridge: Cambridge University Press.

Iyengar, S. (2016), 'Woman-Crafted Shakespeares: Appropriation, Intermediality, and Womanist Aesthetics', in D. Callaghan (ed.), *A Feminist Companion to Shakespeare*, 2nd edn, 507–16, Oxford: Wiley/Blackwell.

Kidnie, M. J. (2000), 'Text, Performance, and the Editors: Staging Shakespeare's Drama', *Shakespeare Quarterly*, 51 (4): 456–73.

Kumar, K. and P. Kour (2019), 'Domesticating Shakespeare: A Study of Indian Adaptation of Shakespeare', *International Journal of ELT, Linguistics and Comparative Literature*, 7 (4): 44–51.

M. (1932), 'Shakespeare Society', *St Stephen's College Magazine*, 25 (1): 45–7.

Manglik, M. (1975–6), 'Stephanian Diary', *The Stephanian*, Annual, 86: 5–8.

Mathur, K. C. (1922), 'The Stage in India: Some Suggestions', *St Stephen's College Magazine*, 75: 13–16.

Padley, W. H. (1925), 'Shakespeare Society', *St Stephen's College Magazine*, 86: 27–8.

Padley, W. H. (1926), 'Shakespeare Dinner', *St Stephen's College Magazine*, 19 (4): 34–5.

Preston, P. (1962), 'From the College Stage', *The Stephanian*, 71 (3): 49–50.

Roy, A. (2011), 'The St Stephen's College Shakespeare Society: A Note', in Vikram Chopra (ed.), *Shakespeare: The Indian Icon*, 152–4, New Delhi: Readers Paradise.

Sen, H. (1973-4), 'The Stephanian Diary', *The Stephanian*, Spring and Annual, 84: 6–10.

'Shakespeare Society's *Comedy of Errors*' (1975–6), *The Stephanian*, Annual, 86: 22–4.

Singh, J. G. and M. Roy (2016), 'Shakespeare in India', *Shakespeare Unlimited*: Episode 40, 27 January. Available online: https://www.folger.edu/shakespeare-unlimited/india (accessed 15 March 2021).

Vepa, A. and S. Vishvanathan (2011), 'St Stephen's College, Delhi, India: History'. Available online: https://ase.tufts.edu/chemistry/kumar/ssc/html/sschis.html (accessed 20 December 2020).

12

Adapting Shakespeare: Directors and practitioners in conversation

Bornila Chatterjee, Sangeeta Datta, Annette Leday, Sreedevi Nair and Preti Taneja

[This roundtable conversation originally took place at the 'Women and Indian Shakespeares' conference at Queen's University Belfast, 2019. The present chapter captures the spontaneity and flow of that conversation, although some aspects have been refined and developed since, with additional questions and voices being added.]

MARK THORNTON BURNETT
  Welcome. We'll start with the following question – what does Shakespeare mean to you?

BORNILA CHATTERJEE
  I am the director of a film called *The Hungry* (2017), a very loose adaptation of *Titus Andronicus*. I never thought that I would ever direct an adaptation of Shakespeare. I came to it

because, back in 2015, to celebrate 400 years of Shakespeare, Film London collaborated with an Indian production company called Cinestaan to fund one microbudget Indian adaptation of a Shakespeare play. So a call for scripts was put out, and they shortlisted three scripts from India and three from the UK; in the end, they chose our script to go into production. The film takes Tamora's story and turns Shakespeare's villain into the hero of our film.

The film was made as part of a microbudget filmmaking initiative; truly, what we did in terms of condensing Shakespeare's characters was because we had very limited resources to make the film. My producers, my co-writers, everybody involved … what was really important was taking the beauty of the written language and figuring out how to translate that cinematically, be it through costumes or the set or music. In doing so, we actually moved pretty far away from the words on the page but, hopefully, we managed to capture the essence of what Shakespeare is trying to say in the play.

MARK THORNTON BURNETT

We move on to our next participant, Annette Leday; would you like to say a few words?

ANNETTE LEDAY

I am one of the co-directors of *Kathakali-King Lear*. I have spent a lot of time in Kerala. I was a scholar from the Indo-French cultural exchange programme from 1978 onwards, and I devoted about ten years of my life to traditional *kathakali*. Then I went on to create a number of productions involving *kathakali* artists, whom I have been connecting with for all these years. We started on the *Kathakali-King Lear* project. The idea came from my then husband, David McRuvie, and he said, 'Start with the best: start by adapting *King Lear* to *kathakali*'.

So I went to my teacher, Padmanabhan Nair Asan, who was the principal of Kalamandalam (University) at that time … and I asked him: 'We have this project; would you agree that the students at Kalamandalam participate in it?' I told him the story briefly in my broken Malayalam (in those days) and, little by little, I could see that he was very interested. At the end of the conversation, I took courage and said: 'Asan, would you consider doing the part of King Lear?'

He said, 'Hmm, let me think about it'.

The next morning, he was organizing everything. Because he was the head of the institution, top artists of the day joined the project and we ended up having a beautiful team of the best actors and musicians of the time. That was in 1989. Another of the great names of the day was Kumaran Nair Asan, who had been my teacher longer, actually; both of them played the role of Lear in turn, and I played Cordelia.

Then I went on to a different approach and did a series of contemporary choreography productions with dancers that had been participating in the *King Lear*, the younger ones. We came back to *Kathakali-King Lear* last year (2018). It toured all over India with a new team of people; some of them had participated in the first production, and we presented it in Paris last April (2019). In this new production, the role of Lear is played by Peesappilly Rajeev. My two teachers are unfortunately no more.

MARK THORNTON BURNETT

Thank you so much. Could I ask Sreedevi Nair to offer a few reflections on your work with Shakespeare?

SREEDEVI NAIR

I come from Kerala in India. I am an academic and a translator. I was working till March 2019 at the Department of English of NSS College for Women, Thiruvananthapuram, which offers B.A. and M.A. programmes in English Language and Literature. I have been teaching Shakespeare to the students of both these programmes. At present, I am with the Samyukta Research Foundation, a small vibrant research centre which focuses on Gender Studies, Translation Studies and Kerala Studies. Besides, I have translated *Two Gentlemen of Verona* and *King John* for *The Complete Works of Shakespeare* (Malayalam) edited by Dr K. Ayyappa Paniker and published by DC Books in the year 2000. I have also done an adaptation for children of *All's Well That Ends Well*. This was published by the State Institute of Children's Literature, Kerala.

At this conference, I'll be presenting a retelling of *Othello* titled *The Stars Still Shine on Desdemona*.[1] This retelling adds just a single detail to the play which overturns the last scene, thus transforming the entire play. In 4.3, Desdemona tells Emilia of her mother's maid, Barbary. In the retelling, Barbary hails from Kerala and she is a trained practitioner of *kalarippayattu*, a form of martial art.[2] As a child, Desdemona is taught *kalarippayattu* by Barbary. So, in the last scene, when Othello tries to smother and kill Desdemona, she pleads, 'Can I live? Can I live for a day? Can I live for an hour? Can I live till I say one prayer?' But when her entreaties are summarily refused, she moves like lightning and strikes Othello at a vital pressure point which makes him go numb and still, on the instant. However, Desdemona doesn't take pride in the fact that she can overpower the valiant General. The moment she feels that she is safe, that is, as soon as she hears the voice of Emilia, Desdemona revives him. But, after this, she decides to leave Othello. She bids him goodbye and leaves – not in anger or in hate but with thankfulness for the heavenly memory of a transient love. Thus, in this adaptation, Desdemona isn't a meek subject but a strong woman of self-esteem and agency.

MARK THORNTON BURNETT

Thank you very much. Could I ask Sangeeta Datta if you would say a few words, about *Life Goes On*, your 2009 film?

SANGEETA DATTA

I think as practitioners, it's important to locate ourselves within the context from which we produce our work. I studied in Loreto Convent and all our English Language and Literature teaching, our first introduction to Shakespeare and many other writers, was handed down to us through our Irish nuns. I was also thinking how special this was that we were introduced to Shakespeare maybe at the age of ten, maybe when we were in class five or six, and from then to sixteen, we learnt the texts by heart, at least four or five of the Shakespearean plays. That was the demand that was made on us.

Shakespeare wasn't ever set on an altar, where we had to look up with great reverence. We come from a tradition in Bengal where literature, and poetry and music is imbibed from a very, very young stage in our lives, and if it is Rabindranath Tagore, if it is Satyajit Ray, if it is Ritwik Ghatak, we were introduced to these writers, and filmmakers and artists. So, if we are able to make connections with Shakespeare and Indian writers or Shakespeare and Indian traditions, I don't think it required a great deal of cerebral work; it happened quite organically, out of the experience and the education that we received in India.

I come from a teaching and academic background and I started writing on cinema before I started making cinema. But I also had the good fortune of working with auteur filmmakers, like Shyam Benegal and Basu Bhattacharya, when I was in Bombay, and teaching at St Xavier's College. Soon after, when I moved to London, I worked on my first documentary, which was on Indian women filmmakers, called *The Way I See It* (1999). It is about the female gaze, it is about how women look at life differently, and that film also travelled extensively to festivals and is now part of the curriculum in many places in the UK and the US.

I also made a couple of documentaries and short films about this, the diaspora culture, because when I moved to live in London, my children were growing up and I was really keen to understand this whole process of what we were going to give these kids in the sense of identity building. So, I made *In Search of Durga* (2001); I made another film which was a contemporary take on Tagore's proto-feminist *A Wife's Letter – Strir Patra* (2008). I worked with the Bengal-based director Rituparno Ghosh as a collaborator, as associate director on many projects, and many of these were adaptations of literature, so: Tagore's *Chokher Bhali* and Tagore's *Noukadubi*, two major novels and very well-known novels, were made into films. O. Henry's short story was translated or adapted into *Raincoat* (2004). *The Last Lear* (2007), which was in a way coming from a play by Utpal Dutt, *Aajker Shahjahan*, was also a film I was involved with before I wrote *Life Goes On*.

I think returning to *King Lear*, the fable-like idea of a father and three daughters – and a father who loves his youngest the most, with whom there is the greatest conflict – that's the sort of base idea with which I started writing *Life Goes On* at a time when there was political turmoil, when there was a great sense of uncertainty really about the diaspora identity in the UK, in Europe at large, even in the US, so we were asking these larger questions about who we are, where we are, but also going back to links which mattered, which were part of our family history, narratives which were never told. So we were able to link Partition, the Bengal Partition, the history in India, link it to the diaspora family around which the story concentrates. I also wrote in the figure of the mother, who doesn't really belong to Shakespeare's *King Lear*, but I felt this idea of loss and the idea of the absent mother in many ways would allow me to look at a world which was potentially then violent and loveless. It was shot largely in London and parts of it were shot in Calcutta and the border town of Taki.

MARK THORNTON BURNETT

Thank you very much. Let's move on now to Preti Taneja.

PRETI TANEJA

My novel *We That Are Young* translates Shakespeare's *King Lear* to contemporary India. It was written in 2010–13 and published in 2017 by the independent small press, Galley Beggar Press. It is a critique of the legacies of colonialism including neoliberalism, of the rise of Hindu fascism and of the ravages that billionaire crony capitalism and its twin disease patriarchy wreak on our world. The novel begins with the division of a vast company by an Indian business mogul between his daughters; through the actions of two families, it follows Hindu India's settler-colonialist tactics which are rooted in British Empire-era laws – towards the occupation of Kashmir.

Shakespeare's work, and particularly *King Lear*, forms part of a core set of texts in my work; it's part of a select personal canon and reference library which consists of plays, poetry, novels and essays, that remind me of what writing is and can do, what I want to do when I write.

MARK THORNTON BURNETT

Thank you for those wonderful initial reflections. Let me move to the next question which is for all our participants: what are some of the challenges in adapting Shakespeare to a different language or medium?

BORNILA CHATTERJEE

For us, obviously the biggest challenge was the language itself, because there is so much poetry there. In a film, the very first thing is how you take that poetry and translate it to a cinematic language: forget about translating it to Hindi or modern English. So in the film we made it very clear that we didn't really want to have that much talk, we didn't even want to get into those sorts of comparisons. Instead, what we tried to do was see how we could do art, how we could take the drama and the texture of Shakespeare's words and translate that to the cinematography, to our costumes. Everybody involved in the film was familiar with *Titus* and everybody had their own ideas on how to translate it into *their* department. We were very much inspired by how Shakespeare describes nature and weather, and we tried to capture that in how we filmed Delhi. We figured the best way to go about it was to take the beautiful poetry of his language and try to transpose that visually.

MARK THORNTON BURNETT

And you have a transposition in terms of the beautiful look of the film because it is full, isn't it, of delicious foodstuffs: kebabs, skewers, scenes of greedy eating, all Shakespearean kinds of scenario.

BORNILA CHATTERJEE

Absolutely. Our mentors pushed us to take the essence of the play and of Shakespeare and try to figure out what that meant for us and how we could capture that on film.

MARK THORNTON BURNETT

Sreedevi Nair, you are a translator, but you are also a performer in the sense that you have written this adaptation with performance in mind, so what were some of the challenges for you?

SREEDEVI NAIR

Well, linguistic challenges are not insurmountable while moving a text from English into Malayalam because, in India, we use English words very liberally in our everyday conversations in the regional languages. Translating images also does not turn out to be too trying. However, the carrying over of Shakespearean poetry as well as certain cultural concepts can, at times, become highly challenging. For example, cuckoldry is quite difficult to translate into Malayalam – the idea that the man will grow horns if his woman is unfaithful is unfamiliar to Malayalis. Such a notion doesn't exist at all in Kerala, maybe also because some powerful communities in Kerala are matrilineal and even matriarchal to some extent. Those women lived in their own homes and enjoyed, to a certain extent, the right to choose their husbands. So, to move the concept of cuckoldry into Malayalam, one may need to gloss it, or even add additional notes.

MARK THORNTON BURNETT

Could you tell us something about Unniyarcha, the heroine that your adaptation of *Othello* is based on?

SREEDEVI NAIR

Unniyarcha lived in the sixteenth century, as did Shakespeare. She was an adept practitioner of *kalarippayattu*. There is a story that Unniyarcha once wanted to attend a festival for which she needed to travel through the forest at night. Everybody dissuaded her as ruffians had marked the place as their territory. However, Unniyarcha decided to go. On the way, she and her husband were attacked by a group of about twenty ruffians who had vowed to abduct her. Her husband ran away and asked her also to flee. In *kalarippayattu*, there is a weapon called *urumi* which is a very long, thin, ribbon-like sword, that can be wound around the hip. Unniyarcha, skilful as she was in the use of the *urumi*, drew it, and confronted the ruffians with it, and they were all floored in no time. Finally, their chieftain begged her pardon to get the men released. The martial art of *kalarippayattu* was commonly practised in Kerala by both men and women until the British banned it in 1804. The British issued an order which stated that anybody who practised *kalarippayattu* would be deported for life. Until then, this martial art was commonly practised in Kerala. So, if we imagine Desdemona's mother's maid as a native of Kerala, it is quite plausible that she was proficient in *kalarippayattu*. Also, if Desdemona had learnt *kalari* as a child, she would have naturally used it to save herself at a critical moment in her life. *Kalarippayattu* has moves which can be used for self-defence but it also has moves which will numb an opponent temporarily or maim him/her for life. In our adaptation of *Othello, The Stars Still Shine on Desdemona*, Desdemona temporarily benumbs Othello and saves herself but, later, leaves him and walks away.

MARK THORNTON BURNETT

Very interesting indeed. Thank you so much. Annette Leday, for you, what would be the challenges? Your website specifies that your overall project in your company is to evolve rare traditional performance techniques towards contemporary creation.[3]

ANNETTE LEDAY

Yes. First of all, putting two masterpieces like Shakespeare and *kathakali* together is in itself a big challenge. I would just mention two challenges. The first is the adaptation of the text, because the literary codes and codification of *kathakali* are very specific and you cannot have a long text because there are different levels of narrative in *kathakali*. There is the text which is sung by two singers; there is the text that is illustrated by facial expression, movements and hand gestures; and there is the improvisational text. So, according to these different levels of text, choices had to be made as to where the text was going to be sung, what was going to be performed, and what was going to be improvised during the play. That forced the adapter to have a very, very tight work and to reduce tremendously Shakespeare's text. I worked a lot with David McRuvie who did the adaptation and the next step was to get it translated, because the text is sung in Malayalam.

Another one is the decision about what types of costumes and makeup were going to be allotted to each character. We just used the *King Lear* plot: Lear and his three daughters, because, otherwise, it would have been too complicated. One of the big challenges was to impose a type of costume for the fool. The fool would be performed as a *kutiyattam vidushaka*. *Kutiyattam* is a more ancient form, it's a Sanskrit theatre form, which appeared before *kathakali*, and there is a character which is exactly the king's fool. So, I thought, 'Well, why not?' It took a lot of discussions with the *kathakali* artists and the *kutiyattam* specialists to get agreement on that.

MARK THORNTON BURNETT

Your productions of *King Lear*, and *The Tempest* involve performers from other cultures and parts of the world, don't they; you have French performers and you have Indian performers and you take your productions on tour?

ANNETTE LEDAY

Yes, in *King Lear*, I was the only Western performer. All the others were *kathakali* performers, professional performers from Kerala. In the new revived production, they are all Indian because I don't perform anymore. [The] *Tempest* was a production done by Bremer Shakespeare Company in Bremen, in Germany, and they invited me to choreograph the island. So, there were a few challenges there too, because I had to fight a lot not to have my dancers put into feathers. I also insisted that the Ariel character would be performed by one of my dancers, and they were all originally *kathakali*-trained dancers who participated.

MARK THORNTON BURNETT

Sangeeta Datta, we were talking yesterday about the lovely imagery in the film ... the colours. We also talked about language. I notice there are some quotations from *King Lear* in the dialogue. For you, what were the particular challenges of approaching *King Lear* in those terms?

SANGEETA DATTA

The biggest challenge was to set it in a contemporary context and to take away those trappings of kingdom, and the regal background or costume and dress, which could have been quite stagy and theatrical, to bring it to a real and contemporary story of an Indian diaspora family in London. Within that, because the youngest daughter is a student of drama, we had a staging of *King Lear*. So, it was a play within the film for which a lot of preparation was required. I spent a lot of time with Professor René Weiss, who teaches English at University College London and is a Shakespearean scholar, and who actually features – he plays King Lear in those scenes. And then I discussed and invited Alison Sutcliffe, the prolific theatre director who was Artistic Director of the Bridge Project at Bridge House Theatre, Warwick. She came down from Stratford-upon-Avon to workshop and direct those stage sections and she also featured as drama teacher. I had a lot of students from RADA and University College London, who were there as part of the cast, and we had great fun working with a group of young people and these three big stars who were brought in from India who come from traditions of theatre: Girish Karnad (Sanjay) is such a well-known theatre person himself, who's written plays, who's revived a lot of traditional literature; Om Puri (Alok), who's the bridge between Indian cinema and the sort of diaspora cinema that we had with the rich tradition of the times in the 2000s, the early millennial films; and Sharmila Tagore (Manju), who comes with the tradition of Satyajit Ray and Rabindranath Tagore and everything within her family and career history. So, it was a wonderful combination of some very experienced, legendary people who came in because they responded to the script, and we had this British-Asian corps of younger actors.

I spent a lot of time on visual planning with my DOP, the Director of Photography, Robert Shacklady, because I did want to make the film – the actual span of the film is those seven days between the death and the funeral of Manju, and I had written it with the idea of cherry blossoms. They only appear for a week in April, and then with the first April shower they are gone. I wanted to capture the transience of life through that. I enjoy a lot of my time on Hampstead Heath, and the particular light that we get in spring and early summer – we shot during that time. So, a lot of planning went into the look of the film.

A lot of the dialogue is in English, but there were bits of Bengali. There was also the process of translating Tagore poetry and song from Bengali into Hindi, which we did with Javed Akhtar, and opened this up for a much larger audience even in India when it was released. So it was negotiating and creating these connections between different languages, cultures, even the look and feel of the film.

MARK THORNTON BURNETT

Could you tell us something about your perception of the ending? You depart from Shakespeare's play ...

SANGEETA DATTA

It doesn't end tragically – it starts tragically, with the death of the mother, and ends with the funeral scene, and within those seven days there are all different crises that the three daughters are going through, all related to identity. The biggest crisis, with the father and the younger daughter, that gets resolved. The funeral is not just a closure but almost a regenerative moment, where there is hope and love again within this family unit. We choreographed the funeral scene, the last release bit with the release of the balloons and the crane shots that we took at that time, using Shakespeare, using lines from *King Lear*, using lines from the *Rig Veda*, using Tagore's theme song, the mother's song, 'Remember Me'. All of that came together, but it was a great deal of planning which went into that rather ambitious sequence.

MARK THORNTON BURNETT

Now may I ask Preti Taneja – what challenges did you face?

PRETI TANEJA

The challenge is to cleave to the text in the way you want to – both to it and away from it – and to be consistent in that. Not to simply rewrite into new language so that the Shakespearean bones show through, or to adapt and update uncritically, but to trust your own relationship with the Shakespearean text, its own modes and movements and your feeling for them. You must write with that alone.

I had to make many intricate decisions about register, tone, linguistic style and voice at the sentence level of my writing. For contemporary appropriators, *King Lear* is an elastic and liberating text. It allows for multiple registers in the same speech; its tension and tragedy is built through puns and epic fragments; it traverses wide emotional and spiritual ground. From the beginning I set out to map as much as I could of the play, from language, plot and themes to the deeper movements of thought and feeling, onto the world I was making in *We That Are Young*, and from that structure I was able to treat Shakespeare's text as malleable, as its presence actually is, in our everyday lives.

MARK THORNTON BURNETT

Thank you. Could I ask each of our speakers just to reflect on this question: in what ways do you think that your work has enabled a new kind of Shakespeare with new meanings and applications to emerge?

SREEDEVI NAIR

Well, I think Shakespeare is a writer for all times and for all people. This is true of all world-class literature. In the classroom, even today when we teach Culture Studies, Gender

Studies, Postcolonial Theory, Queer Theory, Psychoanalytic Theory and many other theories, Shakespeare provides extremely pertinent examples. Likewise, any recent literary, sociological or psychological theory makes yet another, very different, reading of Shakespeare possible. I believe this is why Shakespeare gets rewritten and needs to be rewritten in every age.

At Samyukta Research Foundation, we have come out with a retelling of *Othello* mainly for two reasons. If we make a close reading of *Othello*, we can understand that Desdemona was not unaware of what was going to happen to her. Shakespeare puts words suggestive of her misgivings in Desdemona's mouth several times, especially in 4.3. In this act, when Emilia and Desdemona talk intimately, Desdemona asks Emilia to spread her wedding sheets on the bed that night. She also requests – 'If I do die before thee, prithee shroud me / In one of these same sheets' (4.3.22–3).

Even in the death scene, when Othello is about to kill her and tells her that Iago has killed Cassio, her response is 'O, my fear interprets!' (5.2.72). There are several such instances in the play which give the feeling that Desdemona 'feared' and knew what was going to happen. This is how the play demands its own retelling. Secondly, through the glorification of Desdemona's 'innocent' death at the hands of her thoughtless husband, what ensues is the glorification of the inactivity, the passivity, the frailty and the powerlessness of women. We thought it absolutely necessary to rewrite such a play for the sake of the women of today.

MARK THORNTON BURNETT
Excellent. Bornila Chatterjee, for you – a new kind of Shakespeare emerging from *The Hungry*?

BORNILA CHATTERJEE
Your question made me think about how what is really cool about taking a Shakespearean text and trying to adapt it for other mediums is seeing how there is a lot of room for interpretation. You know, there is, which we faced a lot while making the film. I remember growing up, every year, you had to memorize a new text – in Class Seven it was *The Merchant of Venice*, in Eight it was *Macbeth*, in Nine it was *Othello*. So

our understanding of performance and art is entrenched in Shakespeare, and sort of figuring out how to take it forward. And that's when it is very beautiful.

MARK THORNTON BURNETT
Thank you. Annette Leday, what about for you?

ANNETTE LEDAY
I want to be modest about that; it's a big subject. I just want to say that perhaps *kathakali* has been a sort of a gate towards Shakespeare as well as Shakespeare has been a gate towards *kathakali* for the audience. I feel that *kathakali* has brought a certain extra human dimension to those characters and they fit together very well. When we performed at the Globe Theatre, it was like evidence.

MARK THORNTON BURNETT
Thank you. Next, Sangeeta Datta?

SANGEETA DATTA
Well again, yes, about the reception of Shakespeare, as Bornila was saying. Going to Loreto and learning from the Irish nuns was one route, one channel. But the interesting thing was that when we were younger we were also looking at productions of Shakespeare in Bengali and the folk form *jatra*. It's a larger-than-life performance tradition, and we watched a lot of that. I grew up outside Calcutta in an industrial town called Asansol, Burnpur, and there was a lot of very committed cultural activity happening there. So just as we heard the classical musicians, the masters, every year for the classical conferences, there would be this *jatra*, and they borrowed freely – not just from Shakespeare, work from various international writers. So all of this was coming to us through various traditions.

I must acknowledge my father, who would take me for the film society screenings on Sunday mornings. He was very careless about whether they were adult films or not, but he wanted me to see the classics. We saw the Russian *Lear* (*Korol Lir* [dir. Grigori Kozintsev, 1971]), Kurosawa, Peter Brook, and, with a lot of these, even at a time when I wasn't ready for *King Lear*, you know, we were receiving the text, so these images came to us. It wasn't this pure English canonical tradition coming down to me – *King Lear* came through various traditions, so did *Julius Caesar*, so did *The Merchant of Venice* – all of these came to us through different performative traditions. If you have this very wide range of references at a point when you are beginning to do your own work, you know what you will take and what you won't, and I think that worked for me.

MARK THORNTON BURNETT
Terrific. And now to Preti Taneja.

PRETI TANEJA
I don't think that's for me to answer – the novel is for readers, scholars, critics with their own perspectives and writing in their own traditions to make meaning from. Isn't 'Shakespeare' itself, and all produced Shakespeare, a kind of Shakespeare, in the sense of kindred, in the end?

MARK THORNTON BURNETT
Thank you. For colleagues in the room, please now feel free to ask a question to our participants.

Q1
The question is about visual idiom and the actual words. I think with a lot of these films you find that obviously you can't translate the word-for-word language, but what are some of the visual choices you make?

ANNETTE LEDAY
Well in *kathakali*, the visual is very much to do with the hand gestures and facial expressions. Some of the key parts of the text of Shakespeare, we tried to bring it either in words in the song, or in gestures. And, for example, 'I have nothing to say' – 'nothing'. 'Nothing' comes back, I don't know how many times in this text. And there's no such sign for nothing in the hand gestures of *kathakali*. There is this, which means 'one', and this, which means 'not'; and this (together) means 'nothing'. It's 'one' [+] 'not'. This is an example.

MARK THORNTON BURNETT
Bornila, there are some very striking images in your film: red lips, the goats, the rubbish dump, the fire …

BORNILA CHATTERJEE
It's all there! In our film, actually, one of the main visual idioms were the goats, because, in *Titus Andronicus*, Tamora is the

Queen of the Goths, and we noticed that the Romans would say the word 'goat' by way of insult. So, in a very obvious filmic way, we decided to incorporate that into the visuals of North India that you see.

Q2

Preti Taneja, your book tells of national as well as familial tragedy. Could you please tell us more about how your novel relates Lear's divisions to India's Partition and the ongoing fallout?

PRETI TANEJA

The superstructure of the novel is a direct engagement with Partition, and the book references the accession of the Maharajas, who acceded and so became kings without kingdoms to form the nation, 'India'. It also tracks the division of the kingdom as the subcontinent and the superimposing of capitalism over socialism over a feudalism that has never left. The ongoing conflict in Kashmir is the setting for the novel's endgame. The place of women in the play speaks directly to the way women are treated and perceived in Hindu Indian society – as widows, whores or saints. Dowry, cultural obedience, the use of shame as a weapon of gender control, remain huge social issues for South Asian society.

Q3

I have a specific question for Bornila Chatterjee. The film opens with a very dramatic and startling sequence, early in the film, focusing on the trash mountain. Can you tell us a little more about how you came to the trash mountain and how it represents Delhi for you? What were the links between the play and the adaptation?

BORNILA CHATTERJEE

The film is, or *Titus* is, really about power – a matriarch clashing with a patriarch and how they arrive at this power battle through greed. In basic, simplistic terms – 'trash' is the by-product of greed, and we thought that it would be interesting if the way into this very powerful world of money, if your first way in (as audience) was through that by-product of trash and garbage and the vultures flying overhead. The way I read the text, I'd just be highlighting words like, 'OK, we have to figure out a way to incorporate this somehow'. In

Titus Andronicus, while being very much a play about war, power and battle, Shakespeare uses so many natural allegories, keeps talking about this hole, and snakes, and goats, leaves, water. We thought that that would be a really interesting way to lead you into Delhi's elite.

Q4
Preti Taneja, your work is set in modern-day India and celebrates its particularities in forensic detail, including highlighting a prevailing toxic patriarchy that robs others of agency. Given this setting, could you explain why you chose to make a character gay or have a daughter die at her father's hands?

PRETI TANEJA
The question answers itself.

Q5
A question for all our speakers: what kind of an audience do you visualize? Because you're doing it for a particular audience. What do you think when you translate? Do you want it to be accessible?

SREEDEVI NAIR
When one translates, one usually has a certain audience in mind. When we translate for children, for academics, for common readers, we adopt different approaches. Certain decisions the translators take during the process of translation. Sometimes, when one translates even a writer like Shakespeare, one decides to translate into the modern idiom. Shakespeare, of course, wrote in the sixteenth century – so we can translate his plays into the language that existed at that time but we might also want to translate into the modern language as the translation is meant for the present-day readers. One of my Shakespeare translations is an adaptation for children where I use very simple language and simplify all the complexities in the play to the greatest extent possible. In the other two Shakespeare translations that I did, I have tried to be as close to the original as possible and have retained all the textual peculiarities, but the language used is present-day Malayalam. When I translate, I usually make decisions based on what I think will be the preferences of my target readers.

ANNETTE LEDAY

I generally don't think beforehand about the audience. I think what is more important is what you have and want to do and what you want to say. But working with a very spectacular form, as *kathakali* is, it's going to be spectacular, whatever we do with it. About the audience, we always *hope* that there will be a good audience, that's all.

BORNILA CHATTERJEE

With our film, since it was based on *Titus Andronicus*, we went into it assuming that most people watching the film would probably not be familiar with the play. To that end, it was about making the most accessible version of it possible.

SANGEETA DATTA

Our script was primarily in English, and I wasn't really worried about which audience we would cut off, or which audience we would make this accessible to. We were also quite sure that the film would travel globally and there would be a market for it both in the West as well as in India. I think people are concentrating much more on images, which would create that sort of transportability for us. I just like to go back to the long walk that Lear takes in the storm and what we have on the heath in the actual text over here becomes a sort of surreal walkthrough night-time London, and at one point that geographical space transports to Calcutta, to the Victoria Memorial, evoking British colonial history.

MARK THORNTON BURNETT

Thank you so much to our speakers participating today in this round table. It's been incisive, revelatory and fascinating to hear these insights into the work of art, the processes that lie behind the creation of the work of art and the business of Shakespearean adaptation.

Notes

1   The adaptation can be accessed at: http://sreedeviknair.net/wp-content/uploads/2020/02/The-Stars-Still-Shine-on-Desdemona.pdf (accessed 21 April 2021).

2 For a comparable discussion, see Mark Thornton Burnett and Jyotsna G. Singh's chapter in this volume.
3 The company website is available at: http://annette.leday.cie.free.fr/Keli/History.html (accessed 30 May 2021).

References

Chokher Bhali: A Passion Play (2003), [Film] Dir. Rituparno Ghosh, India: SVF Entertainment.

The Hungry (2017), [Film] Dir. Bornila Chatterjee, India/UK: Cinestaan/Film London.

In Search of Durga (2001), [Documentary] Dir. Sangeeta Datta, UK/India: Stormglass Productions.

The Last Lear (2007), [Film] Dir. Rituparno Ghosh, India: Planman Motion Pictures.

Life Goes On (2009), [Film] Dir. Sangeeta Datta, UK/India: Stormglass Productions.

Nair, S. (2019), *The Stars Still Shine on Desdemona*, Thiruvananthapuram: Samyukta Research Foundation.

Noukadubi (2011), [Film] Dir. Rituparno Ghosh, India: Blue Water Pictures/Mukta Arts.

Raincoat (2004), [Film] Dir. Rituparno Ghosh, India: Shree Venkatesh Films.

Strir Patra – The Wife's Letter (2008), [Film/Dance] Dir. Sangeeta Datta, UK/India: Dance UK/Stormglass Productions.

Taneja, P. (2017), *We That Are Young*, Norwich: Galley Beggar Press.

The Way I See It (2000), [Documentary] Dir. Sangeeta Datta, UK/India: Stormglass Productions.

A SELECTION OF SHAKESPEARE TRANSLATIONS/ADAPTATIONS FROM THE BRITISH LIBRARY NORTH INDIAN LANGUAGES COLLECTION

Priyanka Basu and Arani Ilankuberan

Language	Title	Translated from	Author/Translator	Year	Place
Assamese	*Chandrabali Natak* [14135.f.3.(5.)]	As You Like It	Durgeshwar Sharma	1910	Jorhat
Assamese	*Shakespeare Nataker Galpo* [SAC.1994.a.2542]	Lambs' Tales from Shakespeare	Navakanta Barua	1980	Guwahati
Assamese	*Macbeth* [Ass.B.36]	Macbeth	Devananda Bharati	1924	Golaghat

Language	Title	Translated from	Author/Translator	Year	Place
Assamese	*Desdemona* (extract only) [Ass.B.98]	*Othello*	Hitesvara Barbabaruva	1918	Jorhat
Assamese	*Bhenicara Saoda* [14135.f.10(6)]	*The Merchant of Venice*	Jnanadabhirama Baruva	1926	Guwahati
Bengali	*Jabanara* [VT2716]	*A Midsummer Night's Dream*	Satisachandra Chattopadhyaya	1904	Calcutta
Bengali	*Anangaragini* [14131.a.40.(8.)]	*As You Like It*	Annadaprasad Basu	1897	Calcutta
Bengali	*Sushila-Birsingha* [VT 947(e)]	*Cymbeline*	Satyendranath Thakur	1867	Calcutta
Bengali	*Amara Simha* [VT1374]	*Hamlet*	Pramathanata Vasu	1874	Calcutta
Bengali	*Chandranath* [14131.a.35]	*Hamlet*	Siddheswar Gupta	1894	Calcutta
Bengali	*Hamlet* [14131.a.36.(1.)]	*Hamlet*	Chandiprasada Ghosha	1894	Calcutta
Bengali	*Hyamlet* [14131.aaa.26.]	*Hamlet*	Manomohan Ray	1918	Calcutta
Bengali	*Hyamlet da Prins apha Garanhata* [LP.31.a.308]	*Hamlet*	Bratya Basu	2007	Calcutta

Language	Title	Translated from	Author/Translator	Year	Place
Bengali	*Julius Caesar* [14131.a.46]	*Julius Caesar*	Jyotindranath Thakur	1907	Calcutta
Bengali	*Lear* [14131.aa.3.(1)]	*King Lear*	Yatindramohana Ghosha	1902	Calcutta
Bengali	*Tales from Shakespeare* [VT 1623(b)]	*Lambs' Tales from Shakespeare*	Muktaram Bidyabagish	1852	Calcutta
Bengali	*Lambs' Tales from Shakespeare* [14127.c.1]	*Lambs' Tales from Shakespeare*	Edward Röer	1853	Calcutta
Bengali	*Sekspiyarer Galpa* [14128.a.53]	*Lambs' Tales from Shakespeare*	Sisira Kumara Niyogi	1936	Calcutta
Bengali	*Rudrapala nataka* [VT1323]	*Macbeth*	Haralala Raya	1874	Calcutta
Bengali	*Macbeth* [VT1423]	*Macbeth*	Tarakanatha Mukhopadhyaya	1875	Barahanagar
Bengali	*Macbeth* [14131.aa.4.(1)]	*Macbeth*	Girishchandra Ghosha	1900	Calcutta
Bengali	*Macbeth* (3rd edn) [14131.ccc.45]	*Macbeth*	Nirendranatha Raya	1956	Calcutta
Bengali	*Vinimaya* [VT2941]	*Measure for Measure*	Virendranatha Raya	1909	Calcutta

Language	Title	Translated from	Author/Translator	Year	Place
Bengali	Bhima Simha [VT1322]	Othello	Tarinicharana Pala	1875	Calcutta
Bengali	Othello [14131.a.34]	Othello	Kaliprasanna Chattopadhyay	1894	Calcutta
Bengali	Rudrasena [VT2798]	Othello	Nanilala Vandyopadhyaya	1905	Calcutta
Bengali	Othelo [14131.bb.5.(3.)]	Othello	Debendranath Basu	1919	Calcutta
Bengali	Romeo Ebong Julieter Monohor Upakhyan [14127.d.2.(1)]	Romeo and Juliet (Lambs' Tales from Shakespeare)	Gurudasa Hajra	1848	Calcutta
Bengali	Charumukh-Chittahara Natok [14131.b.12.(1)]	Romeo and Juliet	Harachandra Ghosha	1864	Calcutta
Bengali	Ajaysingh Bilasbati Natok [VT1740]	Romeo and Juliet	Yogendranarayan Das Ghosh	1878	Calcutta
Bengali	Romeo-Juliet [14131.a.36.(2)]	Romeo and Juliet	Hemachandra Bandopadhyaya	1895	Calcutta
Bengali	Romeo and Juliet [279.41.d.17]	Romeo and Juliet	Hemachandra Bandyopadhyaya	1900	Calcutta
Bengali	Shekspiyar [14131.b.24.]	Shakespeare's plays	Haranchandra Rakshit	1896–1900	Calcutta

Language	Title	Translated from	Author/Translator	Year	Place
Bengali	*Shekspiyar* [14131.b.26.]	Shakespeare's plays	Haranchandra Rakshit	1900–1902	Calcutta
Bengali	*Bhramakautuka* [VT930]	The Comedy of Errors	Venimadhava Ghosha	1873	Calcutta
Bengali	*Bhrantavilasa* (2nd edn) [VT1418]	The Comedy of Errors	Isvarachandra Vidyasagara	1875	Calcutta
Bengali	*Bhanumati Chittavilasa Nataka* [279.42.b.54]	The Merchant of Venice	Harachandra Ghosha	1853	Calcutta
Bengali	*Suralata Natok* [VT1319]	The Merchant of Venice	Pyarilala Mukhopadhyay	1877	Calcutta
Bengali	*Saodagar* [VT3550]	The Merchant of Venice	Bhupendranatha Vandyopadhyaya	1915	Calcutta
Bengali	*Lucretia* [14129.a.15.(1.)]	The Rape of Lucrece	Kaliprasanna Vandopadhyay	1880	Calcutta
Bengali	*Nalinivasanta* [279.41.d.17]	The Tempest	Hemachandra Bandyopadhyaya	1900	Calcutta
Bengali	*Jhanjha* [VT 3285(b)]	The Tempest	Nagendraprasad Sarbbadhikari	1913	Calcutta
Bengali	*Madanamanjari* [VT1622]	The Winter's Tale	Anonymous	1876	Calcutta

Language	Title	Translated from	Author/Translator	Year	Place
Bengali	*Rani Tamalini* [VT 3370(d)]	The Winter's Tale	Dhanadacharan Mitra	1914	Calcutta
Bengali	*Sushila-Chandraketu* [VT 963(l)]	Twelfth Night	Kantichandra Bidyaratna	1872	Calcutta
Gujarati	*Vaidyakarya* [14148.cc.12.]	All's Well That Ends Well	Narayan Hemchandra	1895	Ahmedabad
Gujarati	*Ramanasundari* [14148.c.38.(2.)]	Cymbeline	Gopalji Kalyanji Delvarakar	1895	Ahmedabad
Gujarati	*Suryakala* [14148.cc.7.]	Hamlet	Gopaldas Premchand Shah	1895	Ahmedabad
Gujarati	*Hum ja Sijhara, ne hum ja Brutas chum! vanaveli chandamam* [YP.2005.a.870]	Julius Caesar	Hasmukh Baradi	2004	Ahmedabad
Gujarati	*Selected Tales (Lamb)* [14148.a.10]	Lambs' Tales from Shakespeare	Ranchhodbhai Udayarama (Runchodebhai Ooderam)	1867	Ahmadabad
Gujarati	*Measure for Measure* [14148.c.53]	Measure for Measure	Narbheshankar Pranjivan Dave	1906	Bhavnagar

Language	Title	Translated from	Author/Translator	Year	Place
Gujarati	*Romeo and Juliet* [VT2511]	*Romeo and Juliet*	Dosabhai Framji Randhelia 'Delta'	1876	Bombay
Gujarati	*Shekspir Natak Khanda* [14148.b.19.]	*The Comedy of Errors; Hamlet*	Nanabhai Rustamji Ranina	1865	Bombay
Gujarati	*Stri Nyayakala* [14148.c.45]	*The Merchant of Venice*	Narsilal Vanamalidas	1893	Bombay
Hindi	*Shreeman Shakespeare Krit As You Like It* [14158.aa.1]	*As You Like It*	Pandit Gopinath of Jaipur	1897	Bombay
Hindi	*Kusha Kamini* [14157.aa.4.(3.)]	*As You Like It*	Prausaraswathi Priyah	1915	Jabalpur
Hindi	*Apni apni ruche* [14158.a.27.(7.)]	*As You Like It*	Lala Sitaram (Bhupa)	1917	Allahabad
Hindi	*Jaisa Tumа Caho* [Hin B 14575]	*As You Like It*	Rangey Raghav	1962	Delhi
Hindi	*Shakespeare Bhasha Cymbeline* [14158.aaa.7.(4.)]	*Cymbeline*	Lala Sita Ram	1925	Allahabad
Hindi	*Denmark ka raja-kumara Hamlet* [14158.a.25(4)]	*Hamlet*	Lala Sita Ram	1915	Allahabad

Language	Title	Translated from	Author/Translator	Year	Place
Hindi	Khun-I na-haqq nataka [14158.a.21(5)]	Hamlet	D. P. Surat (based on Mahdi Hasan Khan's Urdu)	1915	Benares
Hindi	Hamlet [Hin B 6012]	Hamlet	Sitarama	1927	Allahabad
Hindi	Hemlet [14158.b.36]	Hamlet	Nanak-chand Bhanot	1937	Lahore
Hindi	Haimaleta [Hin B 14581]	Hamlet	Rangey Raghav	1957	Delhi
Hindi	Julius Caesar [Hin B 4934]	Julius Caesar	Sitarama	1925	Allahabad
Hindi	Juliyasa Sizara [Hin B 14579]	Julius Caesar	Rangey Raghav	1961	Delhi
Hindi	Raja Henari panjam [Hin B 8245]	Henry V	Sitarama	1930	Allahabad
Hindi	Said-I bavis [14158.aaa.8(3)]	King John	Avadhesa-Pati Varma 'Khush-dil'	1923	Benares
Hindi	Snehapariksha [14158.a.18]	King Lear	Pandit Badrinarayan	1903	Bombay
Hindi	Kaliyuga Natak [Hin.D.663]	King Lear	Ananda Prasad Khatri	1912	Kashi

Language	Title	Translated from	Author/Translator	Year	Place
Hindi	Raja Lear [14158.a.25(5)]	King Lear	Lala Sita Ram	1915	Allahabad
Hindi	King Lear [Hin B 4941]	King Lear	Sitarama	1925	Allahabad
Hindi	Raja Richard dvitiya [14158.a.25(6)]	King Richard II	Lala Sita Ram	1915	Allahabad
Hindi	Shakespeare katha-gatha [279.51.a.3]	Lambs' Tales from Shakespeare	Jayavijaya Narayana Simha Sharma	1912	Allahabad
Hindi	Nishphal Prem [Hin B 14578]	Love's Labour Lost	Rangey Raghav	1958	Delhi
Hindi	Macbeth (includes 5 plates) [14158.aaa.14(8)]	Macbeth	Sitarama	1926	Allahabad
Hindi	Macbeth ka Padyanuvaad [Hin B 13524]	Macbeth	Baccan	1957	Delhi
Hindi	Maikbetha [Hin B 14577]	Macbeth	Rangey Raghav	1962	Delhi
Hindi	Bagula-bhagat [14158.a.25(1)]	Measure for Measure	Sitarama	1915	Allahabad
Hindi	Measure for Measure [Hin B 5914]	Measure for Measure	Lala Sitarama	1923	Allahabad

Language	Title	Translated from	Author/Translator	Year	Place
Hindi	*Manmohan ka jal* [14158.a.25(3)]	*Much Ado About Nothing*	Lala Sitarama	1915	Allahabad
Hindi	*Much Ado About Nothing* [14158.aaa.7(3)]	*Much Ado About Nothing*	Lala Sitarama	1923	Allahabad
Hindi	*Til ka Tara* [Hin B 14576]	*Much Ado About Nothing*	Rangey Raghav	1960	Delhi
Hindi	*Othello* (Translated from a Bengali version) [14158.a.8.(2)]	*Othello*	Gadadhar Sinha	1894	Benares
Hindi	*Othello ya Venisaka Mura* [14158.a.28.]	*Othello*	Pandit Gobind Prasad Ghildayal	1902	Moradabad
Hindi	*Othello* [14158.a.28]	*Othello*	Pandit Gobind Prasad Ghildial	1916	Moradabad
Hindi	*Othello* [14158.aaa.7(5)]	*Othello*	Lala Sitarama	1926	Allahabad
Hindi	*Athelo* [Hin B 14574]	*Othello*	Rangey Raghav	1962	Delhi
Hindi	*Honabar* [Hin B 298]	*Pericles, Prince of Tyre*	B. Govinda Dasa	1915	Jubbulpore

Language	Title	Translated from	Author/Translator	Year	Place
Hindi	*Premlila* [14158.aa.3]	*Romeo and Juliet*	Pandit Gopinath	1898	Benares
Hindi	*Surendra-Sundari* [14157.aa.2(1)]	*Romeo and Juliet*	Govinda Dasa	1914	Jubbulpore
Hindi	*Prema-kasauti* [14158.df.31(i)]	*Romeo and Juliet*	Lala Sita Ram	1931	Allahabad
Hindi	*Romiyo Juliyata* [Hin B 14580]	*Romeo and Juliet*	Rangey Raghav	1962	Delhi
Hindi	*Bhramjalaka Natak* [14158.b.3.]	*The Comedy of Errors*	Ratna Chanda	1879	Allahabad
Hindi	*Bhul-bhulaiya* [14158.a.25(7)]	*The Comedy of Errors*	Lala Sitarama	1915	Allahabad
Hindi	*Gorakhdhanda* [14158.a.34.(3.)]	*The Comedy of Errors*	Anonymous	1917	Kashi
Hindi	*Bhulbhulaiya: Dhokhbeki Tatti* [Hin.B.2506]	*The Comedy of Errors*	Munshi Brajmohanlal	1920	Calcutta
Hindi	*Bhulbhulaiya* [Hin.B.2780]	*The Comedy of Errors*	Bhupa (Sitaram)	1921	Prayaga
Hindi	*Bhul-bhulaiyan* [14158.a.47(3)]	*The Comedy of Errors*	Mahdi Hasan Khan	1935	Bareilly

Language	Title	Translated from	Author/Translator	Year	Place
Hindi	Bhulabhulaiyam [Hin B 14573]	The Comedy of Errors	Rangey Raghav	1958	Delhi
Hindi	Venice Nagar Ka Vyapari [14158.b.8]	The Merchant of Venice	Arya (Preface in English by Sir Edwin Arnold)	1888	Benares
Hindi	Venis Ka Vyapari [VT2899]	The Merchant of Venice	Khemaraja Srikrishnadasa	1904	Bombay
Hindi	Ek Aurat Ki Wakalat [14158.aa.10]	The Merchant of Venice	Krishna Hasrat	1908	Benares
Hindi	Dil-farosh [14158.a.63(2)]	The Merchant of Venice	Mahdi Hasan Khan	1936	Bareilly
Hindi	Jangal men mangala [14158.a.25(2)]	The Tempest	Lala Sitarama	1915	Allahabad
Hindi	Tempest [14158.aaa.7(2)]	The Tempest	Lala Sitarama	1923	Allahabad
Hindi	Pracanda vata: Seksapiyara krta tempesta ka anuvada [YP.2004.a.7590]	The Tempest	Vinoda Candra Pandeya	2004	Delhi
Hindi	Vyartha sandeha [14157.a.33(5)]	The Winter's Tale	Govinda Dasa	1916	Jubbulpore

Language	Title	Translated from	Author/Translator	Year	Place
Hindustani	*Jam i Ulfat* [14112.bb.8.(3)]	*A Midsummer Night's Dream*	Muhammad Azhar Ali (Kakorawi)	1903	Gorakhpur
Hindustani	*Shekspiyar Dilpazir* [14112.a.44.(3.)]	*As You Like It*	Charan Das Bakshi	1901	Lahore
Hindustani	*Cymbeline* [14112.bb.11]	*Cymbeline*	Muhammad Abd-Al Aziz	1902	Bareilly
Hindustani	*Ainah-yi-Ismat* [14112.bb.21.(2.)]	*Cymbeline*	Dinanath Hafizabadi	1914	Lahore
Hindustani	*Jahangir* [14112.bb.6.(1)]	*Hamlet*	Umrao Ali	1895	Lahore
Hindustani	*Khuni Nahakk* [14112.aa.14.(1)]	*Hamlet*	Mahdi Hasan Khan, Lakhnavi (Ahsan)	1901	Lahore
Hindustani	*Khuni Nahakk* (another edition) [14112.bb.6.(7)]	*Hamlet*	Mahdi Hasan Khan, Lakhnavi (Ahsan)	1902	Lahore
Hindustani	*Hamlet* [14112.aa.15]	*Hamlet*	Muhammad Afzal Khan (Hamdam)	1902	Ludhiana
Hindustani	*Waki'ab i Jahangir i Nashad* [14112.bb.10.(2)]	*Hamlet*	Mirza Nazir Beg, Akbarbadi	1904	Agra
Hindustani	*Gulzar-e-Shekspir* [14112.aa.6]	*Lambs' Tales from Shakespeare*	Tejaram	1899	Lahore

Language	Title	Translated from	Author/Translator	Year	Place
Hindustani	*Yaaron ki mehnat barbad* [14112.bb.9.(1)]	*Love's Labour's Lost*	Muhammad Sulaiman	1899	Patna
Hindustani	*Ja'far* [14112.bb.5.(2.)]	*Othello*	Munshi Ahmad Husain Khan	1895	Lahore
Hindustani	*Bazm i Fani* [14112.bb.12.(1)]	*Romeo and Juliet*	Agha Muhammad Shah (Hashr)	1900	Delhi
Hindustani	*Gulnar Firoz* [14112.bb.6.(6)]	*Romeo and Juliet*	Mahdi Hasan Khan, Lakhnavi (Ahsan)	1902	Lahore
Hindustani	*Ishq i Firoz-lika o Gulnar Siyar* [14112.bb.10.(3)]	*Romeo and Juliet*	Mirza Nazir Beg, Akbarbadi	1905	Agra
Hindustani	*Bhulbhulaiyan* [14112.bb.6.(2)]	*The Comedy of Errors*	Firoz Shah Khan	1896	Moradabad
Hindustani	*Bhulbhulaiyan* [14112.aa.14.(2)]	*The Comedy of Errors*	Lala Sitaram	1906	Moradabad
Hindustani	*Bhul Bhulaiyan* [14112.bb.7.(7.)]	*The Comedy of Errors*	Abd Al-Karun (Kalum)	1912	Ahmedabad
Hindustani	*Gorakh Dhanda* [14112.bb.15.(5.)]	*The Comedy of Errors*	Narayan Prasad (Betale)	1913	Amritsar
Hindustani	*Bhul Bhulaiyon Natak* [14112.bb.26.(2.)]	*The Comedy of Errors*	Munshi Jalal Ahmad (Shad)	1916	Benares

Language	Title	Translated from	Author/Translator	Year	Place
Hindustani	*Chand Shah i Sud Khwar* [14112.bb.5.(1)]	*The Merchant of Venice*	Anonymous	1895	Lahore
Hindustani	*Venis ka Saudagar* [14112.bb.6.(5)]	*The Merchant of Venice*	Saiyyad Ashik Husain	1898	Lahore
Hindustani	*Fardenend O Miranda* [14112.bb.6.(3)]	*The Tempest*	Muhammad Shafi Al-Din Khan, Moradabadi	1896	Moradabad
Hindustani	*Tir i Nigab* [14112.bb.6.(4)]	*The Tempest*	Muhammad Shafi Al-Din Khan, Moradabadi	1897	Moradabad
Hindustani	*Murid i Shakk* [14112.bb.12.(3)]	*The Winter's Tale*	Agha Muhammad Shah (Hashr)	1900	Delhi
Konkani	*Shakspearachea Khellanchi* [Mar B 1068]	*Lambs' Tales from Shakespeare*	Xannai. W. R. Varde Valavilkar	1912	Bombay
Konkani	*Romeo anim Juliet* [Mar B 1133]	*Romeo and Juliet*	J. M. Pinto	1915	Bombay
Konkani	*Romeo ani Juliet* [Mar B 1132]	*Romeo and Juliet*	J. Caetano Francisco D'Souza	1917	Bombay
Konkani	*Twelfth Night* [14140.e.57]	*Twelfth Night*	F. X. Douglas	1911	Bombay

Language	Title	Translated from	Author/Translator	Year	Place
Marathi	*Sangita premamakaranda nataka* [279.55.b.24]	A Midsummer Night's Dream	Ananta Narayana Ukidve	1904	Pune
Marathi	*Sangit Priyaradhana Natak* [14140.e.66.]	All's Well That Ends Well	Vasudev Sadasiv Patwardhan	1912	Pune
Marathi	*Sringaramanjari* [14140.e.24.(2.)]	Antony and Cleopatra	Ananta Vaman Barve	1906	Amaravati
Marathi	*Sangita premagumpha* [279.56.c.38]	As You Like It	Vasudeva Sadasiva Patavardhana	1908	Pune
Marathi	*Tara nataka* [279.55.a.35]	Cymbeline	Vishnu Moresvara Mahajani	1879	Bombay
Marathi	*Tara nataka* [VT2266]	Cymbeline	Vishnu Moresvara Mahajani	1888	Akola
Marathi	*Raja Raghunath Rav* [14140.e.45]	Henry VIII	H. B. Atre	1904	Pune
Marathi	*Vijaya Simha* [VT2267]	Julius Caesar	Kasinatha Govinda Natu	1872	Pune
Marathi	*Bandachen Prayaschitta* [279.58.I.64]	Henry IV	Narayan Gangadhara Limaye	1915	Bombay
Marathi	*Panchama Henry charita* [279.55.c.18]	Henry V	Khanderava Bhikaji Belsare	1911	Bombay

Language	Title	Translated from	Author/Translator	Year	Place
Marathi	*Raja Raghunatharava* [279.58.e.38]	*Henry VIII*	Hanamanta Bapurava Are	1904	Pune
Marathi	*Atipidacharita nataka* (2nd edn) [279.55.c.30]	*King Lear*	Sankara Moro Ranade	1881	Pune
Marathi	*Dhuvanchi paricxa* [Mar B 1068]	*King Lear*	Xannai / W. R. Varde Valavlikar	1912	Bombay
Marathi	*Samansasan* [14140.e.55]	*Measure for Measure*	Anonymous	1910	Pune
Marathi	*Sumativijaya* [Mar D 93]	*Measure for Measure*	Hari Narayana Apte	1910	Pune
Marathi	*Othello* [14140.e.10.]	*Othello*	Rav Saheb Mahadev Govind Shastri Kolhatkar	1867	Bombay
Marathi	*Jhunjarava nataka* [14140. e. 22.]	*Othello*	Govinda Ballala Deval	1890	Bombay
Marathi	*Gore Boilecho callo ghore* [Mar B 1068]	*Othello*	Xannai / W. R. Varde Valavlikar	1912	Bombay
Marathi	*Jayaji Rav Natak* [14140.e.23]	*Richard III*	Bhaskar Ramchandra Nanal	1891	Bombay

Language	Title	Translated from	Author/Translator	Year	Place
Marathi	*Sangit Shalini Natak* [14140.e.43]	Romeo and Juliet	Keshav Vinayak Karmakar	1901	Bombay
Marathi	*Premacha Kalas* [14140.e.50]	Romeo and Juliet	Khanderav Bhikaji Belsare	1908	Pune
Marathi	*Sangit Taravilas Natak* [14140.e.52]	Romeo and Juliet	Dattatreya Ananta Keskar	1908	Pune
Marathi	*Mhatarya vyaparyachi goshta* (2nd edn) [VT2352]	The Comedy of Errors	Ramachandra Vinayaka Oka	1875	Ahmadnagar
Marathi	*Comedy of Errors* [Mar D 290]	The Comedy of Errors	Atmarama Vinayaka Patkar	1876	Pune
Marathi	*Kamedi apha erarsa athava bhrantikrita chamatkar* [14140.f.18.(2.)]	The Comedy of Errors	Anonymous	1878	Akola
Marathi	*Strinyayachaturya* [VT2241]	The Merchant of Venice	Atmarama Vinayaka Patkar	1871	Pune
Marathi	*Mohanechi Angathi* [14140.e.53]	The Merchant of Venice	D. G. Limaye	1909	Khanapur
Marathi	*Venice Nagarcha Vyapari* [14140.e.56]	The Merchant of Venice	Khanderav Bhikaji Belsare	1910	Pune
Marathi	*Chaturgadchya Vinodi Striya* [14140.e.46]	The Merry Wives of Windsor	Panduranga Gangadhar Limaye	1905	Bombay

Language	Title	Translated from	Author/Translator	Year	Place
Marathi	Seras savva ser [VT2277]	The Taming of the Shrew from Lambs' Tales from Shakespeare	Sakharama Parasurama Pandita	1867	Bombay
Marathi	Seras savva ser (2nd edn) [VT2263]	The Taming of the Shrew from Lambs' Tales from Shakespeare	Sakharama Parasurama Pandita	1871	Bombay
Marathi	Tratika Natak [14140.f.33]	The Taming of the Shrew	Vasudev Balkrishna Kelkar	1892	Pune
Marathi	Tratika Natak (2nd edn) [14140.e.28.]	The Taming of the Shrew	Vasudev Balkrishna Kelkar	1894	Pune
Marathi	Tempest [279.58.e.39]	The Tempest	Nilakantha Janardana Kirtane	1875	Bombay
Marathi	Sangit Samasyasambhram Natak [14140.e.30]	The Winter's Tale	Gajanan Chintaman Deva	1895	Pune
Marathi	Premavinoda [Mar B 943]	Twelfth Night	Ananta Viththala Apte	1919	Bombay

Language	Title	Translated from	Author/Translator	Year	Place
Marathi	*Striyanche netrakataksha* [VT2265]	The Two Gentlemen of Verona from Lambs' Tales from Shakespeare	Vinayakarava Govinda Limaye	1886	Bombay
Oriya	*Hamlet* [SAC1986a1543]	Hamlet	Akshay Kumar Bandopadhyay	1934	Cuttack
Oriya	*Premik Premika* [14121.d.30(1)]	Romeo and Juliet	Jagannath Ballabh Ghosh	1908	Cuttack
Punjabi	*Dukhi Raja* [Panj B 985]	King Lear	Balvant Singh	1927	Lahore
Punjabi	*Lal Padsah* [Panj B 1308]	King Lear	Narain Singh	1931	Multan
Punjabi	*Uthelo* [14162.gg.29.]	Othello	Bhai Jivan Singh (Jivan Singh Sevak)	1911	Amritsar
Punjabi	*Heer Ranjha* [07030103 WAV audio recording]	Romeo and Juliet	Banarsidas Jain	1926	Berlin
Rajasthani	*Seksapiyara ki Kahaniyam* [SAC.1986.a.6061]	Lambs' Tales from Shakespeare	Govinda Lala Mathura	1980	Jodhpur
Sanskrit	*Vasantikaswapnam* [14080c.34]	A Midsummer Night's Dream	R. Krishnamachari	1892	Kumbhakonam

Language	Title	Translated from	Author/Translator	Year	Place
Sanskrit	*Yatha te Rochate* [SAC.1986.a.21163]	As You Like It	Ananta Tripathi Sharma	1979	Brahmapuram
Sanskrit	*Shakespeare Natak Katha Chatuskam* [14076.a.123(2)]	Four plays of Shakespeare	Kaudinya Venkateshwara Subramanhya Shastri	1968	Palghat
Sanskrit	*Dinkararajkumar-Hemlekha* [San D 5217]	Hamlet	Sukhamoy Mukherjee	1971	Delhi
Sanskrit	*Chandrasenah Durgadeshasya Yuvaraj* [YP.2008.a.751]	Hamlet	S. D. Joshi and Vignahari Rao	1980	Pune
Sindhi	*Satyani a ji Satya* [Sind.B.342]	Cymbeline	Thakurdasu Bhojraju Hiranandani	1917	Karachi
Sindhi	*Haimletu* [Sind.B.775]	Hamlet	Jethumalu Parsramu Gulrajani	1922	Hyderabad, Sindh
Sindhi	*Shab Iliya* [14164.e.3]	King Lear	Mirza Qalic Beg	1901	Hyderabad, Sindh
Sindhi	*Prem ji Putli* [Sind.B.968]	Selected plays	Nanakramu Dharamdasu Mirchandani	1927	Hyderabad, Sindh
Sindhi	*Husna ain Dildaru* [14164.e.5(1)]	The Merchant of Venice	Mirza Qalic Beg	1897	Hyderabad, Sindh

Language	Title	Translated from	Author/Translator	Year	Place
Sindhi	Shuma ji Shaitanu: ya istri vidya balu [14164.aaa.27(2)]	The Merchant of Venice	Bulchandu Parsramu Punvani	1911	Hyderabad, Sindh
Sindhi	Dingi a zala khe sidho karanu [Sind.B.171]	The Taming of the Shrew	Anonymous	1921	Sakhar
Sindhi	Tufan [Sind.B.1002]	The Tempest	Jethumalu Parsramu Gulraj	1927	Hyderabad, Sindh
Urdu	Qabr-i-Ishq [SAC.1991.a.950]	Antony and Cleopatra	Shahnulhaq Haqqi	1984	Karachi
Urdu	Shahr Se Dur [SAC.1986.a.860]	As You Like It	Akhtar Bastvi	1972	Lucknow
Urdu	Jahangir [VT342]	Hamlet	Muhammad Imtiyaz 'Ali'	1888	Lucknow
Urdu	Songs from Khun-I na-haqq [14112.bb.12(2)]	Hamlet	Mahdi Hasan Khan 'Ahsan'	1900	Delhi
Urdu	Songs from Khun-I na-haqq [14112.a.44(4)]	Hamlet	Mahdi Hasan Khan 'Ahsan'	1901	Amritsar
Urdu	Shakespeare Urdu [14112.a.43]	King Lear	Lala Sitaram	1893	Lucknow

Language	Title	Translated from	Author/Translator	Year	Place
Urdu	*King Li'ar* [SAC.1986.a.27630]	*King Lear*	Majnun Gorakhpuri	1963	New Delhi
Urdu	*Takhliqat-i-Shakspiyar* [SAC.1993.a.1267]	*Lambs' Tales from Shakespeare*	Saqib Razmi	1992	Lahore
Urdu	*Athelo* [SAC.1986.a.26527]	*Othello*	Sajjad Zahir	1966	New Delhi
Urdu	*Ma'shuqah-yi Farang* [306.26.a.17]	*Romeo and Juliet*	Jvalaprasada	1896	Lucknow
Urdu	*Songs from Gulnar Firoz* [14112.a.44(5)]	*Romeo and Juliet*	Mahdi Hasan Khan 'Ahsan'	1901	Amritsar
Urdu	*Bhulbhulayyan* [14112.aa.19.]	*The Comedy of Errors*	Lala Sita Ram	1907	Lucknow

Source: Priyanka Basu and Arani Ilankuberan, compiled using the British Library catalogues

INDEX

Page numbers in italics are illustrations and those followed by n and t are notes and tables respectively

actresses 229–42
  English 23–9
  Indian 29–32
adda (meeting point) 34
Agarkar, *Vikar Vilasta* 31
Ajay-Atul, *Sairat* (dir. Nagraj Manjule, 2016) 162
Akhtar, Javed 253
All India Women's Conference 35
Allana, Amal 36–9
All's Well That Ends Well, children's 245
Amateur Dramatic Clubs 28–9
Ambedkar, B. R. 35, 153, 155
Ambikapathy (dir. Ellis R. Dungan, 1937) 149
Ambikapathy (dir. P. Neelakantan, 1957) 149
Andaman Islands 58
Anderson, Mrs 27
androgyny 74–5
Anglophilia 226, 234, 236
Antony and Cleopatra, Kannaki (dir. Jayaraj, 2002) 113
Arshinagar (dir. Aparna Sen, 2015) 151, 187–205
  'Aami Aami Kore Barai' 199
  'Bari'r Kacche Arshi Nagar' 198–9
  'Kala Paisa Wala' 197, 199

As You Like It
  Aajker Shahjahan 247
  Sharmistha 29
  St Stephen's College, Delhi 231
Asan, Padmanabhan Nair 244–5
Ashoka University 226
Asiatic Journal 27
Auddy, Vaishnav Charan 27

Babri Masjid, 1992 destruction of 198–9
Bahl, Sonia 208
Bahuguna, Urvashi 237–8
Bai, Mehar 30
Bakshi, Kaustav 193
Bandyopadhyay, Tarashankar, *Saptapadi* 47–50
Banerjee, Mamata 146
Bannerjee, Nobin Chandra 44–5
Barbosa, Duarte 119
'Bard in Bombay: Shakespeare in Indian Cinema' conference 2015 182n4
Bardolatry 69–70
Baroda 35
Baroda University 36
Bartholomeusz, Dennis, *India's Shakespeare: Translation, Interpretation and Performance* 79
Basak, Göksel 181

INDEX

Basak, Sohini 237–8
Bassnett, Susan 95
Basu, Debendranath, adaptation of *Othello* 46
Baul music 198–9
Begum, Latifa 30
Bengal
    Mehta, Dr Kumundini Arvind 33, 34
    Othello 45–7
Bengal Partition 248
Bengal Theatre 29
Bengalee 45
Bengali
    adaptations 29–30, 162, 253, 256, 263–7
    femininity 131–48
    studies 69–70
    theatre 85, 225–6
    translations 67–9
    writers 187–8
Bengaliness 187–205
bhadramahila (new urban gentlewoman) 45–7, 50, 59
Bhardwaj, Vishal
    adaptations 3, 6, 57, 140
    hennaed hands 11, 12, 167–84
Bhattacharya, Bhashkar 198, 225–6
Bhattacharya, Rimli 29
Bidyabagish, Muktaram, translation of *Tales from Shakespeare* 67–70, 73–4
Bidyaratna, Kantichandra *Sushila-Chandraketu* 72–4, 73
BJP, '*Jai Shri Ram*' 146
black box proscenium stage 23
bloodshed and henna 167–84
'The Blue Pencil' 228, 236–9
Bollywood 31, 153, 167–84, 188–9, 203, 215
Bombay 28, 30–3, 35

Bombay Legislative Council 35
boy-actors 229–30
Bremer Shakespeare Company, Bremen, Germany 252
BRICS film festival, Delhi 115
Bristow, Mrs Emma 24–5
British Library collections 65–89
    North Indian Languages Collection 66t, 262–84
    South Indian Shakespeare translations 75–85, 76t
British Museum collections 77–8
Buckley, Thea 86n9, 149
bullying 210–13
Bulwer, John, *Chirologia* 181
burlesque 28
Burnett, Mark Thornton 151, 171–2, 178, 197, 201–2, 243–61
Burt, Richard 217

Calcutta 23–9, 70, 137, 139
Calcutta Film Society 187
Calcutta Gazette 23, 24
Calcutta Theatre 24–5
Calvino, Italo, *If on a Winter's Night a Traveller* 237
campus theatrical experiment 225–42
Cannanore (now Kannur) 99
caste system 103–6, 155–7
    Hansaben 35
    Hemanta Katha 97
    Omkara (dir. Vishal Bhardwaj, 2006) 57
    Sairat (dir. Nagraj Manjule, 2016) 161
    Saptapadi (dir. Ajoy Kar, 1961) 48
Censor Board 34
Chakravarti, Paromita 144, 162
Chariar, V. Krishnama 99

Chatterjee, Bankim Chandra 187
Chatterjee, Bornila 243–61
Chatterjee, Partha 72
Chattopadhyay, Bankim Chandra 59
  'Shakuntala, Miranda and Desdemona' 46
chekavar castes 116–18, 120–3, 125–8
Chetsingh, R. 232–3
Chopra, B. R. 53
Chowringhee 24–5
Chowringhee Theatre 25–7
Christian missionaries 70
Christianity 47–51, 193
'cinema of confinement' 57
Cinestaan 244
Clover, Carol 181, 182n6
The Comedy of Errors
  Kannada translations 78
  Malayalam translations 77, 100
  St Stephen's College, Delhi 233–4
  Tamil translation 79
  Tamilized Shakespearean women 83–5
  Viprama Vihasam 83–5, 84
community politics 191–6
Constituent Assembly 35
Constitution of India 35–6
cross-dressing 12, 31, 74–5, 143, 193, 195–6, 198–200, 202, 229–31
Cuppage, Major Willie Adam 28
Cuppage, Mrs 28–9
Cymbeline, Mitra, Dhanadacharan translation of 71–2

Dahiya, Hema 69
Dalit cinema 155–7
Dalits 154
Daniélou, Alain 124

Das, Sisir Kumar 151
Dasgupta, Chidananda 187
Dasgupta, Rohit K. 193
Dasi, Binodini 29–30
Datta, Sangeeta 243–61
Deacle, Mrs 28
decolonization 22
Deleuze, Giles 134
Delhi 36–9, 249, 258–9
Delhi Zakir Husain College 226
Desmet, Christy 134–5
Deval, translation of *Othello* 31
Dhadak (dir. Shashank Khaitan, 2018) 162
dharma 72–3
Dhasal, Namdeo 154
Dil Chahta Hai (dir. Farhan Akhtar, 2001) 208
Dionne, Craig 114
'distant reading' 134
Doniger, Wendy 74
Drego, Sunil 208
Dubai 200
Dumergue, W. 97–8
Dutt, Utpal 46–7, 58, 226
  Aajker Shahjahan 247
Dutta, Michael Madhusudan, *Sharmistha* 29

East India Company 24
Eden, Emily 25
education
  English 66–70, 209
  female 35–6, 75, 82, 92–3, 96–8, 104, 107, 231–2
  Hansaben 35–6
  Marathi 152
  Mukherjee, Bharati 146–7n5
  Noblemen (dir. Vandana Kataria, 2018) 209, 222n4
  Sairat (dir. Nagraj Manjule, 2016) 154

Saptapadi (dir. Ajoy Kar, 1961) 52
theatre and 225–32
Ek Duuje Ke Liye (dir. K. Balachander, 1981) 159
English actresses 23–9
English Civil Services Exam 96
English Education Act 1835 70

Fakir, Lalon, 'Bari'r Kacche Arshi Nagar' 191
'The Falstaff' 228–9
Fandry (dir. Nagraj Manule, 2013) 150, 156
fatalism 58–9
female impersonation by men 23, 30–1
feminine agency 92–3, 96
femininities
   Bengali 131–48
   hennaed hands 170
   and Indian modernities 43–63
   Nair, Mira 234
   performing 140–6
   Veeram (dir. Jayaraj, 2016) 116, 121
feminism
   Allana, Amal 36, 38
   'The Blue Pencil' 238
   Clover, Carol 182n6
   Hansaben 36
   Hemanta Katha 104, 106
   St Stephen's College, Delhi 235
   The Tempest 239–40
   translating 91–2
   A Wife's Letter 247
Fenton, Mary 30
Film London 244
Folger Shakespeare Library 226
Friend of India 45

Galley Beggar Press 248
Gandhi, Mahatma 35, 155
Ganguly, Swati 144
García-Periago, Rosa 169, 226
Garrick, David, *Catherine and Petruchio* 26
gender
   Arshinagar (dir. Aparna Sen, 2015) 188–93, 197–202
   'The Blue Pencil' 237–8
   and colonialism 96–9
   control 258
   Hemanta Katha 92–3, 104–7
   hennaed hands 170
   Macbeth 141–6
   Othello 47, 49
   Ramayana 133
   relations 38
   roles 74–5
   Sairat (dir. Nagraj Manjule, 2016) 153–63
   St Stephen's College, Delhi 232, 234
   translators 96–9
   Veeram (dir. Jayaraj, 2016) 115–16, 121–8
Ghosh, Girish, *Macbeth* 29–30
Ghosh, Harachandra
   Bhanumati Chittabilas 68, 70
   translation of *The Merchant of Venice* 68, 70
Ghosh, Ranjan 57
Ghosh, Rituparno 247
ghost 179–80
Gilani, Benjamin 233
Giri, Madhav Chandra 44–5
Globe Theatre 256
Godayol, Pilar 91
Gokhale, Kamalabai 31
Gokhale, Shanta 32, 143–4
Golding, William, *Lord of the Flies* 208
Gooptu, Sukhalakshmi 237–8
Goswami, Radhika 240
Gowda, H. H. Anniah 95

Grant, Sir John Peter 27
Grant Road Theatre, Calcutta 28
Guattari, Félix 134
Gujarat 2002 riots 199
Gujarati theatres 30–1
Gupta, Arushi 236–7
Guttal, Vijaya 106

Haider (dir. Vishal Bhardwaj, 2014) 167, 169, 178–81
  Jhelum river song 179
Hamlet
  Haider (dir. Vishal Bhardwaj, 2014) 167–9, 178–81
  Irving, Henry 100
  Marathi theatre 31
  St Stephen's College, Delhi 233
  Strange Illusion (dir. Edgar G. Ulmer, 1945) 134–5
  translated into Gujarati verse 35
  Varkki, A. J. 100
  Vikar Vilasta 31
Hamraaz (dir. B. R. Chopra, 1967) 53–7
Hansaben 34–6
  Indian Woman 35
Hansen, Adam 139
Harris, Jonathan Gil 193–4
  Masala Shakespeare 226
Hartley, Andrew James, *Shakespeare on the University Stage* 227
Hatchuel, Sarah 210
Heidenberg, Mike 177–8
Hemanta Katha, Malayalam translation of *The Winter's Tale* 91–110, 98
hennaed hands 167–84
Henry, O. 247
Henry V, Miranda House 232–3
high school drama 207–23, 222n5
Hindi 208, 253

Hindu
  cinema 52–7
  fascism 248
  marriage 44–5
  mythology 134–7, 145–6, 147n8
  womanhood 45–7
Hindu College, Calcutta 68, 225
Hinduism
  Saptapadi (dir. Ajoy Kar, 1961) 47–50
  Vasantayamini Svapnacamatkara Natakavu 78–9
Hinduization, Bengali translations 72
Hindu-Muslim divide, *Arshinagar* (dir. Aparna Sen, 2015) 187–205
Hirematha, S. A., *Vasantayamini Svapnacamatkara Natakavu* 78
Hogan, Lalita Pandit 178
Holland, Peter 227
homosexuality 214–15, 220–1
Hooghly sessions court, Srerampore, Bengal 44–5
Hrid Majharey (dir. Ranjan Ghosh, 2014) 57–9
The Hungry (dir. Bornila Chatterjee, 2017) 243–4, 255–6
Hutcheon, Linda 168

IFFI, Goa 115
illustration 83, 85, 213
In Search of Durga (dir. Sangeeta Datta, 2001) 247
India Office collections 77–8
Indian Civil Services Exam 100–1
Indian Express 178
Indian Women's Rights 35
'Indianization' 69, 76, 79, 83

'indigenization'
  Bengali translations 68–75
  Desdemona 51, 59
  heroines 46
  Othello 55
  Tamil translation 76, 80
  'transculturation of indigenization' 168
insider/outsider dialectic 225–42
Irving, Henry, *Hamlet* 100
Iyengar, K. R. Srinivasa 79
Iyengar, Sujata 134–5, 238–9
Iyengar, Vikram, *Crossings* (2004–11) dance-drama 143–5

Jackson, Russell 219
Jadavpur University 66
Jalote, S. R. 157
jatra performance 256
Jayaraj 57, 113–30
Jhanjha, a translation of *The Tempest* by Nagendra Prasad 71
John, Rebecca Sarah 238–9
Jones, Anne Rosalind 74–5
Julius Caesar
  Bristow, Mrs Emma 24
  films 257

Kalamandalam University 244–5
kalarippayattu (martial arts) 113–28, 246, 250
Kaliyattam (dir. Jayaraj, 1997) 57, 113
Kalyani Kalamandalam theatre group 142–3
Kannada translations 78
Kannaki (dir. Jayaraj, 2002) 113
Kapadia, Parmita 114
Kapoor, Kunal 116, 210, 215
Karim-Cooper, Farah 181
Karnad, Girish 253
Kashmir 248, 258

Kataria, Vandana 207–23
kathakali 244–5, 251–2, 256, 257, 260
Kathakali-King Lear 244–5
Kemble, Fanny 176
Kerala 92, 96, 99, 104, 106–7, 113–14, 116–18, 245–6, 250
Keshavsut 154
Khatau, Kavasji 30
Khote, Durga 31
Khudadad, Urdu adaptation of *Pericles* 30
Kidnie, Margaret Jane 180, 237
  Shakespeare and the Problem of Adaptation 162
Kimmel, Kari 121
King John, Malayalam translation 245
King Lear
  Aajker Shahjahan 247
  Amal Allana's production, 1989, Delhi 36–9
  films 247, 256–7
  kathakali 251–2
  Kathakali-King Lear 244–5
  The Last Lear (dir. Rituparno Ghosh, 2007) 247
  Life Goes On (dir. Sangeeta Datta, 2009) 247–8, 252–3
  Telugu translations 77
  We That Are Young 248, 254, 258
Kolkata 45, 57–9
Kumar, Suresh 118
Kumar, Uttam 52
Kundora Chamundi ('Terrible Mother') 127
kutiyattam 251

Lakshmy Amma, O. M. 91–110
Lamb, Charles and Mary, *Tales from Shakespeare* 67–70, 68, 73–4, 92, 95–7, 99–101

INDEX

Lamb, Mary, *The Winter's Tale* 93–4, 101–4
Lanier, Douglas 134–5, 137, 139, 152
The Last Lear (dir. Rituparno Ghosh, 2007) 247
Leach, Esther 25–7
Lebedeff, Herasim 29
Leday, Annette 243–61
Lehmann, Courtney 150–1
Lei, Beatrice 92
Leventen, Carol 216
Lewis theatre 45
Life Goes On (dir. Sangeeta Datta, 2009) 247–8, 252–4, 260
Lobato, Ramon 208–9, 222n3
localization 36–7, 92–6, 101, 104, 197
Loomba, Ania 96, 105
Lotz, Amanda 209
Lutz, Helma 198

Macaulay, T. B., *Minutes on Education* 70
Macbeth
　Bengali adaptations 131–48
　'The Blue Pencil' 238–9
　Crossings (2004–11) dance-drama 143–5
　Ghosh, Girish 29–30
　Kannada translations 78
　kshatriya 74
　Maqbool (dir. Vishal Bhardwaj, 2003) 140, 167–9, 171–3
　Rajmukuta 31
　Veeram (dir. Jayaraj, 2016) 113–30
　Wife 136–40, 145–6, 146–7n5
Macbeth Mirror (2016) 142
McRuvie, David 244, 251
Madhaviah, A., Tamil translation of *Othello* 81–3, *81*
madness 58–9

Madras (now Chennai) 99, 105
Mahabharata 95–6, 104, 212
Mahanagar (dir. Satyajit Ray, 1963) 50
Malabar 116–18, 121, 128
Malabar Marriage Commission 105
Malayalam translations 77, 91–110, 249–50, 251, 259
　of *The Winter's Tale* 98
Manasu Mallige (dir. S. Narayan, 2017) 162
Mangai, A. 53
Manglik, Mukul 234
Manjule, Nagraj 149–66
Maqbool (dir. Vishal Bhardwaj, 2003) 140, 167, 169, 171–3
　'Jhin min jhini' 172
Marathi
　film 149–66
　poetry and plays 34
　theatre 28, 30–1, 34
Maro Charithra (dir. K. Balachander, 1978) 159
Marshall, Frank A. 100
marumakkatayam 104–5
Mathur, Kali Charan, 'The Stage in India: Some Suggestions' 229
matriliny 104–6
Mayer, Tamar 193, 202
mehndi parties 169–70, 172–3
Mehta, Dr Kumudini Arvind, *English Drama on the Bombay Stage in the late Eighteenth Century and in the Nineteenth Century* 32–4
Mehta, Jivraj Hansa 34–6
Mehta, Vijaya 31
melodrama 51–2, 54–7, 60n6
Menon, Madhavi 221n2
Menon, O. Chandu, *Indulekha* 97–8, 105

The Merchant of Venice Bhanumati Chittabilas 68, 70
'The Blue Pencil' 237–8
films 257
Ghosh, Harachandra 68, 70
Grant Road Theatre, Calcutta 28
Gujarati verse 35
Hansaben 36
Kannada translations 78
Leach, Esther 27
Malayalam translations 77
Noblemen (dir. Vandana Kataria, 2018) 207–23
St Stephen's College, Delhi 230–1
The Merchant of Venice (dir. Michael Radford, 2004) 214, 221
The Merry Merchant of Venice 28
Metcalf, Barbara D. 209
Metcalf, Thomas R. 209
Michael, Joy 231–2
A Midsummer Night's Dream
Kannada stage production 78–9, 78
St Stephen's College, Delhi 237–8
Vasantayamini Svapnacamatkara Natakavu 78
Miranda House 232–3
Mitra, Dhanadacharan, translation of *Cymbeline* 71–2
Mohanty, Sangeeta 100
Mookherjee, Taarini 191, 200
Moretti, Franco 134
Mudaliar, Pammal Sambanda 81–2
mudras (hand gestures) 6, 168, 168, 251, 257
Mukherjee, Bharati, *Wife* 136–40, 145–6, 146–7n5

Mukherjee, Srimati 201
Mukherjee, Urna 237–8
Mukhopadhyay, Swapna 106–7
Muktaram 70
Muruganandan, K. 79–80
Muzaffarnagar 239–40
mythology 177–8
Hindu 134–7, 145–6, 147n8

Nabina (New Woman) 45–7
Naidu, Sarojini 35
Nair, Jayashree Ramakrishnan 94
Nair, Mira 234
Nair, Sreedevi 243–61
Nair caste families 104–5
Nandigram, West Bengal 197
Naresh, Rajiv 235
National Centre for Performing Arts (NCPA) 34
nationalism
Arshinagar (dir. Aparna Sen, 2015) 202
Bengal Partition 70, 72
Dalits 155
and Elokeshi 44–5
female agency 189
and female performers 29
Hindu 199
Hrid Majharey (dir. Ranjan Ghosh, 2014) 58–9
Macbeth 135
Ratha Thilagam (dir. Dada Mirasi, 1963) 53–7
Sangam (dir. Raj Kapoor, 1964) 60n6
NCPA Quarterly 34
Nehru, Jawaharlal 35
neoliberalism 44, 57–8, 248
Netflix 208, 222n3
New Woman 45–7, 51–2
Nabina (New Woman) 45–7
Noblemen (dir. Vandana Kataria, 2018) 207–23

'Northern Ballads', *Vadakkan Pattukal* 114–15, 117–19, 121, 127
NSS College for Women, Thiruvananthapuram 245

Omkara (dir. Vishal Bhardwaj, 2006) 57, 167, 174–8
Orgel, Stephen 104–5
Orkin, Martin 114
Othello
    Bengal 45–7
    Bhimsingha 46
    'The Blue Pencil' 238
    Desdemona 27, 31, 43–63
    Deval's translation of 31
    Hamraaz (dir. B. R. Chopra, 1967) 53–7
    Hrid Majharey (dir. Ranjan Ghosh, 2014) 57–9
    Kaliyattam (dir. Jayaraj, 1997) 57, 113
    Lewis theatre 45
    Malayalam translations 77
    Marathi theatre 31
    Omkara (dir. Vishal Bhardwaj, 2006) 57, 167–9, 174–8
    Ratha Thilagam (dir. Dada Mirasi, 1963) 53–7
    Razu, V. Padmanabha 77
    St Stephen's College, Delhi 235
    Samyukta Research Foundation 255
    Sanskrit translation 100
    Saptapadi (dir. Ajoy Kar, 1961) 47–53, 58
    The Stars Still Shine on Desdemona 245–6, 250
    Tamil translation 77, 80–3, *81*
    Telugu translations 77
    translations 79
    Zunzarrao 31

paanan 114–15, 117, 119, 125–6
Padley, Rev. H. Wilson 230–1
Padma Bhushan 36
Pal, Tarini Charan, *Bhimsingha* 46
Palekar, Amol 34
Paniker, Dr K. Ayyappa, *The Complete Works of Shakespeare* 245
Panja, Shormishtha 2, 4, 201
Pant, Pooja Anna 237, 239–40
Paris Theatrical Company 30
Parsi theatre 1, 30–32, 55
Parsis 28
Partition 193–4, 248, 258
Pati, George 124
patriarchy
    Allana, Amal 38
    androgyny 75
    Arshinagar (dir. Aparna Sen, 2015) 188, 192–3, 198
    Clover, Carol 181
    Desdemona 47
    Elokeshi and the 44–5
    Hemanta Katha 105–6
    hennaed hands 170–1
    The Hungry (dir. Bornila Chatterjee, 2017) 258
    Noblemen (dir. Vandana Kataria, 2018) 216, 220
    Sairat (dir. Nagraj Manjule, 2016) 160–1
    Saptapadi (dir. Ajoy Kar, 1961) 52, 86n10
    translating 91–2, 96, 98
    We That Are Young 248, 259
Paulose, K. G. 92
performative hands 167–84
Pericles
    Khudadad 30
    Malayalam translation 77
    Paraklesarajavinte Katha (The Story of King Pericles) 94–5
Phalke, Dadasaheb 31

Phatak, Nanasaheb 31
  Zunzarrao 31
Philippose, Kalloor Oommen,
  Almarattam (Substitution)
  100
Phule, Jyotibha 155
Pillai, Meena T. 121
'playgoing' 33
Pottan Daivam (low-caste 'loafer'
  or 'idiot') 127
Pradesh, Madhya 210
Prasad, Nagendra 60n6
  Jhanjha 71
Preston, Peter 233
Priyatama (dir. Satish Motling,
  2014) 150
Puri, Om 253
Pursell, Michael 151

Qayamat Se Qayamat Tak (dir.
  Mansoor Khan, 1988) 150,
  159, 192

Raincoat (dir. Rituparno Ghosh,
  2004) 247
Raj playhouses, Calcutta 225
Rajguru, Rinku 154, 162
Ramakrishnan, K. V. 119
Ramayana 95–6, 136–7, 139
Rana, Naintara 236–7
Ratha Thilagam (dir. Dada Mirasi,
  1963) 53–7
Raveendran, P. P. 97
Ray, Satyajit 50, 188, 246, 253
Razu, V. Padmanabha, *Othello* 77
religious differences 47–51, 191
Rig Veda 254
Rink, Mussoorie 28
Romeo and Juliet
  Ambikapathy (dir. Ellis R.
    Dungan, 1937) 149
  Ambikapathy (dir. P.
    Neelakantan, 1957) 149
Arshinagar (dir. Aparna Sen,
  2015) 150, 151, 187–205,
  195
'The Blue Pencil' 236–8
Dhadak (dir. Shashank
  Khaitan, 2018) 162
Ek Duuje Ke Liye (dir. K.
  Balachander, 1981) 159
Manasu Mallige (dir. S.
  Narayan, 2017) 162
Marathi theatre 31
Maro Charithra (dir. K.
  Balachander, 1978) 159
Priyatama (dir. Satish Motling,
  2014) 150
Qayamat Se Qayamat Tak (dir.
  Mansoor Khan, 1988) 150,
  159, 192
Ramyanum Jolitaiyum 105
Sairat (dir. Nagraj Manjule,
  2016) 149–66
Vidyasundar 29
Roy, Ashish 232–5
Roy, Modhumita 226

Sadasivan, C. P., *Shaityakala
  Katha* 101
Saha, Sharmistha 33
St Stephen's College, Delhi 226–42
Sairat (dir. Nagraj Manjule, 2016)
  149–66
Samyukta Research Foundation
  245, 255
San Toy 28
Sanders, Julie 151
Sangam (dir. Raj Kapoor, 1964)
  60n6
sangeet nataks (musical plays)
  30–1
Sans Souci Theatre 26–8
Sanskrit dramatic traditions 74
Saptapadi (dir. Ajoy Kar, 1961)
  43–4, 50–5, 58

Sarbbadhikari, Nagendra Prasad, *Jhanjha* 70–1
Sarkar, Abhishek 178–9
Sastri, S. M. Natesa, *Twelfth Night* 77
sati (ideal wife) 44–5, 49–50
  Anglo-Indian 50–3
Sayed, Asam 168, 178
School of Cultural Texts and Records (SCTR) 66
Schröter, Jens 168
Sen, Aparna 151, 187–205
Sen, Mikhail 235
Sen, Suchitra 50, 52, 58
Sendak, Maurice, *Where the Wild Things Are* 212
Shacklady, Robert 253
Shakespeare Association 67
Shakespeare rhizome 134–5, 137
Shakespeare Society of India 225–42
Shankar, D. A. 95, 101
Sharaby, Rachel 170
Sharma, Tanima 235, 238
shifting identities 207–23
Shirwadkar, V. V. 31
  Rajmukuta 31
'Siddons of Bengal' 25
Simla Gaiety 28
Simon, Sherry 98
Sinfield, Alan 214
Singh, Jyotsna G. 1, 216, 226
Singh, Manohar 37
Singur, West Bengal 197–8
Sino-Indian war 52–7, 60n6
Sisson, C. J., 'Shakespeare in India: Popular Adaptations on the Bombay Stage' 67
Sita (ideal wife) 136–7, 139
SNDT 36
SOAS Library, London 66
South Indian translations 91–110
'The Speeches of *The Tempest*' 228

Sri Vani Vilasini 83
Srinivasiar, S. V., *Ramyanum Jolitaiyum* 105
Srishti Institute of Art, Design and Technology, Bangalore 66
Stallybrass, Peter 74–5
Stam, Robert 189
The Stars Still Shine on Desdemona 245–6, 250
State Institute of Children's Literature, Kerala 245
The Stephanian 232–3
'Stephanian Diary' 234
Stocqueler, J. H., *Memoirs* 25–6
Strange Illusion (dir. Edgar G. Ulmer, 1945) 134–5
Strir Patra – A Wife's Letter (dir. Sangeeta Datta, 2008) 247
Subramanyam, K. 79, 155
supernatural 131–48
Supik, Linda 198
Sutcliffe, Alison 252
Swadeshi (self-sufficiency) 70–5

Tagore, Dwarakanath 26
Tagore, Rabindranath 67, 253
  Bhanusingher Padabali ('The Songs of Bhanusingho') 71
  Chokher Bhali 247
  Noukadubi 247
  'Remember Me' 254
  A Wife's Letter – Strir Patra (dir. Sangeeta Datta, 2008) 247
Tagore, Sharmila 253
Tales from Shakespeare translation, Bidyabagish, Muktaram 67–70, 73–4
Tamil translations 77
Tamilized Shakespearean women 79–85
The Taming of the Shrew
  Catherine and Petruchio 26

Kannada translations 78
Malayalam translations 77, 94
St Stephen's College, Delhi 234
Tamil translation 79
Taneja, Preti 243–61
  We That Are Young 248, 254, 259
Tarasundari 29–30
Teenkori 29–30
Telugu translations 77
The Tempest
  Jhanjha 70–1, 71
  kathakali 252–3
  'The Speeches of *The Tempest*' 228
  St Stephen's College, Delhi 228, 239–40
  Telugu translations 77
Tendulkar, Vijay, *Sakharam Binder* 34
Terry, Ellen 176
Thampu, Rev. Valson 234–5
theyyam performance 57, 127
36 Chowringhee Lane (dir. Aparna Sen, 1981) 60n3, 187
Thirunal, Maharajah Vishakham 96–7
Thosar, Akash 154
Titus Andronicus, The Hungry (dir. Bornila Chatterjee, 2017) 243–4, 249, 255–60
Travancore 96, 99, 104
Trinamool Congress (TMC) 146, 199, 203n3
Trivedi, Poonam 68–9, 178, 181, 182n4
  India's Shakespeare: Translation, Interpretation and Performance 79
Twelfth Night
  Bengali translations 72–4
  Sastri, S. M. Natesa 77
  Sushila-Chandraketu 72–4, 73

'Two Centuries of Indian Print' 65–89
The Two Gentlemen of Verona, Malayalam translation 245

Ugaritic Legend of Baal and Anath 170–1
UN Declaration of Human Rights 35–6
UN Human Rights Conference 35–6
Uniform Civil Code 35
University of Bombay 32, 34
Unni, Chaithanya 97
urban crises, women's bodies and Bengaliness 196–201

Vadakkan Pattukal ('Northern Ballads') 114–15, 117–19, 121, 127
Vadyar, Chidambara, *The Winter's Tale* 96–7
Valmiki, *Ramayana* 131–4
Vandenhoff, Charlotte 175
Varkki, A. J., *Hamlet* 100
Varma, Kerala 96–7
Veeram (dir. Jayaraj, 2016) 113–30
  'We Will Rise' 121
Velu, O., *Paraklesarajavinte Katha (The Story of King Pericles)* 77, 94–5
Venkatacharyar, A, *Viprama Vihasam* 83–5, 84
Venkiteswaran, C. S. 120
Venuti, Lawrence, 'Adaptation, Translation, Critique' 137
Vidyapati 71
Vidyasagar, Ishwar Chandra 187
Vidyasundar 29
Virdi, Jyotika 157
Vivar, Maria Terrera Herrera 198

water 207–8
Waugh, Thomas 220

The Way I See It (dir. Sangeeta Datta, 1999) 247
wedding ceremonies 169–70, 175–6, 179
Weiss, Professor René 252
West Bengal 146
Wetmore, Kevin J. 139
Wheel of Fire dance performance 144
wifely status 136–40
The Winter's Tale
    Hemanta Katha 91–110, 98
    Malayalam translation 77, 98, 100–1
    Vadyar, Chidambara 96–7
'woman's part' 21–42
women
    land and contemporary politics 187–205
    performers 23–4
    as professional performers 29–30
    as warriors 113–30
'Women and Indian Shakespeares' conference, Queen's University Belfast, 2019 243–61
women's bodies
    and community politics 191–6
    urban crises and Bengaliness 196–201
women's liberation movement 182n6
Women's Wrongs 28
Wright, Richard, 'I Have Seen Black Hands' 154

Yegende, Suraj 156

www.ingramcontent.com/pod-product-compliance
Lightning Source LLC
Chambersburg PA
CBHW052150300426
44115CB00011B/1594